The Best Cars

THE
BEST
CARS

A NEW COMPUTERIZED GUIDE TO PERFORMANCE AND EFFICIENCY

William and Michael Stobbs

PELHAM BOOKS

First published in Great Britain by
Pelham Books Ltd
44 Bedford Square
London WC1B 3DU
1981

British Library Cataloguing in Publication Data
Stobbs, W. Michael
    The best cars.
    1. Automobiles – Handbooks, manuals, etc.
    I. Title   II. Stobbs, William
        629.2′222′0212   TL151

ISBN 0 7207 1376 5

Typeset and printed in Great Britain by
BAS Printers Limited, Over Wallop, Hampshire
and bound by Hunter and Foulis, Edinburgh

Contents

List of Cars

Preface

This book is about the classification of cars, mainly on the basis of a simple and, as far as possible, objective approach to the assessment of data mostly made available by the manufacturers. In some instances we have used data from tests carried out by the staff of the magazine *Motor*, and we are grateful to the editor for his permission to use this data.

It is in fact the variability of some of the data quoted from elsewhere that has led us to appreciate the care taken by this magazine in its testing. If we had fuller raw data on, for example, the weight of the car as tested (though *Motor* for their tests provide this) or its performance at half and full load as well as its fuel consumption figures both on the road and stationary on rollers, we could very easily clarify some of the relationships we have used for car assessment, and also reduce some of our uncertainties in the end figures. In one or two places we discuss this problem more fully, on cars such as the Escort 1600 and the Capri 3.0S.

In any event, and despite in general being forced to use a fairly arbitrary addition to the unladen weight, we are of the opinion that the derived data are accurate to within about 5 per cent unless otherwise stated. Our plea to the manufacturers is for the provision of more accurate raw data. The assessment procedure will then yield still more useful results. This will be both to their benefit and to the benefit of the customer.

Every care has been taken in compiling the contents to ensure that they are correct and accurate, but the publishers and authors assume no responsibility for any effect from errors or omissions or from opinions which while made in good faith might be proved to be unsubstantiated. The authors would however be grateful for both comments and potential corrections which might be included in any future edition.

We are grateful to our editors and wives alike for their patience and help, as well as our typists for their care and accuracy. We further offer our sincere thanks to all the manufacturers who have been so understanding in both giving us photographs and data and in allowing us to drive their cars. We are also grateful to John Lambert and Rainer Williams who took additional photographs.

Porsche 911 – non-stop impeccability

Introduction

For most people the car is no longer a luxury but an essential aspect of their way of life, and millions of apparently different cars are manufactured to satisfy this increasingly utilitarian demand. But since the basic engineering principles involved are superficially alike, there are some who say that any method of selection can be only subjective. There is a subjective element in all selection, but it is a demonstrable fact that some cars *are* better than others. A degree of objectivity is possible in the comparison of design, efficiency, dependability, longevity, and integrity, though not perhaps in how grand, expensive or spectacular a car might be.

Horseless carriages driven by internal combustion engines, based on the Otto four-stroke principle, have been in use since the 1880s, and they have been improving steadily in almost every respect. As time goes by, they go faster, ride and handle better, require less maintenance, break down less often, start and stop better, and progress from here to there more quickly and with more precision.

Annually they become more automatic and require less servicing. More elements become sealed for life. Electronic ignition timing is programmed to remain unchanged through the life of the engine. Indeed those with electronic systems should not be able to maladjust themselves. We would appear to be living in the best of all possible dream-car worlds, so why this present concern to differentiate between the best and the worst?

It is because the best are becoming increasingly safe and more serene, and the worst are becoming more uneconomic and potentially dangerous. If it were a matter of the elite versus the honest workhorse it would be another matter. It is, however, more a question of which cars have integrity and which do not.

A central theme in this book is the use of a new pair of relationships which can be used to judge a car's performance and efficiency with accuracy. Our basic formula introduces the concept of a 'Performance Dimension' or PD and uses only four manufacturer's statistics: maximum speed, acceleration, bhp and

weight. If we take as a measure of performance the product of the car's maximum speed and its acceleration, and compare the value obtained with the maximum power output divided by the car's weight, we find that all cars fall on or about a roughly straight line relationship as shown in the graph opposite. Those above the line are, in a clear sense, poorer than average and those below the line are better than average. The latter do more for their power to weight ratio than their brethren.

The further a car is beneath the line the more superior is its performance. Thus the Porsche 911 Turbo, Lotus Esprit Turbo, Daimler-Jaguar Double Six, Lotus Esprit (Dellorto) and Austin Mini Metro 1.3 are all above average while the Caterham twin cam, despite its explosive acceleration, is on these overall grounds below average. The whole graph shows the Performance Dimensions for about 350 cars. More facts on the Performance Dimension (PD) formula are outlined in Chapter 2 'The Measure of Performance'.

Cars are, however, for driving. In the end many of their qualities and faults can only be discovered by so doing. Statistics, while providing useful evidence, cannot exclusively predict the best. This is because the car is a complex synthesis of the individually comparable power train, aerodynamic envelope, steering, suspension geometry, and brakes in an invariably experimentally determined combination. A good quality mixture produces a car which rides and handles well.

The decisions in this book are based on science, engineering and driving. For this reason we have road tested not only nearly all the cars described here, but many others not represented. We have in no way attempted to usurp the car testing attitudes of the major magazines. Our road testing has mainly been confined to those aspects of our comparisons for which figures are not enough and driving in as many different conditions as possible is essential. While handling and comfort speak for themselves as clearly as the ease or difficulty of seeing an instrument or an oncoming cyclist, we have addressed ourselves more carefully to each car's personality. It is this, after performance and handling, which makes a car a winner or a loser.

A car when first driven either feels right or is rebellious: it has a pleasing feel which itself contributes to safety, or it feels insecure or uncertain, which detracts from safety. It is not really surprising that national characteristics still appear in cars. Italian cars in the main have visual flair with vibrant personalities, German cars often achieve perfection without any demonstrative features, and French cars have been taught over the years to stay bolted together whether treated with Gallic verve or total diffidence. It is interesting to note with what tenacity the people of many countries continue to use their native products and swear by them. The idea of a world car is always in the air and never materializes, although VW and Ford have both come near to it. We have attempted in this book to accept without bias of any kind all cars from all countries and all manufacturers who are able to allow us to road test and analyse their vehicles.

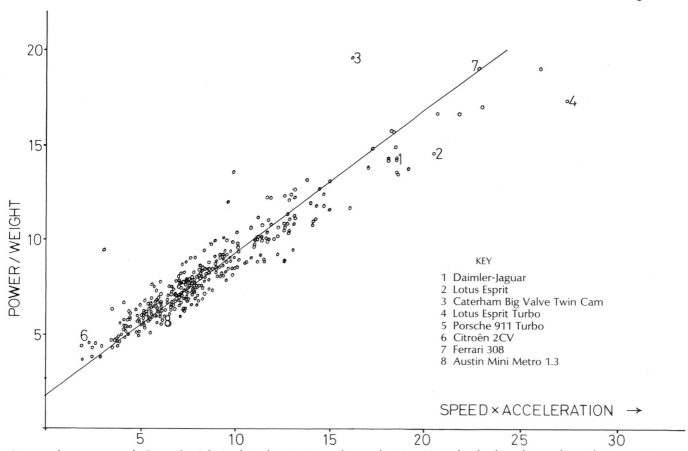

A car performance graph. Power/weight is plotted against speed x acceleration. Note that both scales are linear but are not dimensioned, the form of the graph being unit size independent. A full explanation of the graph and approach is given in 'The Measure of Performance', p 30

KEY
1 Daimler-Jaguar
2 Lotus Esprit
3 Caterham Big Valve Twin Cam
4 Lotus Esprit Turbo
5 Porsche 911 Turbo
6 Citroën 2CV
7 Ferrari 308
8 Austin Mini Metro 1.3

1 Beyond the Facia

Let us try to put it in the tiniest of nutshells. When the ignition key is turned fully, electric current flows to two places: the starter and the ignition coil. The motor in the starter engages its gear with the flywheel and turns it. The flywheel pushes round the crankshaft and in turn all the moving parts in the engine. One of these is the fuel pump, feeding petrol from the tank into the carburettor. The carburettor's job is to mix petrol with air, and this mixture is drawn along to the engine's inlet valves. The camshaft, which like everything else is driven by the crankshaft, pushes the inlet valves open at the appointed time.

Once through the inlet valves, the mixture is sucked in at the top end of the cylinders by the pistons as they withdraw down the cylinders, and then compressed as they rise up on the return stroke, the inlet valve having meanwhile closed tight. As the piston squeezes the volatile and powerful mixture into a small space, the time approaches for the mixture to be ignited.

Ignition then occurs. The electricity has also flowed to the ignition coil, which increases the voltage from 12 volts to a shattering 20,000 volts. This high tension current passes, as a spark, across the gaps of the sparking plugs at the correct times with the aid of a distributor, which is also geared to the camshaft. The mixture catches fire from the spark, burns and expands, thrusting with the power of ten or more horses on each piston.

Work has now commenced, and will continue while there is fuel to burn. The starter motor has disconnected itself by cleverly disengaging its pinion from the flywheel.

Once running, the engine becomes a paragon of co-ordinated self-help. It drives a fan to cool itself, an impeller to circulate water around its furnace-like hot parts and an oil pump to spray oil on every moving part. It also continues to pump petrol from the tank to the carburettor, and drives the alternator which, once the motor is running, generates electricity for the ignition coil, spark plugs and lights, and for recharging the battery.

The engine is running, but the car is stationary. The gear lever is in neutral, so the engine's power can reach no further than the gearbox. The driver presses the clutch down, and this disconnects the engine from the gearbox altogether while a gear is being engaged. Power can now pass through the gearbox, along the propeller shaft to the final drive. Here it branches in two ways, to left and right driven wheels; but on its way it passes through a differential, which is quite indispensable if you think for a minute: on a corner the two wheels will travel different distances and at different speeds, and so will need different amounts of power, or else skid. The differential takes the engine's power and shares it out between the wheels, each according to its needs.

The 'dif' might be cunning, but the electrics are truly magical. First of all, the battery, as we know, hands over to the alternator once it has started the engine, and the alternator tops up the charge in the battery in return. The battery (traditionally based on the lead–sulphuric acid cell) contains positive and negative electrodes immersed in dilute sulphuric acid. The electricity is produced in a reaction between the acid and the electrodes, and charging puts the reaction into reverse.

The ignition system is the wonderful part. The ignition coil is the source of firing voltage. It consists of a rod-shaped laminated core, wound round with 15,000 to 30,000 turns of thin copper wire. Outside a layer of insulation, this winding is surrounded by a few hundred turns of thick copper wire. The thick wire is called the primary coil and the thin wire the secondary coil.

Now it is one of the ways of electricity that when a low voltage is supplied to the primary coil and suddenly interrupted, a momentary impulse at a much higher voltage is induced in the secondary coil. The 12 volts from the battery are interrupted in the primary coil, and 20,000 volts come leaping out of the secondary coil, to be taken to the sparking plugs and make these live up to their name.

Allied to the coil are two mechanisms. The contact breaker keeps on interrupting the electrical circuit at the right times; and the distributor passes the bursts of high-tension current out to the sparking plugs in the firing order. Timing is the crucial factor in this action, and both the distributor and the contact breaker (which is situated in the head of the distributor) are driven by the camshaft, which in turn is driven by the crankshaft, so ultimately the electrical timing and the movement of the pistons are both parts of the same mechanical chain of action.

When cars will not start, or behave in an erratic manner, it is often due to faulty electrics, but it is neither difficult nor expensive to have the points and plugs seen to, or the battery charged. The engine itself is, in the main, very durable. Exhaust valves sometimes need replacing, and this is no surprise because their working temperature is about 1,500°C; but nowadays it is comparatively rare for such disasters to occur as the connecting rods breaking through the crankcase, or other catastrophes of the vintage period.

There are engines and engines of course, as we all know: the best engines which always work efficiently, the mediocre ones which have attacks of hysteria or asthma and break down spasmodically, and the really bad ones which create chain reactions of mechanical misery, beyond imagination until they happen. Quite soon, you will know how to avoid the bad ones, and it is important that you do so because they have demanding habits. When you have bought them a new battery and exhaust system, a set of tyres and a few new valves, two constant velocity joints and a radiator, they feel they have a permanent place in your life. They feel certain that after such an investment they can demand a replacement engine, which would be cheaper than a new car, and you could start a new and wonderful life together and drive to the Himalayas without a care in the world.

So choose a really good car in the first place, and that is what this book is about. And when you have, do not expect it to last forever. It is in the nature of motorcars not only to rot and rust away, but to be made obsolete by the ceaseless innovations of the motor industry.

INTRODUCING BHP

James Watt, one of the inventors of the steam engine, also invented the concept of horsepower, which he used to assess the power output of steam engines, in about 1780. The unit was determined by the rate at which an average horse was supposed to work; Watt estimated this to be 550 ft/lb wt per second, a ft/lb wt being the energy that will lift one pound one foot. A known weight was suspended down a well, over a pulley, and a horse was harnessed and encouraged to pull the weight up, the time being measured with a stop watch.

Horsepower later came to be measured on a dynamometer, which resists the effort of an engine with a spring and registers the result on a dial where the horsepower can be read off. It was found, incidentally, that James Watt must have had a rather strong horse: most horses can only manage at best about 0.75 'horsepower'. The unit has nonetheless remained as Watt had created it, a tactful gesture towards the animal kingdom.

Most large garages now possess a dynamometer. The car is driven onto it, and the wheels rest on rollers. When the engine is started and put in gear the car remains stationary, and drives the rollers round. These are braked by a cylinder, but in the process the power the car is exerting on this brake is registered on the dial, and so the units are known as brake horse power (bhp).

Torque is the effort of turning something round an axis. In a car, it is the measure of the leverage that the engine exerts, via the transmission system, on the driving wheels.

The speed of the engine is recorded by the tachometer, which gives the revolutions of the crankshaft per minute (rpm). The performance of the engine varies with the rpm of the crankshaft and this is usually shown by a power curve on a graph, together with a torque curve.

Engine designers try to obtain a balanced engine with good figures in both brake horse power and torque. It is torque which provides power at low and medium revs, and high brake horse power which provides high maximum speeds. If you look at a power graph in this book you will see that both the curves rise and fall, and their peaks occur at different rpm. Using these you can start doing your own research, by observing which engines manage to get these two curves close enough together to provide useful torque and bhp across a wide range of rpm.

You can relate all this to your own car as you drive along, if you choose an opportunity to stay in second gear for a stretch and accelerate steadily, rising towards the engine's peak revs. You will notice that at some point, usually about 20 per cent below peak rpm, the rate of increase of speed decreases, although the engine is still accelerating: this means that you are now on the downward turn of the bhp curve. Do not over-rev the engine; watch the tachometer if you have one.

The power-weight ratio is another important characteristic of a car, which you can work out from manufacturer's data with your pocket calculator. It simply means the ratio of the bhp to the weight. Naturally, if the weight is excessive, the speed will fall and the fuel consumption will rise, but if the weight is too small the vehicle may lack structural stability and be as safe as a Japanese lantern. This ratio used to be shown in bhp/ton, but with the change to metric units the current method is kW/tonne; a metric tonne being 1000 kg and about 2 per cent smaller than an imperial ton which is 2240 lb.

POWER IN THE METRIC SYSTEM

Nowadays it is common enough for output to be expressed both in bhp and in its metric counterpart, the kilowatt, which is converted at the rate of 1 kW = 1.341 bhp.

In the metric system force is expressed in terms of the Newton (N) which has an imperial equivalent of 7.233 poundals (lbal) or 0.2248 lb wt.

When a force of one Newton is moved through one metre, one Newton metre (Nm) of work is done. This is a Joule. Power expresses a rate of doing work and one Watt (W) is one Joule per second or 1 Nm. One kilowatt (kW) is one thousand Watts.

SAE AND DIN

These are the two most commonly used test procedures for measuring the power of motor vehicles. The SAE method is that for America's Society of Automotive Engineers while the DIN (Deutsche Industrie Normen) standard is more commonly used in Europe. SAE figures include the effect of the gear train and are thus lower than those derived on the DIN approach.

Class 1 500-1200cc

INTRODUCTION

Engineers do not like engines of this size because they can not only achieve more torque and bhp if the capacity is slightly larger, but also better fuel consumption. There are utility vans of 500 cc in existence in Japan which *do* have phenomenally good fuel consumption figures, but in order to make them safe for passengers the added weight would probably bring the figure down. It seems possible, however, that the future might hold micro-minis, if sufficient attention was given to radically new technology in all areas, because so far as fuel consumption is concerned, we have been running on the spot since the 1930s when the Fiat Topolino could achieve 55 mpg.

The small cars of the twenties and thirties existed for a different reason. There was no thought then of a shortage of fuel, it was a shortage of money. Manufacturers were producing cars which everyman could afford to buy in the first place, and then afford to run. Herbert Austin's legendary Seven came out in 1922 and achieved a phenomenal success. It cost £100 and the 747 cc engine developed 13 bhp and in a supercharged form won the Brooklands 500 mile race in 1930. It also rescued Herbert Austin from the receiver. It is interesting to note that this engine was built under licence by car manufacturers all over the world, such as BMW in Germany where it was called the Dixie, Rosengart in France, Bantam in the USA, and Datsun in Japan.

Other small popular cars of the 1920s included the Citroën 856 cc 5CV, the Opel Laub Frosch (tree frog) 851 cc, and the Renault KJ type.

Then, just as now, people, engineers and manufacturers moved up to 1000 cc. The Austin 10, Morris ten, Ford ten and the Citroën 7CV traction-avant were perhaps the most significant European cars of the thirties. 'Petite Rosalie' a 10 hp Citroën broke 300 international class records while covering a distance of 301,875 km (187,500 miles) at an average speed of 93.4 km/h (58 mph). Fiat sensibly continued with the small car theme with the Topolino, an engine of 570 cc returning 55 mpg.

So, fifty years of research and technological development later, we are still managing to achieve around 50 mpg when really trying. At least we are not retrogressive. The Ford Escort 1100 and the Suzuki SC 100 GX of course are better in every respect than the Fiat Topolino – they go faster, handle better and stop much more effectively.

The problems to be solved are still the same. A car which must not cost too much initially. The Austin Seven cost £100 and the Morris Eight £125 in 1930. At the time of writing (mid-1981) small cars were all priced between about £2500 and £3000. But does everything cost 30 times more than it did in 1930? No; the 12.8 litre Bugatti Royale exhibited at Olympia in 1932 had a quoted price of £6500 (× 30 = £195,000).

Also, the service costs must not be too high, and in this respect most modern cars have used the latest technology to very good effect. The new Ford Escorts are serviced once a normal 12,000 mile year only, and then within a one hour period, and the number of units which are sealed for the life of the car or require no servicing has grown remarkably, with most manufacturers.

Suzuki SC 100

AUSTIN MINI METRO ID, E, L & HLE

The Metro has formidable rivals: VW Polo, Ford Fiesta, Renault 5, Peugeot 104, Opel Kadett, Citroën Visa Super and Ford Escort 1100. The engine is derived from the original A series power unit introduced 30 years ago, 803 cc developing 28 bhp in 1950 and 998 cc developing 46 bhp in 1980. It has the same basic format with a three bearing crankshaft and vertical valves with push-rods, siamesed ports and bath-tub combustion chamber, as developed by Harry Weslake.

The gearbox is also the same, and the suspension and steering similar, but the brakes are more sophisticated. Fortunately, the original from which it is derived was a good fore-runner, and efficient. The co-ordination of engine/gearbox above each other was good for the Mini, and the Mini, with some attention from Cooper, won the Monte Carlo rally several times.

There are also two redoubtable precedents for continual development on a basic design – the VW Beetle and Rolls-Royce 20/25 and 25/30 engines.

The improvements to the Metro engine include an inlet air temperature control device, a crankshaft torsional damper, nimonic exhaust valves, a hydraulic timing chain tensioner, stiffening ribs to the cylinder block, larger drive belt pulleys, a special new SU carburettor, improved piston rings, new contact breaker points and a redesigned oil filter.

The design of the Metro's bodyshell followed a convoluted path of two major changes of basic design, three design directors, the employment and rejection of two well-known designers, Michelotti and Pininfarina, and the final acceptance of a design by home grown David Bache which is the best of them all. This design took eight years from its inception in 1972.

There were two uppermost factors in the brief – a good fuel consumption figure and generous space, and both have been realised. The torsional stiffness of the bodyshell is 5900 ft/lb per degree, which is better than average. The Metro has two sub-frames, front and rear, rubber mounted to the body structure, and designed for noise and vibration suppression.

That well-known engine, developed still further

Austin Mini Metro Base, L and (HLE)

Engine: A+ overhead valve 4 cylinders in line transverse
Capacity: 998 cc
Bore; stroke: 64.6 mm   76.2 mm
Compression ratio: 9.6 to 1 (10.3 to 1)
Carburation: HIF 38
Max. power at 5400 (5600) rpm: 45 (47) bhp   33.6 (35) kW
Max. torque at 3000 (3250) rpm: 53 ft/lb   71.9 Nm

Transmission: 4 speed manual. Final drive ratio is 3.44 for the HLE compared with 3.647 (giving 16.3 mph/1000 rpm in top) on the Base and L

Suspension: Hydragas suspension all independent.
Front: unequal length upper and lower arms with anti-roll bar
Rear: trailing radius arms and coil spring helpers

Steering: Rack and pinion 3.3 turns lock to lock
Turning circle: 33 ft 6 in   10.2 m

Brakes: Dual circuit with 8.3 in (21 cm) discs on front, 7 in (17.8 cm) drums on rear

Dimensions:
Length: 11 ft 2 in   3.4 m
Kerb weight: 1638 (1646) lb   743 (747) kg

Performance:
Maximum speed: 87 (88) mph   140 (141) km/h
0–60 mph: 16.6 (18.2) sec
Fuel consumption
   at 56 mph: 53.1 (58.3) mpg   5.3 (4.8) litres/100 km
   at 75 mph: 38.5 (41.7) mpg   7.3 (6.8) litres/100 km
   urban: 38.4 (41.5) mpg   7.4 (6.8) litres/100 km

Insurance Rating: 2

Derived Data:
bhp/litre (kW/litre): 45.1 (47.1)   33.6 (35)
bhp/ton (kW/tonne): 52.9 (56.2)   39.4 (41.8)
Speed × acceleration: 5.24 (4.83)
Performance Dimension: 9.9 (8.6)
Petrol consumption/ton at 56 mph (10/F): 6.4 (1.56)   (5.8 (1.72)
Change in petrol consumption between 56 & 75 mph: 38% (40%)

The American PSE (Passenger space efficiency) ratio, in which the sum of the maximum front legroom and the couple distance (between the hip joints of front and rear passengers) is expressed as a percentage of the overall length of the car, shows the Metro in a good light:

	PSE ratio (%)
Metro	50.0
Fiat 127	47.2
Ford Fiesta	48.9
Renault 5	47.4
VW Polo	47.1

The Metro has a larger boot than any of its rivals, and more legroom and shoulder room. It is efficient in its use of space because it capitalizes on Issigonis' engine over gearbox design, and the rear subframe allows a low flat floor and small wheel arch intrusions. The heating and ventilation are good, the instrumentation clear and the ride and handling as good as the overall design.

The most panoramic of the small cars, and elegant with it

17

FORD ESCORT 1100

We see in the latest Escort a typical example of the Ford company's efficient and direct attack on demand. For its overall size the car is remarkably spacious with a comfortable and relaxed position for the driver, and more than adequate accommodation generally for all but the most demanding of passengers. Again the car is marketed in five forms from the most spartan and utilitarian to the most viciously sporting as an XR3.

As usual with Ford, one over-simplifies to say there are a mere five versions to choose from. It might be amusing to note that there are some 2^{40}, or roughly a million million potentially different versions of the basic saloon alone to choose between. While Ford are clearly over optimistic if they think they are ever likely to sell all possible varieties, they have, we think, hit something of a winner in the Escort. It has the cleanest of lines and now handles with great solidity: a safe and yet delightfully driveable car. After early problems the suspension, all independent, gives a very good ride and in even the much more powerful versions of the car, the

best handling that could be expected.

Interesting comparisons can be made, both with the Fiesta and between the various engined forms of the Escort. Here we are interested primarily in the 1117 cc engined car which, on Ford's basic data, has a performance dimension very similar to, but clearly better than, that of the Fiesta. The more marked difference between the cars is apparent on examining the ratified figures for the cars' fuel consumptions. Not only are the figures for the Escort at all speeds and in urban driving better than those of the Fiesta, but given the added weight of the car under review it is clear, on comparing fuel efficiency with performance that considerable improvements have been made in the Escort's efficiency.

A major part of the improvement in efficiency undoubtedly centres on the Escort's cleaner lines, this being the more apparent when it is realised that the gross frontal area of the Escort is about 10 per cent greater than that of the Fiesta. It will be remembered

Left: *Ford bodyshell designs have been improved steadily and now have such good features, visually, that they probably will not date so noticeably as they used to. This is the estate version*

Right: *Simple and easy to service, the engine can be maintained quite readily by an enthusiast*

Ford Escort 1100 L/GL

Engine: Four cylinders in line, ohv transverse, cast iron block and head
Capacity: 1117 cc
Bore; stroke: 74 mm   65 mm
Compression ratio: 9.0 to 1
Carburation: Ford
Max. power at 5700 rpm: 55 bhp   41 kW
Max. torque at 4000 rpm: 60.7 ft/lb   82.4 Nm

Transmission: Four speed manual, front wheel drive

Suspension:
Front: independent MacPherson struts with coil springs.
Rear: independent swinging arms and coil springs with tie bars

Steering: Rack and pinion, 3.69 turns lock to lock
Turning circle (kerbs): 32 ft 11 in   10.03 m

Brakes: Dual line, servo assistance optional. 9.5 in (24 cm) discs on front and 7 in (17.8 cm) drums on rear

Dimensions:
Length: 13 ft 3.5 in   4.05 m
Kerb weight: 1752 lb   795 kg

Performance:
Maximum speed: 90 mph*   145 km/h
0–60 mph: 13.6 sec*
Fuel consumption
   at 56 mph: 49.6 mpg   5.7 litres/100 km
   at 75 mph: 36.2 mpg   7.8 litres/100 km
   urban: 34.9 mpg   8.1 litres/100 km
*Ford computed data

Insurance Rating: 3

Derived Data:
bhp/litre (kW/litre): 49.2   36.7
bhp/ton (kW/tonne): 62.3   45.8
Speed × acceleration: 6.6
Performance Dimension: 10.6
Petrol consumption/ton at 56 mph (10/F): 6.46   (1.55)
Change in petrol consumption between 56 & 75 mph: 37%

that for a given drag factor and speed the force due to air resistance is proportional to the frontal area.

The Escort in even the 1117 cc engined form is generally a nippy and enjoyable car to drive. It stands out extraordinarily however in the way in which its Performance Dimension is steadily improved as its power is increased. With the CVM 1300 cc engine it attains a PD figure of 11.3, while the XR3, with an acceleration time of only 8.6 seconds to 60 mph, is a genuine sports car attaining a figure of 13.4. The standard 1.6 litre CVH engined model has the intermediate PD of 12.2, while even more remarkable is the fact that the cars' figures are maintained almost unchanged for the estates.

Our feeling, however, is that much of the cars' appeal is lost in estate form while sufficient and sensible use of the very adequate storage space of the Escort saloon is made with the hatchback. The car can incidentally be bought in both three and five door form. If it were not for the remarkable conservatism of the average car buyer,

it's difficult to see how this added option would not finally drive the Fiesta owner to the Escort, even if he did not appreciate the latter car's generally more graceful lines. The Escort is perhaps a little bit more ashamedly a small 'big car' rather than a genuine baby, so perhaps those who insist on sticking to the established performer will hang on to the more genuine small car image of the Fiesta for a little longer.

For us the Escort is an exceptional car in many of these classes. It gives performance with potential reliability, being modern but not wickedly *outré* either mechanically or in style. At the same time it does not hang on to old fashioned approaches to anything like the same degree as the average unbreakable Japanese machine. The latest Escort will do well deservedly.

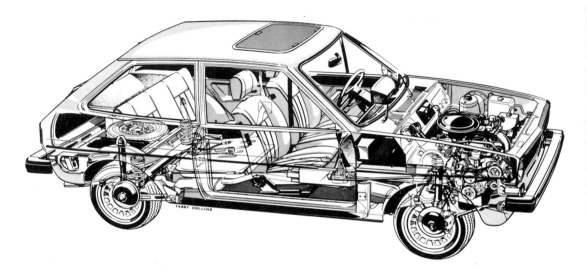

FORD FIESTA 1100 GL

Ford have the knack of seeing a need in the market place and filling it efficiently. The Fiesta, as a three-door hatchback in one form or another, has been doing well for five years: in the first four years of production alone over 1.5 million were built. The car nominated in the 500–1200 cc class is the relatively recently introduced GL version of the 1117 cc engined model, but whether the new car buyer gets an L, the S, a Ghia or the basic saloon, is fairly immaterial.

To keep to the spirit of the business we would suggest that the serious minded should stick firmly to the basic saloon, but there are probably some arguments for the plusher versions. Secondhand values in the longer term certainly tend to remain a little higher for 'extra' cars, and given the number generally available they are also usually easier to sell. The more careful purchaser might also note that, neglecting colour and trim, there are a further thirty or so option variations between the five models mentioned.

Much more important is the choice of engine size.

Generally one finds that a car performs well with only one particular size of engine. The Fiesta is however fairly unusual in that performance dimensions for the 950 cc and 1100 cc engined cars are virtually identical. At the set speeds the 950 cc engine gives marginally better fuel efficiency, but under normal circumstances one would suspect that the average driver would tend to need that little more power which the 1117 cc engine, even if a little long in the tooth, can give.

The data for the 1300 cc version are given above for comparison and it is clear that not only is the performance improved substantially in absolute terms by the incorporation of the still larger engine but so too is the behaviour of the car relative to the average performance behavioural line. A PD of 11.3 for a relatively small car is fairly exceptional. We see from the figures for fuel economy that this is only achieved with a decrease in economy.

A comparison of the positions of the two versions of the car on the efficiency versus PD graph shows that the

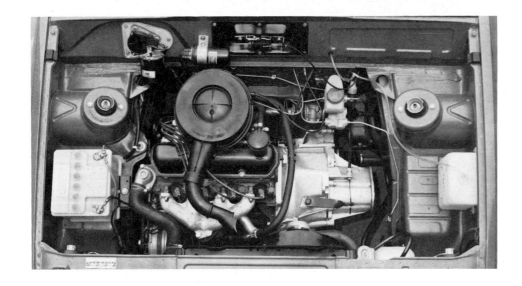

Opposite: *Strength and simplicity can be seen in the design and construction*

Right: *Clean, competent and very compact, the Fiesta engine lends itself to DIY maintenance*

Ford Fiesta 1100 GL (1300 GL)

Engine: Four cylinders in line, ohv transverse cast iron block and head
Capacity: 1117 (1298) cc
Bore; stroke: 74 (81) mm 65 (63) mm
Compression ratio: 9.0 (9.2) to 1
Carburation: Ford single venturi downdraught (Weber 32/32 DFT)
Max. power at 5700 (6500) rpm: 53 (66) bhp 39.5 (49.2) kW
Max. torque at 3000 (5000) rpm: 59.3 (68) ft/lb 80.5 (92.3) Nm

Transmission: Four speed manual, front wheel drive

Suspension:
Front: independent MacPherson struts with coil springs.
Rear: dead beam axle with five link location by trailing arms and Panhard rod, coil springs and anti-roll bar

Steering: Rack and pinion, 3.4 turns lock to lock
Turning circle: 29 ft 11 in 9.1 m

Brakes: Dual line diagonally split servo assisted. 8.7 in (22.1 cm) front discs and 8 in (20.3 cm) rear drums

Dimensions:
Length: 11 ft 8 ½ in 3.57 m
Kerb weight: 1609 (1769) lb 730 (802) kg

Performance:
Maximum speed: 90 (95.4) mph 145 (153.5) km/h
0–60 mph: 13.7 (11.3) sec
Fuel consumption
  at 56 mph: 47.1 (44.1) mpg 6.0 (6.4) litres/100 km
  at 75 mph: 33.6 mpg 8.4 litres/100 km
  urban: 32.1 (31.4) mpg 8.8 (9.0) litres/100 km

Insurance Rating: 2

Derived Data:
bhp/litre (kW/litre): 47.4 (50.8) 35.4 (37.9)
bhp/ton (kW/tonne): 64.8 (74.2) 47.5 (54.4)
Speed × acceleration: 6.6 (8.44)
Performance Dimension: 10.1 (11.3)
Petrol consumption/ton at 56 mph (10/F): 7.33 (7.2)1.36 (1.38)
Change in petrol consumption between 56 & 75 mph: 40% (31.2%)

---

trend between the two is about midway between the CD and AB types of behaviour. If one was thinking of breaking with the hairshirt syndrome, it's difficult to see how one could avoid buying the Escort 1300 rather than the bigger engined Fiesta, clearly good though the latter car is. The 1117 cc Fiesta is however by no means a total sloucher. While the whole point of the car is perhaps to avoid the tendency to the racing gear change, it's difficult to see why Ford persist with what can best be described, at least subjectively, as a rubber gear lever, though the clutch is pleasantly positive.

Essentially however, while the GL package can give one a whole host of 'in car entertainments' from cigarette lighters to vanity mirrors and a carpeted luggage compartment, perhaps the major attribute of the car is the surprisingly open unclaustrophobic feeling it can give, coupled with a simplicity appropriate to the car's class. By comparison with the small engined Escort it is not a modern looking car, but nor is it ostentaciously old fashioned.

Similarly, mechanically there is little in the Fiesta that could be described as brand new in concept, though this has the distinct advantage of lending, at least potential, reliability. As a car to drive the Fiesta could hardly be described as exciting, but despite having fairly limited feel, the car's handling is essentially good if not excellent. It certainly hangs on to corners with little roll and a lot more positive assurance than appearances might lead one to expect.

All in all the Fiesta is popular for good reason. It's a sound and sensible car, clean of limb, far from flashy and solidly sensible without being heavily dated.

OPEL KADETT 1.2 IC 4 DOOR

It was always going to be interesting to see what General Motors would come up with once they set about the front wheel drive hatchback market. They seem to have examined the German market and the VW Golf rather more carefully than the perhaps brighter and lighter potential rival, the Fiesta.

The new Kadett comes in a number of different forms though the same body profile serves the 2 and 4 door saloons as well as the 3/5 door hatchbacks. The bodyshell is undoubtedly efficient with a drag coefficient of 0.39 and the front view of the car is as clean limbed as this figure might imply. From the rear however the car has a slightly hunched appearance perhaps as a result of the rear window being relatively shallow, by comparison with that of many other hatchbacks. The all round visibility is however generally very good.

The Vauxhall Astra as a 3 or 5 door hatchback is extremely closely related to the Kadett and is also built in Germany. In 1.3 litre form the cars use identical engines and while the Astra is marginally heavier it

seems surprising that the Kadett achieves acceleration figures, as reported by *Motor*, so much better than those for the Astra.

The differences are rather larger in the 1.2 litre form of the two cars of interest to us here, and the Astra then retains a higher bhp and compression ratio with marginally better fuel economy. In fact it's probably only on the relatively purist grounds that the smaller Kadett came first that it is preferred here to the Astra.

Both cars are somewhat heavier than their competitors, and it is mainly for this reason that neither manages to outperform either the small Fiesta or the new smaller engined Escorts. It is for other reasons that the Kadett is included here. The extra weight would appear to have gone to sensible use. When for example we examine the MacPherson strut front suspension of the Kadett we find it particularly unusual in that the front wheels are set forward, with the drive shafts angling back from the wheel hubs to the differentials.

The anti-roll bar is operated by short push rods from

Opposite above and below: *A possible contender for the small world car title, the Kadett has the simple, rugged strength of a car which has been designed to accept everyday wear and tear without losing its quality*

Right: *Simplicity of layout belies the well-designed engine with chain-driven camshaft*

Opel Kadett 1.2 litre N (4 door)

Engine: 4 cylinders in line, transversely mounted, cast iron head and block. Chain driven high level cam
Capacity: 1196 cc
Bore; stroke: 79 mm   61 mm
Compression ratio: 7.8 to 1
Carburation: Solex 30 PDSI
Max. power at 5400 rpm: 53 bhp   39 kW
Max. torque at 3400 rpm: 60.4 ft/lb   82 Nm

Transmission: 4 speed manual gearbox. Front wheel drive with asymmetric drive shafts with two homokinetic joints

Suspension:
Front: independent with MacPherson struts, torsion bar stabilizers optional.
Rear: compound crank rear suspension with miniblock progressive rate springs

Steering: Rack and pinion 3.9 turns lock to lock

Brakes: Diagonally split dual circuit, assisted, with front discs and rear drums

Dimensions:
Length: 13 ft 1.5 in   4 m
Kerb weight: 1837 lb   833.3 kg

Performance:
Maximum speed: 89 mph   143 km/h
0–60 mph: 15.1 (18.5) sec
Fuel consumption
    at 56 mph: 44.8 mpg   6.3 litres/100 km
    urban: 29.7 mpg   9.5 litres/100 km

Insurance Rating: 3

Derived Data:
bhp/litre (kW/litre): 44.3   32.6
bhp/ton (kW/tonne): 57.6   41.7
Speed × acceleration: 5.89   [4.8]
Performance Dimension: 10.5   [8.5]
Petrol consumption/ton at 56 mph (10/F): 6.85   (1.45)
[ ] manufacturer's data

the lower wishbones, which are also swept back so that the wheel hubs are well ahead of the inboard pivots. The rear suspension has very wide semi-trailing arms rather like the Polo, and the conical variable rate coil springs look very effective in this configuration. The result of the endeavour is undoubtedly extremely good handling. At high speeds the feel is satisfyingly neutral and in the wet it is both remarkably forgiving and very solid. A tendency to mild understeer is immediately countered in a well balanced way by easing off the power. In a sense the smaller engined cars have handling characteristics which far outstrip their general performance, though this can hardly be a fault!

The plusher larger engined versions of the Kadett are still by no means as well equipped as many of their rivals, and the small Kadett is, if hardly spartan, certainly fairly basic. In this it should suit the tastes of the determined small car driver, but it's a pity that the car, despite looking generally well put together, is rather on the noisy side.

Where the car's simplicity really scores is in the functional and clearly styled facia. The instruments are few but they are clearly legible and free from reflection while the warning lights are simple and readily interpretable. The stalk controls, too, are well above average, and we generally liked the siting of the subsidiary lighting and heating controls in the centre of the facia.

This is a car which is undoubtedly better in larger engined form but must be retained in our smallest car class mainly for its handling and cleanliness.

SUZUKI SC 100 GX IGH

This is a relatively new and interesting rear engined car, a bit reminiscent of a Honda in its apparent bulkiness, which in fact belies its small frontal area and low height. The car is remarkably cheap and perhaps on that basis comparison with older designs of potential European rivals shows it up too well. Given the universal acclaim the car testing fraternity has given this recent Japanese import, it might be as well to examine it more closely.

Starting with the car's good points, it undoubtedly handles extremely well, with a responsive and delightfully light rack and pinion steering. This in itself, given the rear engine, says a lot for the fairly conventional suspension. The car's performance is also very good, with both top speed and acceleration figures far superior to those for cars like the 850 Mini, Fiat 127, or Renault 4. Equally, the car's fuel consumption is far from bad, and particularly good at lower speeds. Furthermore the car is generally well equipped and finished for its class, and not uncomfortable if a little cramped: luggage space in particular is rather hard to find.

What then is the problem? Essentially it is that it ought to work still better than it does. The car is very light indeed for its engine power. Admittedly it is not an easy car to assess in terms of its basic data: errors, for example, associated with the differences between unladen and kerb weight and 'weight as tested' rear their head. It will be remembered that the weight used in our performance dimension is the kerb weight plus 224 lb, a figure generally less than that for most car tests but fair, given the way we have used the figure comparatively. Given our general surprise at the car's figures, we have however used in this case both our standard addition, to give an effective weight of 1613 lb, and the weight as actually tested by *Motor* (1803 lb). Figures in brackets in our derived data refer to the use of this latter figure. Also in this case DIN figures for the brake horse power and torque were not available, only SAE values which, being subject to gear train losses, are lower. Admittedly, for such a small car, the DIN values will not be much larger than the figures known, so we

Opposite: *A spirited and extremely economical small car*

Right: *The silhouette is noticeably Japanese*

Suzuki SC 100 GX

Engine: 4 cylinders in line, alloy head with sohc belt driven. Transverse rear mounted
Capacity: 970 cc
Bore; stroke: 65.5 mm   72 mm
Compression ratio: 9.0 to 1
Carburation: Mikuri 30 PHD
Max. power at 5000 rpm: 47 (SAE) 50 bhp   37.3 kW
Max. torque at 2500 rpm: 61.3 (SAE) 65 ft/lb   88.2 Nm
DIN figures estimated as $\sim$ 6% higher than SAE

Transmission: 4 speed manual

Suspension:
Front: coil springs. Independent by double wishbone with anti-roll bar acting as lower forward link.
Rear: coil springs. Independent by semi trailing arms

Steering: Rack and pinion 3.1 turns lock to lock
Turning circle: 27 ft 6 in   8.4 m

Brakes: Dual circuit splint front/rear with 7.5 in (19.1 cm) discs on front, 7.1 in (18 cm) drums on rear

Dimensions:
Length: 10 ft 6 in   3.2 m
Weight unladen: 1389 lb   630 kg
Weight as tested: 1803 lb   818 kg
Performance:
Maximum speed: 82 mph   132 km/h
0–60 mph: 17.3 sec
Fuel consumption
   at 56 mph: 56.5 mpg   5.0 litres/100 km
   at 75 mph: 40 mpg   7.1 litres/100 km
   urban: 41.9 mpg   6.7 litres/100 km
Insurance Rating: 2
Derived Data:
bhp/litre (kW/litre): 51.5   38.5
bhp/ton (kW/tonne): 69.4 (62.1)   50.9 (45.6)
Speed $\times$ acceleration: 4.74
Performance Dimension: 6.8 (7.6)
Petrol consumption/ton at 56 mph (10/F): 6.9 (6.2)   1.44 (1.61)
Change in petrol consumption between 56 & 75 mph: 42%
(Bracketed figures use weight as tested)

have taken the minimum difference we think fair, estimating a 6 per cent increase in both figures, to give the DIN values.

A glance at the derived data is sufficient to make the point. The car's very high power to weight ratio means that its performance figures, although far from bad, give it a performance dimension of 6.8 which is really fairly appalling. Even if we use the as-tested weight, which is unfair to the car's competitors, but serves to demonstrate the maximum error in the approach, the figure is still only raised to 7.6.

Again, while a fuel consumption of only 5 litres/ 100 km at 90 km/h is pretty good, as a figure/ton at between 6.9 and 6.2 litres/100 km/ton the fuel consumption is far too high for the performance if the car follows the likely CD behavioural line common to small economy cars of this type.

These comments will be better understood on examination of the performance graphs in the Summary (p. 28). It would seem extremely unlikely that this car does not follow the general trends which we have shown to be followed by all cars whose data we have examined, so on this basis we can only conclude phenomenologically that the car should have a lower petrol consumption and have better performance figures than it has.

Perhaps the most sensible attitude to take at this point is, 'so what?' The car *is* economic and *does* perform well and *is* fun. It would thus appear that Suzuki have managed all this, not necessarily by pristine engineering so much as by making the car very light; perhaps with the added advantage of making it at least potentially (as an under-performer) rather reliable.

The Polo is in many ways the best of the VW bodyshells. Designed at Bertone, it has a simple grace which some of the other cars in the range lack

VOLKSWAGEN POLO GLS (E)

The Polo, like the Fiesta which it slightly predates, has been around for some time. It can still be purchased with the original 895 cc engine but the 1093 cc unit has been used in the LS and later GLS model since 1977. Most of the changes over the last year or two have been essentially cosmetic. After all the Polo is essentially sound, handles well, and is perhaps fractionally up market of most of its rivals even if it marginally under-performs them.

The introduction of the new E class in 1981 has thus been interesting. The changes throughout the VW range are fairly drastic, and in the smaller car somewhat overdue in view of the increasing competition from cars such as the Escort and Metro on fuel economy grounds.

It is first worthwhile noting that there is not an E for 'Economy' version of the 895 cc Polo: it's in general much easier to improve the slightly bigger cars, as we have already noted for other makes of car in the class. The GLS is by no means thirsty as it stands. With a performance dimension of 10.8 (using figures based on

the half laden weight which is perhaps a little charitable) and a fuel efficiency figure of 1.45, it's already doing rather better than the Fiesta, but nowhere near as well as either the Escort all round or the Metro in terms of economy.

Fortunately for VW, they had an easy first move to make with the engine, and this was to increase its compression ratio, thus naturally increasing its efficiency. The problems with compression ratios world wide are really to some extent political: higher values demand high octane petrol with lead additions to prevent preignition, and it is interesting that the figure has been taken as high as it has for the Polo.

The designers could, of course, then have gone all-out for the improved performance, which would have naturally become available with an appropriately ratioed gearbox. Instead, and presumably in the face of market demand and competition, the performance figures, at least for the Polo, have been carefully stage managed to be the same as in the lower compression

An acceptable facia, well designed and practical. It could never be dated to the point of ridicule because it is so functional

---

Volkswagen Polo GLS (E)

Engine: Four cylinders in line, transverse front mounted, ohc belt driven
Capacity: 1093 cc
Bore; stroke: 69.5 mm   72 mm
Compression ratio: 8.0 to 1   (E 9.7 to 1)
Max. power at 5800 rpm: 50 bhp   37 kW
Max. torque at 3500 rpm: 57 ft/lb   77 Nm

Transmission: Four speed manual gearbox (4th gear on E is overdrive)

Suspension:
Front: suspension struts and lower wishbones combined with transverse stabilizer.
Rear: torsion beam, centre coupled trailing arm axle

Steering: Rack and pinion
Turning circle: 31 ft 6 in   9.6 m

Brakes: Diagonally divided dual circuit with discs at front, drums at rear

Dimensions:
Length: 11 ft 10 in   3.6 m
Weight unladen: 1510 lb   685 kg
½ laden weight: 2073 lb   940 kg

Performance:
Maximum speed: 90 mph
0–60 mph: 15.4 sec
Fuel consumption
at 56 mph: 44.1 (55.4) mpg   6.4 (5.1) litres/100 km
at 75 mph: 32.5 (39.8) mpg   8.7 (7.1) litres/100 km
urban: 31 (40.4) mpg   9.1 (7.0) litres/100 km

Insurance Rating: 3

Derived Data:
bhp/litre (kW/litre): 45.7   33.8
bhp/ton (kW/tonne): 54.1   39.3
Speed × acceleration: 5.84
Performance Dimension: 10.8
Petrol consumption/ton at 56 mph (10/F): 6.9 (5.5)   (1.45) (1.81)
Change in petrol consumption between 56 & 75 mph: 36% (39%)

GLS model, while the gearing overall has been altered to allow third gear to give the car's top speed, fourth gear thus becoming an overdrive.

The changes in fuel efficiency for a number of the VW models are fairly dramatic in their Economy suiting, but it could be argued that in most cases the petrol consumption has simply been brought into line with that of the competition. This is not the case for the new 1093 cc engined Polo. Clearly other radical changes have been made to the carburation, combustion chamber design and camshaft, to achieve the exceptional fuel economy figure of 1.81. It is thus in a way a pity that the designers didn't follow through their engine improvements with a five speed gearbox, thus allowing improved performance as well. Presumably, however, the pressures of market competition have dictated their approach, and there isn't anyway a great deal of point in giving the car much added performance, given the other models in the VW range.

The further changes in the E cars include a very

sensible stop-start electronic control system for use in traffic. As news releases have somewhat enigmatically noted: 'extensive studies by VW engineers have shown that fuel can be saved by switching off the car engine completely in traffic if the stop is for more than five seconds'. The system, operated by a button on the steering column stalk, very sensibly only operates when the car is at a standstill, and is cancelled by depressing the clutch and touching the accelerator. The formula E models also have a gear change indicator to educate the driver, and a consumption gauge telling him his rate of fuel consumption when in the appropriate gear.

The Polo, by the standards of some of its rivals such as the Metro or Escort, looks a little rounded and dated, but it handles well and in the GLS form has sufficient performance and excellent handling. The formula E modifications put the car back into serious contention, certainly making it the most economic (and least polluting) car in its class for its performance.

500–1200 cc: SUMMARY

Most of the major manufacturers have dabbled in the baby car market at one time or another. Rather surprisingly, as we have seen in the introduction to this section, the criteria balance defining 'the best' is rather difficult to sort out. We are certainly not concerned solely with cheapness and lowness of running costs. Indeed a number of buyers in the area would often appear to be exhibiting at least a degree of inverted snobbery: their car being an advertisement for how little they care about such trivia.

The continued popularity of the 2 CV, Dyane, Fiat 126 and the old Renault 4TL would perhaps have something to do with this; though we admit to a fair amount of affection for the first and the last in this list. The 2CV in particular is both surprisingly roomy and comfortable and endearingly bizarre.

We really ought, however, to assume that we are not dealing exclusively with masochists or car haters. On that basis we must turn to the more rational approach that purchasers in the range are interested in: a convenient 'about town' car, economical in all ways, with a reasonably nippy traffic behaviour, adequate space for the shopping, but definitely neither the room nor the comforts to take granny and all the children to Moscow except in dire emergency.

Those that really want to travel a reasonable distance regularly really ought to consider spending a little more initially. It is, after all, because most people do so that the next size range, of the 1200–1500 cc cars, tends to be both considerably better value for money and in general rather better engineered. That this in turn is so is not entirely a result of supply and demand: the smaller the size of a car, the more difficult it is to provide the essential requirements, without the power to weight ratio becoming so appalling that the car has to be flogged to death to get it up the drive into the garage.

Furthermore while petrol efficiency can be good at low speeds, simply because the engine is even then run at high efficiency, increased speeds result in disproportionate increases in petrol consumption. Again the generally relatively high power to cubic capacity ratios required for even adequate performance suggests engine stresses which make one somewhat nervous about reliability.

With these points in mind a surprisingly large number of the thirty or so cars in the class can be discounted from our choice of the 'best' with ease. The old Mini, though ridiculously good for its vintage, just has to be mothballed, if only on the grounds that we ought to be able to do better by now.

The relatively new Visas are interesting, but the smaller engined version is not much better than the 2CV and the super E with its 1124 cc power plant, though acclaimed by many, does not do as well as it ought to. The same can be said for the Daihatsu Charade and Suzuki 100GX, since the two Datsun Cherries are both lower powered, and both perform more respectably. Fiat, with typically Italian gusto, manage to have the two cars in the range with the poorest and best performance, and the 127 Sport certainly has good standards of roadholding, but are they good enough? We find the car a bit frightening, despite the packaging being tempting.

The Peugeot 104 GL and ZR have rather more to offer in smoothness, though for this sort of firm if somewhat noisy ride perhaps one ought to be French. Again the Renault 5TL, though perfectly adequate if a bit more utilitarian, and certainly more interesting to look at, only just creeps onto the good car side of the average performance line. Toyota, though giving a reasonable amount for the money, don't manage this feat either, and the VW Derby and Talbot Sunbeam are both system designed for more powerful engines and thus don't come off in the class.

On grounds of efficiency, and this in many ways must, at least logically, be of primal concern in this group, the cars that stand out are the Metro L, the 957 cc and 1117 cc powered Ford Fiesta, the smallest engined Ford Escort, the Opel Kadett L and the VW Polo in its E package. Data for the Golf in both standard and Economy form are given in the article on the Golf GTi, and presented in our graphs of the data. This car is perhaps more properly a member of the larger engined classes.

Opel Kadett.

The Metro, much to our surprise, really is rather good, if having the poorest performance in our 'best' group (excluding the rather odd Suzuki). Its space utilization is excellent, the suspension works to give excellent handling and roadholding and it should last.

The Opel Kadett is a somehow typically good product of this manufacturer, making the older Chevettes seem positively cantankerous and cheap. Interestingly, its fuel efficiency figure splits that of the Escort and Fiesta, though its performance in absolute terms would appear to be poorer than that of either of the Ford cars. For those with a more rugged approach, the smallest engined Escort is exceptional, if only in that this is one of the few cars which remain efficiently engineered for the full range of engine sizes used (if, that is, we accept Ford's performance figures).

The two best cars in the group are undoubtedly the Ford Fiesta and the VW Polo, particularly in E format where the car's fuel efficiency with retained performance is staggering. Both engine sizes in the Fiesta outperform their counterparts in the Polo, but the latter car feels more solid and smooth. With tendencies towards comfort one would buy the Polo E; with a bit more firmness and chastity, the 1117 cc Fiesta.

Class I   Data Summary

Datum Point		Perform-ance	Power/Weight	PD	FE
A	Austin Mini Metro L	5.2	53	9.9	1.56
B	Austin Mini Metro HLE	4.8	56	8.6	1.72
C	Ford Escort 1100	6.6	62	10.6	1.55
D	Ford Fiesta 1100	6.6	65	10.1	1.36
E	Opel Kadett 1.2	5.9	58	10.5	1.45
F1	Suzuki SC 100 GX	4.7	69	6.8	1.44
F2	Suzuki SC 100 GX	4.7	62	7.6	1.61
G	VW Polo GLS	5.8	54	10.8	1.45
H	VW Polo E	5.8	54	10.8	1.81

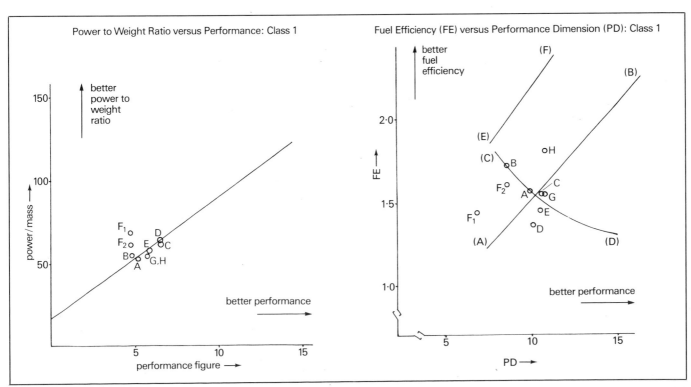

2 The Measure of Performance

We have already seen that if we multiply a car's maximum speed by its acceleration, the result is, on average, linearly related to the maximum power output per ton. It was for this reason that we introduced in Chapter 1 the Performance Dimension (PD) as the ratio of these quantities or, in a sense, a measure of what a car will do for what it's got. While performance alone should rarely be the sole reason for the choice of a particular motor car, our PD can potentially tell us a lot. We must thus examine rather carefully what the formula means, and whether it is a reliable guide to an individual car's performance. We must also explain the relationship sufficiently so that the keen DIY enthusiast with a pocket calculator can compare his latest purchase with his old and trusted push-rod overhead inlet, side valve exhaust that always seemed to go so well.

In order to do this we will need to understand how to express the terms we are using, like work and power, in terms of simpler 'properties' such as mass (M), length (L) and time (T). This threesome are commonly described as 'fundamental dimensions' in the sense that individually they cannot be described in terms of any other property. It is easy, however, to see how other properties can be described, and thus related, using these fundamental dimensions. For example, how do we work out the speed of a car? It is the distance travelled, L, divided by the time taken, T: it must have the dimensions L/T. Similarly, 'acceleration' is the rate at which speed is increased and is therefore expressable as speed divided by time or L/T^2. Through our common experience we are also aware how an object of a given mass can be accelerated by applying a 'force' to it. The force needed will depend on the mass of the object and on how big an acceleration we wish to produce. Thus we can express the dimensions of a force as mass times acceleration or ML/T^2. If a force acts for a given distance on a mass, either to accelerate it or to move it at a constant speed against other forces which would otherwise slow it down, 'work' is done and 'energy' used. Both these terms then have the dimensions of force times distance, or ML^2/T^2. But how do we define the 'power' of a car engine? Power, P, is the amount of work the engine can do per second, so this too can be expressed in terms of our fundamental threesome by saying that P has the dimensions: ML^2/T^3. We can now immediately see the dimensional relationship of interest here. If we rewrite P as

$$M \times \frac{L}{T} \times \frac{L}{T^2}$$

it becomes clear that a car of power P and mass M has a 'power to mass ratio' of P/M, and that this has the dimensions of speed times acceleration. That this is so does not, however, mean that there *has* to be a relationship of the type we have discovered. Indeed at maximum speed the power of a car is being used to overcome friction in the drive train, against which work will be done at a rate which will tend to be proportional to the speed, and wind resistance. The retarding force which the air exerts is roughly proportional to the square of the speed or L^2/T^2. In neither case is the mass of the car directly relevant. By contrast, at low speeds the rate at which a car can be accelerated would be expected to be inversely proportional to its mass while the maximum torque which can be applied as a function of both the engine and drive train characteristics might appear to be more important than the maximum power available.

However, a car designer generally wants both good acceleration and a high maximum speed and this requires a balancing act. While the shape of a car is just about irrelevant in considering its acceleration, the frontal area is very important in determining the air drag forces. Again there is a limit to which the mass can be reduced to improve the acceleration: the car has to have structural integrity and a sufficiently strong gear train to transfer the power to the road wheels. Furthermore it is perhaps particularly important to take note of another result from our common experience which might be conveniently expressed as: 'Nobody ever got anything for nothing.' What this boils down to is that work cannot be done without using at *least* an equal amount of energy. The more nearly the two turn out to be equal the greater the efficiency with which the job is done.

Table I	Manufacturers' Data				
	A	B	C	D	E
	Speed (mph)	Acceleration (seconds to 60 mph)	Mass (cwt)	Capacity (cubic cm)	bhp
Pram	71	18.8	13	950	40.5
Mouse	91	11.8	15	1300	61.2
Armadillo	110	12.3	21	2200	104.6
Chiaroscuro	113	9.5	18	1600	92
Bullet	118	9	19	2100	114.4
Windjammer	103	8	14	1500	100.8
Tub	129	8.3	20	2100	161.7

Table II	Derived Data					
	F	G	H	I	J	K
	bhp/ litre	P/M power to mass ratio	$L/T \times I/T^2$	Perform- ance Dimen- sion	Deviation from average as bhp	J as % of G
Pram	42.6	54	41	0.76	−4	−7.4
Mouse	47	72	77	1.07	+4	+5.5
Armadillo	47.5	91	89	0.98	−5	−5.5
Chiaroscuro	57.5	92	119	1.29	+17	+18.5
Bullet	54.5	109	131	1.20	+8	+7.3
Windjammer	67.2	126	129	1.02	−10	−7.9
Tub	77	147	155	1.05	−11	−7.1

Considering a more pragmatic approach, if we take all the car data and plot P/M for each car against its maximum speed multiplied by its acceleration, we find that all the points lie on or around a straight line. Bearing in mind the discussion above, it is then clear that the extent to which a particular car lies off the average line gives a fundamental measure of a car's quality. If it is better than the average, i.e. it lies below the straight line, it is giving more for a given power to mass ratio than expected, and is thus more efficient, better designed and engineered.

The principles involved in this form of car comparison are perhaps most easily understood by examining the data for seven hypothetical cars. In table I the 'manufacturer's' data for each of our imaginary group seem, at first sight, to be fairly standard. Most, however, have some exaggerated feature which we will see is brought to the surface when we make a comparison of their PD figures. If, of course, we were interested in speed or acceleration alone we would examine columns A and B and pick, depending on our preference, the Tub or the Windjammer. However, after very little work with the pocket calculator we could derive a few more figures from the basic data. We might then pick our car on the basis of engine stress: the Pram has the least power output/litre, but does this mean it is going to be reliable, or is it just badly designed or out of date? Alternatively we might guess that column G might provide an answer, and here the Tub again claims the

honours with the best power to weight ratio. On the other hand, taking the attitude that a bit of both is best, the product of the performance figures, in column H, suggests that the Bullet might strike home. The Chiaroscuro comes to the front only when we compare a car's performance (H) with its power to mass ratio (G). This is made abundantly clear by plotting H against G for all our hypothetical cars. The line is the average line for all cars and we see that, while the Mouse and Bullet aren't bad, it is the Chiaroscuro which gives the most for what it's got. It is this that suggests that this motor car is fundamentally better engineered and designed than the others.

To emphasize the point it might help to picture each of the cars from their basic data. The Pram in its day was indeed a good small car, but is now out of date. Similarly the Mouse, while more modern, is essentially ordinary while the Armadillo has long since past its prime. We imagined the Tub to be a Bullet with a bolt-on turbo conversion: this meant that a car with reasonable performance was thus unbalanced and while undoubtedly this improved its speed and acceleration, it ended up less good overall. The Windjammer is another conversion: this time we imagine a Mouse with bored out engine and lowered suspension stripped of just about anything removable. We now have fantastic acceleration, a sickeningly low engine life, and fairly bad all-round performance. This would again be because such a conversion could not retain the overall balance of the original design to make a fundamentally better car of improved performance we would have had to have started again, and this is what we have done for the Chiaroscuro.

In columns J and K in table II, showing the derived data, we have given figures for the difference of each of the cars from the average performance line. This is the best way of quantifying the data, but it is a bit complicated. When we describe how real cars behave throughout this book we give for each only the PD, because generally the bigger this is the better. It must, however, be remembered that bigger PD figures tend to be the rule for higher powered cars: the average performance line does not pass through the origin of our graph. In general, however, we compare cars of similar sizes in our classification scheme, so within each class comparisons of PDs alone are adequate.

Those readers who like to dip in and out of a book will gain a further understanding of the PD by reading our discussion of fuel efficiency (p. 92). To summarize this later chapter, we have found that if we compare a car's PD with the rate at which it uses fuel at constant speed we can get still more information. In general there are two trends, which can be seen in all the graphs in the class summaries throughout the book. There is a class of car which gains added performance relative to its power to weight ratio by using more fuel. (Or conversely can have a better fuel consumption only by making the PD worse.) This is the trend C–D. There is also a family, for which the engineers can only be praised, which manages improved fuel consumption and improved performance: the line A–B (paralleled in general for diesels by the trend E–F). We feel that this further emphasizes the Performance Dimension as a measure not just of performance but of overall engineering excellence.

Class 2   1200-1400cc

INTRODUCTION

These are the cars for those who have escaped from the smallest, or have never seen the point of being jolly and small. They want to travel, and not just shop, and yet have no wish for too many grand extras to be carried tortoise like around them. Ideally, the best cars should be not so slow as to drive passengers and driver alike mad on the motorway, have sufficient space for a bit of luggage and yet be small enough to nip in and out of the busy high street parking places. They should also, of course, be efficient in their use of fuel and be easily resaleable without too great a loss.

The main danger here of course is that we seem to be talking about a car which is neither one thing nor the other, and manufacturers and purchasers alike are liable to fall between two or perhaps three stools. A car, for example, which might appear to be nippy if a little noisy about town, but certainly pleasing and adequately roomy in such a mode, could well be singularly frustrating for that long journey. Alternatively, the slightly smoother, more comfortable, and generally larger vehicle, might use more petrol and depreciate more rapidly than might be desirable.

In general the current attitude to maximizing space in a small car is to have front wheel drive, while the 'hatchback' approach really can give that added flexibility in usage without the car becoming an estate. While we see hatchbacks in other groups, this is logically the type of usage and size of car to which the approach is best suited.

Already a popular size, undoubtedly there will be an increasing number of cars in this capacity in the near future because of the continuous rise in petrol costs. With a more positive leaning towards fuel efficiency and economy, there will probably be less emphasis on performance. Reduction in weight by the use of new materials will eventually improve the power/weight ratio and consequently both performance and efficiency. At the time of writing the new materials necessary were still prohibitively expensive.

Opel Kadett – rugged, well designed and reliable

CITROËN GSA CLUB and PALLAS SALOON

It might be hoped that the current minority of car buyers who admire the innovative in engineering design and style will increase. Like all Citroëns, the GSA is nothing if not ingenious and totally idiosyncratic, and that despite a production run in one form or another which now approaches a decade. Actually the car has changed quite a bit over the years and the GSA now has a large hatchback, although there is also an estate. Incidentally the much talked about GS Special range would appear to be essentially the older smaller engined GS in smartened up form: admittedly more economic than its older counterpart at the magic speeds, but lacking the performance of the GSA.

Performance is not, however, even the GSA's strongest point. While the car cruises well and smoothly at 70 mph and will wind up like most Citroën engines, as the long country miles roll by, one still has the strong impression of thrashing about and driving the car hard. It is then far from quiet.

As may be seen from our data the performance is more than adequate for a car in this size range, though the maximum speed and acceleration figures are those of *Motor* and rather poorer than claimed by Citroën. However, from our experience over the years with these cars, they improve if carefully tuned and, if anything, like a good Burgundy, develop with a little age.

The improved fuel economy of the car, as well as its marginally poorer performance compared with the old GSX-3, would appear to be a function of the changed gear ratios and five speed box of the GSA, though the hatchback's added weight will not have improved the car's acceleration. The five speed box is however well ratioed: while the fifth gear is essentially an overdrive, the third gear is about right for overtaking.

We have discussed the general disadvantages of automatic transmissions elsewhere (p. 126) but Citroën's C-matic system is a good one and the performance and economy reductions with this optional extra are not as bad as one might expect.

Leaving aside the car's performance, we are attracted

Opposite: *Designed with an interest in power/weight ratio, the body stays together without any over-emphasis on strong build quality*

Right: *Able to withstand a continual thrashing, the engine provides good accessibility to all essential elements*

Citroën GSA Club and Pallas Saloon

Engine: Flat four-cylinder with belt driven ohc, air cooled, light alloy
Capacity: 1299 cc
Bore; stroke: 79.4 mm 65.6 mm
Compression ratio: 8.7 to 1
Carburation: Twin choke Weber 30 DGS
Max. power at 6500 rpm: 65 bhp 48.5 kW
Max. torque at 5000 rpm: 72.2 ft/lb 98 Nm

Transmission: Five speed manual (four on estate). Front wheel drive via double constant velocity drive shafts. (The C-matic torque converter semi-automatic is also available)

Suspension: Hydropneumatic, independent and self-levelling with load by wishbones (front) and trailing arms (rear)

Steering: Rack and pinion
Turning circle: 31 ft 8.3 in 9.66 m

Brakes: Dual circuit fully powered discs on all four wheels

Dimensions:
Length: 13 ft 9.2 in 4.19 m
Kerb weight: 2105 lb 955 kg
Payload: 882 lb 400 kg
Performance:
Maximum speed: 98 mph 158 km/h
0–60 mph: 14.6 secs
Fuel consumption
  at 56 mph: 40.9 mpg 6.91 litres/100 km
  at 75 mph: 31.7 mpg 8.91 litres/100 km
  urban: 30.1 mpg 9.38 litres/100 km
Insurance Rating: 4
Derived Data:
bhp/litre (kW/litre): 50 37.3
bhp/ton (kW/tonne): 62.5 47.4
Speed × acceleration: 6.7
Performance Dimension: 10.7
Petrol consumption/ton at 56 mph: 6.64
Change in petrol consumption between 56 & 75 mph: 29%

---

to it mainly for its sheer style and the excellence of its ride when cruising. The hydro-pneumatic suspension is excellent and the handling at reasonable speeds light and responsive if a little heavy at low speeds or when cornering hard, though this is perhaps not the thing to do at least after a good French lunch. The car's tendency to roll while it tenaciously hangs on to the tightest bend, despite anti-roll bars front and rear, remains off-putting but appears to be the price one pays for the otherwise excellent ride.

Citroën, in adding the hatchback, have in no way lost the car's excellent and distinctive lines, which are if anything improved with the new version's slightly increased length. Other additions include more prominent bumpers, a new grille and side protection mouldings as well as a front underchin spoiler.

Internally the car is generally distinctly comfortable with a good driving position. The controls and rather floppy if pleasingly direct gear change are well to hand, though perhaps old Citroën owners should not mistake

the handbrake on the facia for the gear lever. While the instrumentation is adequate and includes a rev counter, the English version of the car has, until recently, shown its age in this department. We gather that the Special's new facia has now been incorporated on right hand drive GSA models and is a great improvement, though the 'satellite' controls need a fair bit of familiarization, particularly since they are unilluminated at night.

All in all the GSA remains an excellent and comfortable motorway cruiser for a car of its pretensions, and is aesthetically pleasing and efficient.

FORD ESCORT 1.3

The driving position is good with excellent controls, but the facia lacks a tachometer. The space is well thought out, with room for the passengers. The boot is large but the rear seat does not fold down properly to make extra room. The large glass area makes visibility better than in many cars, and this with the well organized space makes for a comfortable medium sized car which can cruise at 70 for long periods with no problems at all.

As mentioned elsewhere (1600 and XR3) this much vaunted engine is very good indeed but not the magical device one would have expected after so much time and money spent on research and development. It is still the best engine in this section however, with a Performance Dimension figure of 11.3, whereas the VW Golf 1300 has a figure of 10.7. All the same, however good the hemi-head is in the combustion business, there's a lot of harshness going on elsewhere in the engine and gearbox.

So far as handling and roadholding are concerned, although the initial skittering, turbulence and rolling due to damping deficiencies and mistakes have been ironed out, the situation is by no means right yet, as although it is possible to find a good Escort 1300 with a suspension which really works, there are others which behave very badly. Even the best of them do not have the sharp and crisp handling of the Kadett, which has no bodyroll, no understeer, and is the best of all the cars in this section on handling, the brakes being better as well.

The Escort's heating and ventilation system is very adequate, except that it is linked in a way that makes it impossible to keep a cool head and warm feet, which most Japanese cars provide. Despite the fact that the engine has not really produced anything radically new, and despite the enormous teething troubles with the suspension and damper settings, the new Escort is a well designed car with a pleasant bodyshell and comfortable and spacious interior. It also has a capacity to cruise quietly and economically, presumably for a year between services, which *is* a step forward.

Above: *As this phantom picture shows, the bodyshell conceals no startlingly original features. The research went into the engine*

Opposite above: *The Escort is a practical car while also providing a shape which is attractive and aesthetically satisfying*

Right: *It's a small world full of small cars, and the front of the Ford has many similarities with the Opel Kadett*

Ford Escort 1.3

Engine: 4 in line, transverse 'CVH' engine
Capacity: 1296 cc
Bore; stroke: 80 mm   64.5 mm
Compression ratio: 9.5 to 1
Carburation: Ford
Max. power at 6000 rpm: 69 bhp   51.5 kW
Max. torque at 3500 rpm: 73.8 ft/lb   100.1 Nm.

Transmission: Four speed manual gearbox, front wheel drive

Suspension:
Front: independent MacPherson struts with coil springs.
Rear: independent swinging arms and coil springs with tie bars

Steering: Rack and pinion, 3.69 turns lock to lock
Turning circle: 32 ft 11 in   10.03 m

Brakes: Dual line, servo assisted 9.5 in (24.1 cm) discs on front and 7 in (17.8 cm) drums on rear

Dimensions:
Length: 13 ft 3.5 in   4.05 m
Kerb weight: 1796 lb   815 kg

Performance:
Maximum speed: 98 mph   158 km/h
0–60 mph: 11.3 sec
Fuel consumption
   at 56 mph: 47.1 mpg   6.0 litres/100 km
   at 75 mph: 36.7 mpg   7.7 litres/100 km
   urban: 30.4 mpg   9.3 litres/100 km

Insurance Rating: 4

Derived Data:
bhp/litre (kW/litre): 53.2   39.7
bhp/ton (kW/tonne): 76.4   56.1
Speed × acceleration: 8.67
Performance Dimension: 11.3
Petrol consumption/ton at 56 mph (10/F): 6.64   (1.5)
Change in petrol consumption between 56 & 75 mph: 28%

Easily adjustable, the hatchback can be a four-seater plus boot or, with the rear seats folded, a boot as large as a three-litre sedan

OPEL KADETT 1.3

The Kadett is larger than most of its competitors in the 1.3 litre category. The outline is crisp, and the design of the whole vehicle has the same no-nonsense decisiveness. The front-drive effect, usually obvious, is virtually undetectable. The handling qualities in fact are as outstanding, in an unobtrusive way, as those of the Senator and Monza. It is not surprising that the Opel Kadett won the 'Golden Steering Wheel' award, in 1980, sponsored by the West German newspaper *Bild am Sonntag*, with a nine-nation, 23 member judging panel, the VW Jetta and Mitsubishi Colt being some way behind.

The 1297 cc in line four-cylinder engine of the Kadett develops 75 bhp and 74.5 ft/lb torque. Naturally there are hydraulic tappets, as GM invented them; an alloy cross-flow head, overhead camshafts and a twin-choke down-draught carburettor by GMF (General Motors France). The top speed of 98 mph and 0–60 acceleration of 11.7 seconds are creditable and well above average for 1300 cc. (Even the legendary Alfa Romeo 1.5 Ti takes

10.9 seconds.) A superb little engine like this needs, deserves and should have a tachometer. The fuel consumption of 35.0 mpg is reassuringly constant. In a 600 mile drive through London twice, outward and return, to the West country, encompassing city driving, motorways and Devon and Cornwall's twisting donkey roads, the Kadett had a lot more to offer than economical fuel consumption. The fast and smooth gearchange, 80 mph cruising, splendid suspension and sense of inherent safety make it a most satisfying small car. Passengers are well cared for with space, large windows and comfortable seating. Heating and ventilation are simple to control and adequate.

The Kadett is a natural spartan due partly to cost, but it is a spartan with fire, muscle, longevity and real economy. Noise suppression is needed to make it a world beater for which it has the potential.

Top: *The traveller version is totally functional*

Above: *The distinctive Opel nose*

Well-filled, *the engine compartment still leaves room for manoeuvres and adjustments*

Opel Kadett 1.3 GL

Engine: 4 in line, transverse, cast iron block, aluminium head. Sohc, belt driven.
Capacity: 1297 cc
Bore; stroke: 75 mm 73 mm
Compression ratio: 9.2 to 1
Carburation: GMF Varijet II downdraught
Max. power at 5800 rpm: 75 bhp 55.9 kW
Max. torque at 4500 rpm: 74.5 ft/lb 101 Nm

Transmission: 4 speed manual

Suspension: Anti-roll bars front and rear.
Front: independent by MacPherson struts, coil springs.
Rear: trailing arms with torsional cross beam and coil springs

Steering: Rack and pinion

Brakes: Dual diagonally split, servo assisted 9.3 in (23.6 cm) discs on front and 7.9 in (20.1 cm) drums on rear

Dimensions:
Length: 13 ft 1.5 in 4.0 m
Kerb weight: 1927 lb 874 kg

Performance:
Maximum speed: 98 mph 158 km/h
0–60 mph: 11.7 sec
Fuel consumption
   at 56 mph: 46.2 mpg 6.1 litres/100 km
   at 75 mph: 34 mpg 8.3 litres/100 km
   urban: 30 mpg

Insurance Rating: 4

Derived Data:
bhp/litre (kW/litre): 57.8 43.1
bhp/ton (kW/tonne): 78.1 57.3
Speed × acceleration: 8.37
Performance Dimension: 10.7
Petrol consumption/ton at 56 mph (10/F): 6.36 (1.57)
Change in petrol consumption between 56 & 75 mph: 36%

The Peugeot 104 is simple and elegant. It shows individuality in a world full of small hatchbacks

PEUGEOT 104 ZS

The first Peugeot 104s were launched in 1972, but in 1979 they were completely restyled by Paul Bracq, an ex-BMW designer. The 104 ZS has the largest and most powerful engine and the highest price for this range and it is certainly well equipped. Naturally, it has the best power/weight ratio in our data summary, as this is its most obvious feature, but the Fords and Opel Kadett outperform it. The performance dimension is the lowest and the fuel efficiency is not outstanding, so there is no way that it can be given an accolade for technical merit in this company. Nevertheless, it is a solid, sensible and well-designed small car which we feel would stand up well to many thousands of miles of everyday motoring. Look down any high street and you will see cars parked there which are downright sordid. Rust-bitten and lopsided with the travail of it all and worrying more than their owners about their next MOT, they show how undurable cars in general can be. We feel that the Peugeot 104 ZS would not be one of these and in fact this is proven because in 1981 one sees the 1972 models

about looking reasonably fit and well.

The 1360 cc engine develops 72 bhp and 79 ft/lb torque; it is the same as that used in the Renault 14 TS, and gives a top speed of 98 mph and 0–60 mph in 12.0 seconds. The suspension by omnipresent MacPherson struts and trailing arms is lively because of the sporty damper settings, and handling is of an acceptable standard. The 104 is a small car. Its very short wheelbase is only 87.6 inches and consequently it accommodates four people somewhat awkwardly. As a two seater with a splendid boot it is successful.

The driver's seat is adjustable, the stalk arrangement on the steering wheel is from the 505, and the instrument panel with rev counter is similar to the 305. Heating and ventilation are adequate. In general, the ZS is well equipped, with electric windows, a digital clock and reversing lights, some of which we would swap for a standard rear window wash/wipe. There is some gear whine and a lot of wind noise. A neat, modest shopping car for two, with good performance and economy.

Above right and left: *Fore and aft, the same simple elegance*

Below: *Disarmingly, the spare wheel obliterates the engine which continues to aspirate with its twin-choke solex*

Peugeot 104 ZS

Engine: 4 cylinders in line sohc
Capacity: 1360 cc
Bore; stroke: 75 mm   77 mm
Compression ratio: 9.3 to 1
Carburation: Twin choke Solex 32/35
Max. power at 6000 rpm: 72 bhp   53.7 kW
Max. torque at 5000 rpm: 79 ft/lb   107 Nm

Transmission: 4 speed manual

Suspension: Anti-roll bars front and rear.
Front: independent by MacPherson struts with coil springs.
Rear: independent by trailing arms and coil springs

Steering: Rack and pinion

Brakes: Dual circuit front/rear with 9.5 in (24.1 cm) front discs and 7.1 in (18 cm) rear drums

Dimensions:
Length: 10 ft 11 in   3.32 m
Weight unladen: 1702 lb   772 kg

Performance:
Maximum speed: 96 mph   154 km/h
0–60 mph: 12 sec
Fuel consumption
  at 56 mph: 47.9 mpg   5.9 litres/100 km
  at 75 mph: 35.8 mpg   7.9 litres/100 km
  urban: 30.7 mpg   9.2 litres/100 km

Insurance Rating: 4

Derived Data:
bhp/litre (kW/litre): 53   39.5
bhp/ton (kW/tonne): 83.7   61.5
Speed × acceleration: 8
Performance Dimension: 9.6
Petrol consumption/ton at 56 mph (10/F): 6.85   (1.46)
Change in petrol consumption between 56 & 75 mph: 34%

RENAULT 14 LS and TS

The Renault 14 was introduced in mid 1976 and aimed at the mid range sector of the European hatchback market. The TS became available in the United Kingdom in late 1979 and the LS with the same larger engine as the TS but with slightly lower level of equipment, as in the TL, appeared in 1980.

In TS form the car is remarkably well equipped with, for example, central locking and electric windows. There is plenty of space in the car too and the seats are comfortable, if not in the front as supportive as their shape suggests they should be. The car has a distinctive, somewhat large bottomed appearance which is not, with acquaintance, unpleasant. It is also generally well made, handles effortlessly and safely, and is relatively well priced in a competitive corner of the market.

A feature of the car is its engine which like the transmission, is Douvrin built and generally smooth and quiet, giving fairly effortless cruising in the 80 mph region. The unit is all alloy with a single overhead camshaft and differs from the 1218 cc in having a much larger stroke. The increase in bhp from 57 to 70 seems to produce surprisingly little low speed improvement in performance and Motor's figures are, for 0–60 mph times, poorer than might be expected on comparison with the behaviour of the smaller engined car.

On these tests the car has a PD of 10, which actually seems rather low in view of both the increased power and the generally well designed engine. For once one rather hopes the car as tested was not up to scratch, in our opinion the car certainly feels generally much more lively than the figures indicate. Be that as it may, the car is not intended to be all that sporty, and we like it anyway for its individuality, good ride and solidity.

Opposite: *There is a large, competent design department at Renault making positive and often original bodyshells and interiors*

Above: *The quality of engineering by Douvrin is backed up by an engine bay where everything is solid, dependable and accessible*

Renault 14 LS and TS

Engine: 4 cylinders in line, all alloy sohc chain driven. Transverse mounted
Capacity: 1360 cc
Bore; stroke: 75 mm 77 mm
Compression ratio: 9.3 to 1
Carburation: Solex 32CIS A Twin choke
Max. power at 6000 rpm: 70 bhp 52.2 kW
Max. torque at 3000 rpm: 78 ft/lb 106 Nm

Transmission: 4 speed manual

Suspension: Anti-roll bars front and rear.
Front: independent by MacPherson struts, coil springs.
Rear: independent by trailing arms and transverse torsion bar

Steering: Rack and pinion

Brakes: Dual circuit servo assisted. 9.5 in (24.1 cm) discs on front and 7.1 in (18 cm) discs on rear

Dimensions:
Length: 13 ft 2 in 4.01 m
Weight unladen: 1904 lb 864 kg

Performance:
Maximum speed: 98.5 mph 158 km/h
0–60 mph: 13.3 sec
Fuel consumption
    at 56 mph: 44.1 mpg 6.4 litres/100 km
    at 75 mph: 32.5 mpg 8.7 litres/100 km
    urban: 31 mpg 9.1 litres/100 km

Insurance Rating: 4

Derived Data:
bhp/litre (kW/litre): 51.5 38.4
bhp/ton (kW/tonne): 73.7 54.1
Speed × acceleration: 7.4
Performance Dimension: 10
Petrol consumption/ton at 56 mph: 6.7 (1.48)
Change in petrol consumption between 56 & 75 mph: 36%

Above and opposite: *One of Giugiaro's bodyshells which is already known throughout the world: a fine amalgam of aesthetics and function*

Left: *Classically simple, this could be the back of a much more expensive car*

VOLKSWAGEN GOLF LS (1.3)

One of the main troubles with an extremely good car like the Golf is that it's rather difficult to put it into any single category with ease. We find it mentioned in the 500–1100 cc class, mainly on account of the very marked improvements which have been made, in the E range, to the 1.1 litre engine. Perhaps as strikingly, we see the GTi in the 1400–1700 cc group as a genuinely high performance small hatchback saloon. The appearance of the car with a 1272 cc engine thus rings the changes to the full. In many ways the size of the car might suggest that this is where it should have started, and there is no doubt that with the mid-sized engine it performs as well as ever, if perhaps a little more fussily than the GLS, with a 1457 cc engine, at higher speeds.

This car provides a convenient opportunity to discuss the effect on the derived data, such as the Performance Dimension, of the slightly different inputs that can result from using either manufacturer's or hard external test data. A general problem is that for manufacturer's data the weight as tested is rarely given, though for the VW

range as a whole we have taken the '½ payload' approach which is general for better German specifications.

Normally the data are processed using the unladen weight with the addition of a fairly arbitrary, but at least generally fair, 224 lb. What one would like to do in all cases would be to use the weight as tested, and the results of external tests, if accepted by the manufacturer, and process these figures.

In this specific case we have done just this. The bracketed data and derived data refer to a *Motor* test of December 1979. It will be seen that *Motor* were unable to attain the claimed maximum speed of the car, but beat VW's acceleration figures by a very large margin. At first this might appear subjectively to be due to different approaches to the car's weight as tested, but close examination makes this extremely unlikely. Here we have a manufacturer who essentially appears to play extremely safe, an attribute which is not mirrored uniformly throughout the trade. We thus have for VW

Volkswagen Golf 1.3

Engine: 4 cylinders in line, transverse front mounted, sohc, alloy head
Capacity: 1272 cc
Bore; stroke: 75 mm   72 mm
Compression ratio: 8.2 to 1
Carburation: Solex down draught with manual brake
Max. power at 5600 rpm: 60 bhp   44.7 kW
Max. torque at 3500 rpm: 69.9 ft/lb

Transmission: 4 speed manual gearbox

Suspension:
Front: MacPherson struts and lower wishbones.
Rear: combined trailing arm torsion beam axle

Steering: Rack and pinion
Turning circle: 33.8 ft   10.3 m

Brakes: Dual diagonal circuit. Front discs and rear drums

Dimensions:
Length: 12 ft 6 in   3.81 m
Kerb weight: 1775 lb   805 kg

Performance:
Maximum speed: (91) 93 mph   150 km/h
0–60 mph: (13.2) 14.6 sec
Fuel consumption
   at 56 mph: 42.8 mpg   6.6 litres/100 km
   at 75 mph: 31.7 mpg   8.9 litres/100 km
   urban: 26.9 mpg   10.5 litres/100 km

Insurance Rating: 5

Figures as manufacturer: bracketed data from *Motor*.
Bracketed data on basis of *Motor* figures and weight as tested (2171 lb). Other figures use VW data and weight at half pay load (2254 lb)

Derived Data:
bhp/litre (kW/litre): 47.1   35.1
bhp/ton (kW/tonne): (61.8) 59.6   (45.4) 43.7
Speed × acceleration: (6.9) 6.36
Performance Dimension: (11.1) 10.7
Petrol consumption/ton at 56 mph: (6.8) 6.6   (1.46) 1.52
Change in petrol consumption between 56 & 75 mph: 35%

and *Motor* respectively figures of 6.4 and 6.9 for performance (a difference of 8 per cent); of 59.6 and 61.8 for power to weight ratio (a difference of 3.5 per cent); and of 10.7 and 11.1 for the Performance Dimension (a difference of 3.75 per cent).

These differences are fairly typical of the uncertainties which result in not having a uniform form of testing procedure. In fact divergences from the idealized figures given, for the average motorist, at a function of the leadenness of his foot, lightness of hand, and weight of his children will be about as large as the differences between the figures we have quoted.

Given that we have taken, as far as possible, a uniform attitude to the data, comparisons in general are as fair as we can currently make them. Obviously, however, we are not helped by manufacturers who are over optimistic. We are, for example, relatively worried about the currently available data for the Ford Escorts, as has been mentioned in the preface and further discussed in our article on the Capri 3.0 S (page 106).

It will also not have escaped the notice of the new Golf owner, or prospective purchaser, that whereas we have given the data and derived data for both the base 1090 cc engined Golf and its 'energy conscious', E, sister with higher compression ratio engine and slightly improved drag coefficient, we have not given the results for the E versions of the larger sized Golf cars.

We suggest that the reader gets out his pocket calculator and follows our procedure, thus discovering the delights of being reasonably objective about his choice of car. He will discover that the E class of Golf in general does indeed leapfrog the average economy behaviour of most other cars, but not to the exceptional degree that we saw for the smallest engined version of this generally exceptional car.

To conclude, the 1.3 Golf is a sensible and good family hatchback with remarkable accommodation for its size, reasonable equipment and good instrumentation: a desirable motor car.

1200–1400 cc CARS: SUMMARY

This is the size of car that most of us have aimed at, at one time or another. The depressing point is that most people try to escape to get either a bigger or a sportier car – though a few do determinedly gravitate to the economic 'smallest'. Thus if we are to summarize our discussion of the group we should look out for the cars which are likely to break this trend: the vehicle which once bought is, if not cherished, at least liked sufficiently to ensure that the next car bought is likely to be of the same make and size.

As always, there are grand old names as well as newcomers which would fit the bill. The Citroën GSA Club is certainly the type of car which is either liked or loathed. Further, while its performance is not staggering, both it and the Golf have many of the attributes we discussed in the introduction to this class. While both have relatively poor absolute performance figures, both have intermediate, if not good, performance dimensions. For their weight neither is too uneconomic, and the reader with a pocket calculator will rapidly discover that the Golf in E form is in fact quite remarkably frugal in its fuel demands.

A car which handles well and is clearly competitive with perhaps better performance is the Kadett, though the same could be said of the bigger engined Fiesta. The Fiesta, however, for its weight uses rather more fuel, and anyway is sufficiently sensible and spartan to be a good buy in our 'smallest car' group rather than here. The Metro too makes a healthy attempt at escaping from the small car brigade with its bigger engine, but arguably is small enough to be out of place on our criterion for what is required in this class.

The two French cars selected, the Peugeot 104 ZS and the Renault 14 LS, do have a lot to recommend them, and tend to be liked by their owners, but on paper don't come out well.

Glancing at the classes above and below this one, we see a few escapees, as was bound to be the case given our over-simplified classification in terms of engine size. Notably in the 1400–1700 cc group we see the Peugeot 305 SR and the Lancia Delta. While the former car is not really to our taste, though it too has its admirers, the Lancia Delta is, for us, one of the most enjoyable small cars we have had the pleasure of driving. Strictly on its performance dimension, we should cast it savagely aside, but find ourselves unable to do so. We like it as a car with style and poise: a driver's car.

We now come to the major problem car in the group: the Escort 1300. If its performance figures are indeed as good as Ford claim, the 1.3 CVM engine has done surprisingly well. This, too, is a car with style, and it certainly has all the attributes which look to make it a winner in the group. It looks clean and functional. We hope it is as good as it seems to be – if it is, it emphatically returns the Metro to the 500–1200 cc class and should rule the roost here with ease.

We rather expected to find the Golf more clearly ahead on paper in the group, and in fact in E form it very nearly tops the list: find out for yourselves. We like the car to drive, but find that this car's best place is in the sportier 1400–1700 cc group, as the quite exceptional GTi.

Clearly something can be said for all the cars in the group, and perhaps this is not surprising since in general here we are almost certain to be hopping from one aspect of the requirements to another. Our own preferences are for the Citroën GSA, Escort and Golf.

Class 2   Data Summary

Datum Point		Perform-ance	Power Weight	PD	FE
A	Citroën GSA Club	6.7	63	10.7	1.51
B	Ford Escort 1.3	8.7	76	11.3	1.5
C	Opel Kadett 1.3 GL	8.4	78	10.7	1.57
D	Peugeot 104 ZS	8.0	84	9.6	1.46
E	Renault 14 LS	7.4	74	10	1.48
F1	VW Golf 1.3 LS (VW figures)	6.4	60	10.7	1.52
F2	VW Golf 1.3 LS (*Motor* figures)	6.9	62	11.1	1.46

Citroën qualities in aerodynamic design together with hydropneumatic suspension and untiring engines deserve a larger share of the market.

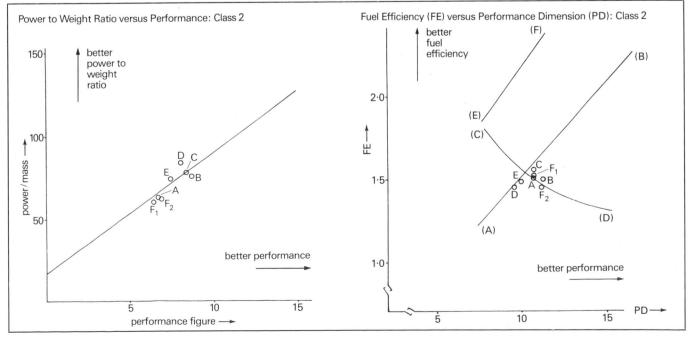

Class 3   1400-1700cc

INTRODUCTION

Cars of this size are at the heart of the matter. The conjectural 'World Car' will probably emerge having an engine within this capacity because it is large enough to develop sufficient power and small enough to retain an acceptable fuel efficiency. With world petrol prices moving irresistibly higher this is essential.

The seventies had a positive influence on redirections in both the design and production of cars. When Sheikh Yamani welded the Organization of Petroleum Exporting Countries (OPEC) into a power block influential enough to dictate terms to the industrialized west, oil prices quadrupled and the shock started a worldwide recession. The oil-consuming countries also quietly acquiesced to an unparalleled transfer of wealth from the West to the Middle East and this, as a trivial spin-off, created a new market for the exotica and fabulous cars. Much more potent effects were headlong declines in sales and the rise of Japanese imports in almost all countries. It is interesting to note that the hysteria caused by these two facts had no effect on Mercedes-Benz and BMW whatsoever who both continued at full capacity and even with waiting lists.

The world is now preoccupied with an international car production war, and the facts are only too well known. Japan has dominated the world market in cameras, radios and motor cycles and has now turned to the car. They are now second in the world table for production after the USA, and also very high in the annual car efficiency tables published by the German TUV and ADAC, both of which keep statistics of breakdowns.

The eighties are already showing, after the various debacles of the previous decade, a general pattern of the strong becoming stronger and the weak becoming weaker. Various companies have combined to achieve some kind of strength, and even the strong ones have been hedging their bets. With Japan selling three times as many cars as West Germany and twice as many as the rest of the world combined to the USA alone, buying shares in their bonanza is certainly one answer, but this book is concerned with engineering, not the world stock exchange.

This introduction started with the idea that should a new world car arise, its engine would probably be within the 1400–1700 cc capacity. The world car haunts the minds of industrialists because of the unimaginable millions which it could earn. It also hypnotizes engineers because they know that to achieve this position it would have to be original in concept and almost faultless. The nearest to the world car, the VW Beetle, had been discontinued, only to be put into production again in Brazil, with a FWD engine. The Beetle had broken Ford's sales records by 1972. It was originally produced with an unburstable (because understressed) horizontally opposed four cylinder rear engine of 1131 cc capacity, driving the rear wheels with a cruising and top speed of 100 km/h (62 mph), and including an unbreakable torsion bar suspension with a classical tear drop body for a low Cd, together with a total solidity of construction. It had been dismissed after World War II by both Ford and a British engineering consortium as worthless. We, the authors, have had eleven of them and you, the reader, must have driven them too. Our current VW caravan, with a Cd like that of a double-decker bus, is powered by the 1600 cc version of the boxer-four engine and cruises effortlessly at 105 km/h (65 mph) all day, returning 25 mpg. On driving it in the Arctic Circle, going to the North Cape of Norway, it was serviced and given a fan belt, clutch cable and two spare light bulbs, all of which it gratefully accepted and used, but never stopped involuntarily.

The Beetle, although now almost obsolete, is the exasperating yardstick which few cars can stand up to, primarily because of its total integrity. It is almost unbreakable. Hitler asked Porsche to design a car which would stand up to arctic and equitorial conditions which he did. Hitler then fumed because it was too expensive to produce, so after a twenty minute speech full of rich invective, to which Hitler listened, Porsche *did* make it simpler, and also easier and cheaper to manufacture. The ten prototypes were made, impeccably, by Mercedes-Benz at Porsche's suggestion, and in a freakishly short, record time. Then millions of miles of road testing were carried out by army drivers, organized by Ferdinand Porsche, to try out modifications.

The eight cars in this category all produce more brake horse power and have higher top speeds. Three of them are also VWs, and this is not surprising as after a small hiccough on the termination of the Beetle, which shook the whole German economy as VW staggered towards bankruptcy, they finally produced the Golf engine range and this coupled with a bodyshell by Giugiaro is a serious contender for the new world car.

As we point out, the Audi 80 is also an outstandingly good car. There is also the Lancia Delta, produced by Fiat-Lancia-Autobianchi-Ferrari who have enough resources and brilliant engineers to produce a world car, but we do not think the Delta is strong enough. The Ford Escort 1.6 has an engine which is certainly good enough to be the world car's heart, but the remainder of the car lacks something. The Alfa is brilliant but not worldly enough and the Peugeot is sound but not really brilliant. These appraisals are related to the idea of their feasibility as a world car, which is something which occurs very rarely. Simply as cars they are outstanding.

This class is where we see in the main sportier versions of the small hatchbacks and, occasionally, smaller engined versions of the bigger, more traditional cars. We must clearly thus cater for two tastes in this group, which are genuinely mutually exclusive, and bear this in mind in our summary.

On the one hand we have the traditional and generally, but not necessarily, more sedate needs of the conventional car buyer. He likes the three box concept and neither wants to spend a ridiculous amount of money nor requires exceptional performance, despite doing a fair amount of travelling and thus needing to get about comfortably and efficiently.

On the other hand we have the far from sedate driver who can see the sense in the hatchback concept, doesn't want a big car, but likes driving. This is where we should really look for efficiency, design and engineering expertise.

Golf GTi

ALFA ROMEO   ALFA SUD SPRINT VELOCE

Alfa Romeo introduced the smaller engined Suds in the early 1970s and in many ways they got it right first time. It is not just the name which attracts those who like to admire engineering. As a car to look at, too, the Sud has steadily improved over the years, and the coupé as the Sprint Veloce has some of the looks of the GTV without pretending to be bigger than it is.

Equally, however, the Veloce is a genuine four seater with more than adequate leg room and genuinely supportive seating. Admittedly there aren't too many of the luxuries that seem to be forced into many cars currently, but they aren't what the Veloce buyer is likely to be looking for anyway. Our Alfa buyer likes style and he likes good handling with adequate power.

The Veloce's handling qualities remain exceptional. Indeed they remain for the mid to small sized front wheel drive the standard against which all else is tested. Perhaps on this subjective level care is required; there is, after all, the equivalent danger faced by the boxing referee, and world champions generally have to be

knocked out! Be that as it may, great care continues to go into the car's suspension, though the front independent suspension is by modern standards essentially normal. The rear suspension, giving longitudinal and transverse stability by a Watts parallelogram linkage and Panhard rod respectively, is interesting and particularly effective in stabilizing the car on heavy braking. The car, however, owes its handling characteristics as much to its excellent weight distribution and wide wheelbase.

The four-cylinder horizontally opposed engine has a number of good features too, not least of which is the positioning of each of its two twin choke carburettors directly over its own cylinder bank, to give extremely responsive throttle control. The gearbox is as precise and quick as always, though now with the added power given by the increased compression ratio and improved aspiration there is no longer the need to stir the pudding so much.

There are two less well liked features of the Sud range.

Opposite: The Sprint Veloce is a very beautiful small car

Right: The flat-four and its two Webers, giving 63.7 bhp/litre. The ohc Alfa engines look more grand but this one provides intense and continuous power

Alfa Romeo Alfa Sud Sprint Veloce

Engine: Four cylinders horizontally opposed, with belt driven sohc per bank, cast iron block. Alloy head.
Capacity: 1490 cc
Bore; stroke: 84 mm 67.2 mm
Compression ratio: 9.5 to 1
Carburation: Two Weber twin choke downdraught
Max. power at 5800 rpm: 95 bhp 70.8 kW
Max. torque at 4000 rpm: 96 ft/lb 130 Nm

Transmission: 5 speed manual front wheel drive

Suspension: All coil springs.
Front: independent MacPherson struts transverse link and anti-roll bar.
Rear: beam axle by Watts, parallelogram linkage and Panhard rod for cross control

Steering: Rack and pinion

Brakes: Twin circuit servo assisted. Discs front 10.2 in (25.9 cm) and rear 9.2 in (23.4 cm)

Dimensions:
Length: 13 ft 2 in 4.02 m
Kerb weight: 2017 lb 915 kg

Performance:
Maximum speed: 109 mph 175 km/h
0–60 mph: 10 sec
Fuel consumption
  at 56 mph: 39 mpg 7.25 litres/100 km
  urban: 22.7 mpg 12.4 litres/100 km

Insurance Rating: 6

Derived Data:
bhp/litre (kW/litre): 63.7 47.5
bhp/ton (kW/tonne): 95 69.7
Speed × acceleration: 10.9
Performance Dimension: 11.5
Petrol consumption/ton at 56 mph: 7.24 (1.38)

The more trivial of these is sound insulation, and although a considerable amount of care has clearly gone into this, with sound and vibration damping couplings and the use of foam, the car is not all that quiet. But then the engine does make rather a pleasant noise!

As current old Alfa owners, our more major interest lies with what has been done on rust prevention. One is always liable to be a bit pessimistic about Italians ever understanding the problems of an English winter, but they certainly seem to be trying harder now, with zinc coated sheeting for many of the panels and plastic sealants over welded joints. Generally, however, the level of finish on the Veloce, although far from bad, does not show the care which lends new confidence in this area.

The Veloce is not really the car for over gentle town motoring; its character demands that it be driven, and all its good qualities come to the fore on the open road. It there stakes its claim as the mid-sized coupé which,

although now bettered on pure performance by a few competitors, remains unrivalled in terms of the satisfaction it can give.

The engine is delightful to see, hear and drive. Several times in this book we have discussed the world car with conjectures as to size and shape, but it will certainly not resemble this rooster. The Alfas still have the same riotous blood flowing in their veins that they had right from the start: all their engines, whatever the capacity, are demanding. This Veloce in particular needs to be, and wishes to be, driven.

AUDI 80 GLE

The real beauty of the Audi GLE is in its engine. This four-cylinder in-line 1588 cc unit is unquestionably one of the best in the world for its size, and naturally VW/Audi make widespread use of it – in the VW Golf GTi, Scirocco (GLi and Storm), Passat and the GLi Jetta. With carburettors it produces 75 or 85 bhp and with fuel injection 110. The carburettor versions give maximum speeds of up to 100 mph, and the injected engines 110 to 113 mph.

This engine, which is mounted in-line rather than transversely as in the Golf, drives the front wheels through a five speed gearbox, the fifth being in the nature of an overdrive/economy gear. Suspension is by MacPherson struts at the front with a dead torsion beam axle and coil springs at the rear. Steering is by unassisted rack and pinion, and the steering wheel is too large. Brakes are servo assisted discs at the front and drums at the rear. Although they do their work, they fail to impart a sense of the very highest confidence. Performance, handling and road holding are all of a high standard.

The interior space is more than adequate and this comes as no surprise as the body shell is a noticeably large 'three-box' saloon. The seats are ergonomically acceptable and provide no lumbar aches at the end of a long journey, but nevertheless they are dated. There are better seats which hold people still and peaceful when the bodywork is whirling. The pilot can find or make a reasonable seating position, because the steering column is adjustable for rake and the seat for height and reach, but the lateral support is insufficient and the accelerator pedal is too high off the floor.

Equipment is in the near-luxury class. Tinted glass, manual sunroof, electric windows, central locking, five speed box, and a decor which is simple and in good taste. The VW Scirocco GLi has been mentioned in these despatches as one of the best of the 'new spartans' and the Audi 80 GLE is a brother spartan sharing the same engine. The Audi is an honest piece of engineering, offering space for the family and their luggage, performance, handling, comfort, good design

Opposite: *This one is a competitor for the Fords, designed for everyday use by families as well as travellers*

Right: *Today's engine bay shows something very different from the old self-effacing little power units. The Bosch K-Jetronic unit is in the foreground and the oil filter just beyond*

Audi 80 GLE

Engine: Four cylinders in line, sohc, transverse front mounted
Capacity: 1588 cc
Bore; stroke: 79.5 mm   80 mm
Compression ratio: 9.5 to 1
Injection: Bosch K-Jetronic
Max. power at 6500 rpm: 110 bhp   82 kW
Max. torque at 5000 rpm: 103 ft/lb   139.7 Nm

Transmission: Manual five speed gearbox, front wheel drive (the lower compression ratio carburated GLS (85 bhp) has an optional automatic transmission). The fifth gear is an economy overdrive on the GLE.

Suspension: Progressive rate coil spring.
Front: MacPherson struts and lower wishbones.
Rear: negative roll radius torsion crank axle

Steering: Rack and pinion
Turning circle: 34 ft 1 in   10.4 m

Brakes: Diagonally divided and servo assisted. Front discs, rear drums

Dimensions:
Length: 14 ft 6.5 in   4.44 m
Weight unladen: 2094 lb   950 kg

Performance:
Maximum speed: 110 mph   177 km/h
0–60 mph: 9.3 sec
Fuel consumption
   at 56 mph: 39.2 mpg   7.2 litres/100 km
   at 75 mph: 30.7 mpg   9.2 litres/100 km
   urban: 23.5 mpg   12 litres/100 km

Insurance Rating: 6

Derived Data:
bhp/litre (kW/litre): 69.3   51.6
bhp/ton (kW/tonne): 106.3   78
Speed × acceleration: 11.8
Performance Dimension: 11.1
Petrol consumption/ton at 56 mph (10/F): 6.96   (1.44)
Change in petrol consumption between 56 & 75 mph: 28%

---

everywhere from engine and body shell to all the minor details, but it is expensive.

The Audi 80 GLE has one very special feature. It is economical to run. Over a 600 mile drive including the Snowdonia mountains, motorways, and country B roads, it provided irreproachable performance in all road categories and 35 mpg. All three passengers were happy, comfortable and relaxed.

Simple and satisfying efficiency, especially in the heating and ventilation system

FORD CORTINA 1.6 GHIA

Since the dark ages Ford's have made practical and sensible cars. Admittedly once in a while since the era of the Model T, mistakes have been made, and back countless years ago it was suicidal to take a well loaded Mk 2 Cortina out on an icy road. Progressively, however, the Cortina concept has improved. There is certainly not much in the Mk 4 suspension or general layout which could be described as violently innovatory. There aren't any mistakes either, and the hardened suspension of the Ghia gives the predictable and safe, if somewhat harsh, handling characteristics beloved of those who like just a little hard footed oversteer in the wet.

It would have been thought that by the time the Ghia nametag had been appended, the number of options would have fallen to manageable proportions, but despite the car being fairly lavishly equipped this is not the case. This particular model is not, however, included here for reasons of comfort. We have chosen it because it is on this car that one gets the remarkable 1600 cc 2v

ohc engine. Not too many 1600 cc cars have better than 100 mph top speeds and 0–60 mph times of better than 11 seconds, and still fewer which are as heavy as the Cortina.

In its class, the car's performance dimension of 11.8 is quite exceptional, and bettered in the whole Cortina range only by the now distinctly long in the tooth 2 litre ohc engined car, with a figure of 12.3. Perhaps the truly remarkable point about the Cortinas is that they do reasonably well on our comparisons with any of their engines. Even the 1300 cc engine gives it a PD of 10.1 while the 70 bhp 1600, though of course much slower off the mark than the Ghia, gives a very laudable figure of 11.5.

This is rightly a popular car, functional, cheap to run and fairly economic given its weight. Laudable though innovation is, it is no use unless the end result is an improvement. While it is difficult to imagine the series not undergoing some radical change soon, one can only hope the car's successor is as good.

Opposite: *The Ford of the 1980s is commendably smart, especially the Ghia models*

Above: *The engine is superficially much as always but we know this one develops 90 bhp and there will be no need to bother with it much of the time, except for a dipstick check*

Ford Cortina 1.6 Ghia (Manual)

Engine: Four-cylinder 1600 2V overhead camshaft
Capacity: 1593 cc
Bore; stroke: 87.7 mm   66 mm
Compression ratio: 9.2 to 1
Carburation: Ford
Max. power at 5700 rpm: 90 bhp   67.1 kW
Max. torque at 4000 rpm: 91.9 ft/lb   124.7 Nm

Transmission: Four speed manual, rear wheel drive

Suspension:
Front: independent, short and long arms, coil springs and anti-roll bar.
Rear: four-bar link variable roll coil springs and anti-roll bar

Steering: Rack and pinion, 3.7 turns lock to lock
Turning circle: 32 ft 9.5 in   10.1 m

Brakes: Dual line servo assisted 9¾ in (24.8 cm) discs on front, 8 in (20.3 cm) drums on rear

Dimensions:
Length: 14 ft 3 in   4.34 m
Kerb weight: 2354 lb   1070 kg

Performance:
Maximum speed: 101 mph   162 km/h
0–60 mph: 10.9 sec
Fuel consumption
    at 56 mph: 39.2 mpg   7.2 litres/100 km
    at 75 mph: 30.4 mpg   9.3 litres/100 km
    urban: 25.5 mpg   11.1 litres/100 km

Insurance Rating: 4

Derived Data:
bhp/litre (kW/litre): 56.5   42.1
bhp/ton (kW/tonne): 78.2   57.4
Speed × acceleration: 9.3
Performance Dimension: 11.8
Petrol consumption/ton at 56 mph (10/F): 6.26   (1.60)
Change in petrol consumption between 56 & 75 mph: 29%

Above: *A Ghia with its distinctive international styling*

Opposite, near right: *Section of the engine, showing the compound valve head with belt-driven camshaft, and sensible arrangement of auxiliary drives*

Far right: *Combined gearbox and final drive*

FORD ESCORT 1600

The new Ford engine is designed for long life, minimal maintenance, fuel economy, noise suppression and a light weight, all within legal emission standards, together with computer-aided calibration of all control systems.

Research confirmed the known theoretical fact that a pure hemisphere is the most efficient chamber shape. Twin cams were rejected on the grounds of expense and complexity. A single overhead camshaft is used. The valves are kept tangential to the hemi-surface, with the stem canted at a compound angle to the cylinder axis. This allows each valve to be operated with its own cam, by an angled rocker. It is from this part of the design that the engine gets its name – CVH – Compound Valve-angle Hemispherical chamber.

Maintenance-free hydraulic tappets are used, similar to those of General Motors (see diagram). Clearances due to wear are automatically taken up by the oil in the tappets, so no valve adjustment is required after initial assembly.

The grey-iron sand-cast cylinder block extends only to the crankshaft centre-line, for easy access to the bearings. The patterns of external webbing for strengthening were developed by using model analysis of a compound stress model at Leuven University, Belgium. The same research also reduced engine noise level by 3 dB (A), halving the sound energy produced.

The auxiliary drives are all simplified. The distributor is mounted to the end of the camshaft. The oil pump is mounted directly on the crankshaft nose with no intermediate skew gears. The fuel pump is driven by an eccentric boss on the camshaft. The toothed-belt drive to the camshaft also powers the water pump. Cooling for the radiator is by electrically powered fan. The alternator alone is driven by a conventional veebelt.

A breakerless ignition system is used which requires no maintenance. The voltage output at the coil is increased by 30 per cent, the spark energy is six times greater, and the spark duration doubled. A new design of HT cable was developed, using a carbon impregnated

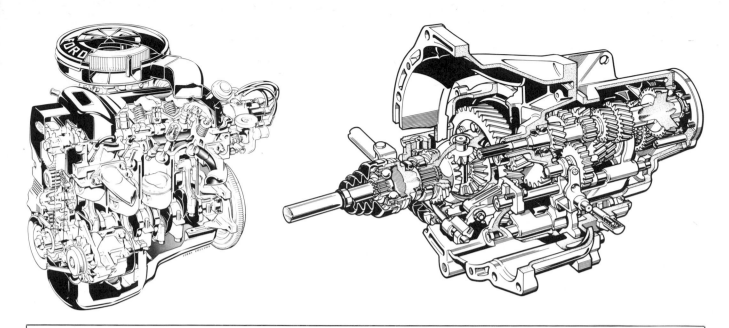

Ford Escort 1600 Ghia

Engine: Four cylinders in line, CVH overhead valve, transverse mounted cast iron block and head
Capacity: 1597 cc
Bore; stroke: 80 mm   79.5 mm
Compression ratio: 9.5 to 1
Carburation: Ford
Max. power at 5800 rpm: 79 bhp   58.9 kW
Max. torque at 3000 rpm: 92.6 ft/lb   125.6 Nm

Transmission: Four speed manual gearbox, front wheel drive

Suspension:
Front: independent MacPherson struts with coil springs.
Rear: independent swinging arms and coil springs with tie bars

Steering: Rack and pinion, 3.69 turns lock to lock
Turning circle: 32 ft 11 in   10.03 m

Brakes: Dual line servo assisted. 9 ½ in (24.1 cm) ventilated front discs, 7 in (17.8 cm) rear drums

Dimensions:
Length: 13 ft 3 ½ in   4.05 m
Kerb weight: 1962 lb   89 kg
Performance:
Maximum speed: 104 mph*   167 km/h
0–60 mph: 9.7 sec*
Fuel consumption
   at 56 mph: 44.1 mpg   6.4 litres/100 km
   at 75 mph: 34.4 mpg   8.2 litres/100 km
   urban: 30.7 mpg   9.2 litres/100 km
*Ford computed data
Insurance Rating: 5
Derived Data:
bhp/litre (kW/litre): 49.5   36.9
bhp/ton (kW/tonne): 80.9   59.4
Speed × acceleration: 11.4
Performance Dimension: 14.1
Petrol consumption/ton at 56 mph: 6.56   1.52
Change in petrol consumption between 56 & 75 mph: 28%

---

glass fibre core, sheathed in silicon, insulated with a new plastic, with an extra outer cover of Hypalon which provides resistance to oil and engine heat degradation. A new design of spark plug was needed because of the high flame temperatures. This consists of a copper core case in nickel-chromium-iron alloy.

The CVH engine requires a service time of less than one hour per *year* for the 1100 version, and 45 minutes for the breakerless ignition 1300 and 1600 engines.

Engine efficiency can be expressed in various ways – mechanical, volumetric and thermal. In mechanical efficiency, determined mainly by the friction of the pistons, bearings and valve gear, the 1100 version recorded 79.3 per cent. In thermal efficiency, the CVH showed a 6 per cent improvement on the best previous Ford engine, the ohc 2 litre RS 2000. In volumetric efficiency, that is the amount of air drawn in compared with the swept volume, the CVH showed an efficiency of 82.8 per cent because of the new combustion system.

While there are no new developments in the suspension of the new Ford Escorts, the aerodynamic shape of the bodyshell is good. The engine produces 60.15 bhp per litre which is not the exceptional figure one would have expected after such a long gestation period in research and development. The VW 1600 GTi produces 69.26 bhp per litre, and yet the dimensions are almost identical. The Escort 1600 has a bore and stroke of 80/79.5 mm. The VW 1600 has a bore and stroke of 79.5/80 mm. It would be interesting to see how much more bhp the Escort would produce if fitted with a fuel injection system.

LANCIA DELTA

There are many front wheel drive cars of this size which are outstandingly mediocre. The Lancia Delta has no mundane features at all. It is like a large quality car which has been reduced in size but retains the distinguished ambience and refinement. Giugiaro designed the body and this is noticeable inside and out. It is a pleasure to look at from any angle.

It is also a driver's delight. The basically Fiat Ritmo engine, with a belt-driven ohc, has been given 10 more bhp by means of a higher compression ratio, Weber carburettor, larger intake manifolds and electronic ignition. The five speed gearbox has no flaws – the ratios feel right for this size and weight; and ninety mph seems a right and proper cruising speed.

The excellent roadholding is retained at all speeds and in all conditions, however vivid the driving or appalling the weather. There is such a faultless balance of power and suspension that one has a tendency to drive the car to its reasonable limits all the time, resulting in fuel consumption of only about 26 mpg, and

so losing all that was gained by the scaling down in size. Thinking harder about fuel economy, but still getting a lot of pleasure because of the splendid harmony of the design, 35 mpg is easily possible.

This car was included in the book more for the qualities which it showed when being driven than from its performance figures. If you look at the data summary you will see that it has statistics which fall short of several of the others. This is partly due to the fact that it is 100 cc less in capacity, and this is crucial when it is performance which is being weighed in the balance; nor can it offer exemplary fuel economy. It is the quality of all round design, lively performance and excellent road holding which make it outstandingly good.

Economy is necessary in all matters in the 1980s, fuel of course, but basic costs as well. There are many who are giving up the kind of large vehicles that are costly to buy and to run. The Lancia Delta will make them feel very much at home with the same refinements for a smaller outlay.

Above: *A Giugiaro side elevation, with sills sloping upwards towards the rear*

Opposite: *In our opinion this is one of the best looking of the small cars, with efficiency to match*

Right: *Simple and extremely comfortable*

Lancia Delta 1500

Engine: Four cylinders in line with belt driven sohc, transverse front mounted
Capacity: 1498 cc
Bore; stroke: 86.4 mm   63.9 mm
Compression ratio: 9.2 to 1
Carburation: Weber 34 DAT8
Max. power at 5800 rpm: 85 bhp   62.6 kW
Max. torque at 3500 rpm: 90.4 ft/lb   123 Nm

Transmission: Five speed manual gearbox via integral differential to front wheels

Suspension: MacPherson strut independent coil spring suspension all round with front anti-roll bar

Steering: Rack and pinion
Turning circle: 34 ft 5.5 in   10.5 m

Brakes: Dual diagonally split servo assisted front discs and rear drums

Dimensions:
Length: 12 ft 9 in   3.88 m
Kerb weight: 2150 lb   975 kg

Performance:
Maximum speed: 99 mph   159 km/h
0–60 mph: 12.2 sec
Fuel consumption
    at 56 mph: 40.3 mpg   7 litres/100 km
    at 75 mph: 30.2 mpg   9.4 litres/100 km
    urban: 28.4 mpg   10 litres/100 km

Insurance Rating: 5

Derived Data:
bhp/litre (kW/litre): 56.7   41.8
bhp/ton (kW/tonne): 80.2   58.1
Speed × acceleration: 8.1
Performance Dimension: 10.1
Petrol consumption/ton at 56 mph (10/F): 6.6   (1.51)
Change in petrol consumption between 56 & 75 mph: 34%

PEUGEOT 305 SR

Many manufacturers have been keen to offer cars with full specifications to buyers who are considering trading down to achieve greater economy and lower running costs, and the Peugeot 305 SR is one of them. It is in the same category as the Alfa Romeo Giulietta 1.6, Renault 18 GTS, and the Ford Cortina, all of which offer performance which is superior, so why has it been included in our selection?

The answer is that the Peugeot 305 is a dependable, no-nonsense car with space, comfort and economy built into it. It has the worst performance figure and the worst power/weight ratio, but the best fuel efficiency figures in our data summary. It is a solid, simple car for the Mr Everyman who has other things on his mind than performance, and who would feel uncomfortable in the Alfa Romeo Sprint Veloce. Looking round at our friends we find that several of them own Peugeot 305s.

The Peugeot 305 SR, as a four door medium sized saloon, was introduced in 1978, and with its relatively recently designed, though small, engine is a leading

contender in the market. For the traditionalist who prefers a proper car to a hatchback this is the area where British Leyland will have to contend with cars such as this, the Renault 18 and the better performance 1.6 litre Cortinas: a difficult job.

The Peugeot is an easy car to drive, commendably safe with reasonable feel and little understeer even on hard cornering. It also shows less roll than its French competitors, and the gearchange for a transverse mounted front wheel drive engine is precise and quick.

As may be seen from the derived data, it does not perform too badly and is very close to the average behavioural line: not a bad achievement for its engine size. It does better, however, for its weight when we examine its fuel economy.

We include the 305 here not for exceptional performance, but as a reasonably well equipped and comfortable car. It's safe and unflappable, with more than adequate seating for four adults conscious of their comfort and of driving in a well finished car.

60

Above: *The engine bay is dramatically basic*

Right and opposite: *Peugeot made a name for themselves years ago for a co-ordination of dependability, simplicity and strength. All three can be seen in these pictures*

Peugeot 305 SR

Engine: 4 cylinders in line, transverse mounted with sohc
Capacity: 1472 cc
Bore; stroke: 78 mm   77 mm
Compression ratio: 9.2 to 1
Max. power at 6000 rpm: 74 bhp   55.2 kW
Max. torque at 5000 rpm: 86 ft/lb   116.7 Nm

Transmission: 4 speed manual

Suspension: Anti-roll bars front and rear.
Front: independent by MacPherson struts, coil springs.
Rear: independent by trailing arms and coil springs

Steering: Rack and pinion

Brakes: Front discs, rear drums

Dimensions:
Length: 13 ft 10.5 in   4.23 m
Weight: 2128 lb   965.3 kg

Performance:
Maximum speed: 95 mph   153 km/h
0–60 mph: 13.2 sec
Fuel consumption
   at 56 mph: 45.5 mpg   6.2 litres/100 km
   urban: 31.7 mpg   8.9 litres/100 km

Insurance Rating: 4

Derived Data:
bhp/litre (kW/litre): 50.3   37.5
bhp/ton (kW/tonne): 70.5   51.7
Speed × acceleration: 7.2
Performance Dimension: 10.2
Petrol consumption/ton at 56 mph: 5.9   (1.69)

VOLKSWAGEN GOLF GTi

Volkswagen have progressively introduced higher compression ratio versions of their engines for the performance cars like the GTi and Scirocco. They have also leapfrogged their rivals in terms of fuel economy: while the older low compression ratio cars gave much poorer than average fuel efficiency for their weight, the new cars do rather better.

Before discussing the Golf GTi we consequently include here, for direct comparison, data for both the five door Golf L and Golf LE. It is in fact with the 1093 cc engine that the most radical improvements have been possible, as has been mentioned in our discussion of the Polo. The Golf, despite being at least in length and with the 1093 cc engine officially in our 500–1100 cc class, does not match PD or fuel efficiency figures for the Polo even in E form.

The car is more suited to its natural mid-size hatchback class. It can figure in the 1200–1400 cc class with the 1272 cc LS with a very creditable PD of 11 but with poor fuel efficiency. It still more appropriately

appears in the class under discussion as the 1457 cc engined GLS (again with a reasonable PD of 11 and a now rather better fuel economy figure of 1.52) but by far its best form is as the distinctly high performance GTi.

Essentially, having pushed up the compression ratio, the only way to go to improve performance with retained reasonable fuel consumption was to change to fuel injection. This Volkswagen have done, with the Bosch K-Jetronic system, to achieve a fairly phenomenal power output of 110 bhp at 6100 rpm. The torque figures, too, peak at the satisfyingly high rpm of 5000, so with the car's naturally light weight body we have a car approaching the sports car class. Certainly its maximum speed of 112 mph is about the same as that of the Escort XR3.

Its acceleration times are, however, poorer. This gives some hint of the retained economy attitude in the Volkswagen stable. While recent improvements have led to a lowering of the Golf's drag coefficient from 1.41 to 1.38, this figure is higher than that for the new Escort.

Opposite: *Trendy yet practical, the convertible has only one small fault (see text)*

Right: *The GTi power unit is fuel injected. Eventually, all cars will be fuel injected because it is more efficient*

Volkswagen Golf GTi and (Convertible)

Engine: Four cylinders in line, transverse front mounted sohc
Capacity: 1588 cc
Bore; stroke: 79.5 mm   80 mm
Compression ratio: 9.5 to 1
Injection: Bosch K-Jetronic
Max. power at 6000 rpm: 110 bhp   82 kW
Max. torque at 5000 rpm: 103 ft/lb   139.7 Nm

Transmission: Manual five speed gearbox, front wheel drive

Suspension: Anti-roll bars front and rear.
Front: MacPherson struts and lower wishbones.
Rear: combined trailing arm torsion beam axle

Steering: Rack and pinion
Turning circle: 33 ft 9.5 in   10.3 m

Brakes: Dual, diagonally divided, servo assisted. 9.4 in (23.9 cm) ventilated discs on front, 7.1 in (18 cm) rear drums

Dimensions:
Length: 12 ft 6 in   3.81 m
Weight unladen: 1852 (2072) lb   840 (940) kg

Performance:
Maximum speed: 112 (106) mph   180 (170) km/h
0–60 mph: 9.1 (10.2) sec
Fuel consumption
   at 56 mph: 38.2 (38.7) mpg   7.4 (7.3) litres/100 km
   at 75 mph: 29.7 (30.4) mpg   9.5 (9.3) litres/100 km
   urban: 26.7 (23.3) mpg   10.5 (12.1) litres/100 km

Insurance Rating: 6

Derived Data: (using weight at ½ payload (2337 lb))
[ ] figures for GTi weight + 0.1 ton
bhp/litre (kW/litre): 69.3   51.6
bhp/ton (kW/tonne): 105.4 (101.1) [118.7]   77.4 (74.2)
Speed × acceleration: 12.3 (10.4)
Performance Dimension: 11.7 (10.3) [10.4]
Petrol consumption/ton at 56 mph (10/F): 7.09 (6.7)   1.41 (1.48)
Change in petrol consumption between 56 & 75 mph: 28% (27%)

Gear ratios have been kept on the long-legged side, so that despite having a lower weight and much higher bhp than the Escort, the GTi manages only 9.1 seconds to 60 mph, by comparison with the startling 8.6 seconds claimed for the XR3.

The Golf handles well, and is well balanced under the hardest of cornering treatments. The stiffening lent to the GTi by anti-roll bars front and rear gives a still firmer feel, and as front wheel driven cars go it is much more of a pleasure to drive than most: the gear change in particular is quick and crisp and the clutch light and smooth.

The Golf range is not lavishly equipped. At the same time the cars are comfortable and sensibly appointed. The Golf now has as standard, for example, a rear wash/wipe system, and the GTi has more supportive front seats, halogen headlights, and a very readable rev counter paired with an equally well designed speedometer. The facia is elegant and unobtrusively well designed.

There really would appear to be no way a car the size and weight of the GTi can manage to feel as smooth at high speed as a larger performance car. The Golf GTi is a well designed fast car, of about the smallest size compatible with its performance. We like it as a functional and unfussy driver's car.

The Golf convertible is essentially a GTi with the top sawn off and the body held together again by a massive and sensible central roll bar. The car tends to turn all eyes, and it's perhaps symptomatic of its market that we first came across it in a rather swish central Italian village on a hot summer's day in 1980.

The convertible's performance figures, although impressive, don't match those of the more aerodynamic GTi. Although the hood can be put up and down with great ease, when it is up rear vision is not too good and wind noise is obtrusive. This is, however, a sensible small convertible and for those fortunate enough to live in sunny climates a very enjoyable alternative to the GTi.

VW SCIROCCO

The Scirocco, with a power/weight ratio of 139 bhp/ton, is quick. The Bosch injected engine, with electronic ignition, develops not only 110 bhp, but 140 ft/lb torque at 5000 revs, which is what makes it so different from, and better than, the average 1600. There is a fine balance between this power and the suspension, with a minor quibble about the brakes, which are not in quite the same category as the assertive power. As for ride, the Scirocco has agility and precision which brings no criticisms from the back seats.

The interior is well designed and completely equipped. The noise level is not like a limousine's, because to obtain it would have added weight, and this would have upset the ratio, and that would remove the crackerjack performance. Silence is expensive. Heating and ventilation are clinically efficient.

In the manufacturer's analysis, look at the prices of the major items and see whether there have been economies. See where the money has been used. With the Scirocco, the alternator and starter motor are both

expensive and first class – costing three times as much as the average – and with a reputation for long life. Engine, gearbox and clutch are well below average in cost because VW have a good exchange system worldwide. As for maintenance, the cost of major servicing, clutch renewal, new exhaust and front disc pads are all *below* the average, due to good design and well organized service departments.

The power and torque of this engine will be realized by comparing it with the Renault 18 Turbo:

VW	Renault	
110/6100	110/5000	bhp
140/5000	134/2250	torque ft/lb

The Scirocco was the forerunner of a new generation of spartans – dazzling in engineering efficiency and refinement, civilized in every detail, but luxurious in none.

The bodyshell, designed by Giugiaro, was the forerunner of today's generation of 'down to real

Opposite: *This is one of the most taut designs for a bodyshell in the world today, and as functional as it looks*

Right: *Engineering at its best – 110 bhp without fuss or power bulges*

Opposite below: *An impeccable spartan interior which makes many others look blowzy*

Volkswagen Scirocco GTi and Storm

Engine: Four cylinders in line, transverse front mounted
Capacity: 1588 cc
Bore; stroke: 79.5 mm   80 mm
Compression ratio: 9.5 to 1
Injection: Bosch K-Jetronic
Max. power at 6100 rpm: 110 bhp   82 kW
Max. torque at 5000 rpm: 103 ft/lb   139.7 Nm

Transmission: Five speed manual gearbox and front wheel drive via double joint drive shafts

Suspension: Progressive coil springs. Anti-roll bars front and rear.
Front: MacPherson struts and lower wishbones.
Rear: combined trailing arm torsion beam axle

Steering: Rack and pinion
Turning circle: 33 ft 9.5 in   10.3 m

Brakes: Servo-assisted diagonally divided. Front ventilated discs, rear drums

Dimensions:
Length: 12 ft 9 in   3.81 m
Weight unladen: 1764 lb   800 kg

Performance:
Maximum speed: 115 mph   185 km/h
0–60 mph: 8.7 secs
Fuel consumption
   at 56 mph: 38.7 mpg   7.3 litres/100 km
   at 75 mph: 30.7 mpg   9.2 litres/100 km
   urban: 23.3 mpg

Insurance Rating: 7

Derived Data: (using ½ full load weight (2216 lb))
bhp/litre (kW/litre): 69.3   51.6
bhp/ton (kW/tonne): 111.2   81.6
Speed × acceleration: 13.2
Performance Dimension: 11.9
Petrol consumption/ton at 56 mph (10/F): 7.38   (1.35)
Change in petrol consumption between 56 & 75 mph: 26%

---

essentials' cars, so that the interior looks utilitarian. Driver's seat, wheel, facia, pedals and visibility are all good and workmanlike. Handling is smooth, efficient and without quirks of any kind, and performance as good as most 2 litre cars and better than all other 1600 cc cars.

The fuel consumption, now more of a priority with VW than ever, was 31 mpg while dealing with tests, and a handsome 34 mpg over a 650 mile drive to the Northumbrian moors up the neglected A1, and back down the Pennines, showing its dynamic qualities on roads designed for carts and horses and in weather for sou'wester hats.

VW showed good sense in amalgamating their outstanding engine and suspension system with Giugiaro's bodyshell, and other German manufacturers could do likewise, asking Gandini to do them the honour of turning their estimable engineering into works of art.

Engine plus suspension; a co-ordination which is balanced and works well

1400–1700 cc: SUMMARY

We will deal first with the requirements of our more traditional car buyer, looking for good value in a well known guise. We must expect him to recognize good engineering but not want it either too dear or in too flamboyant a form.

We don't have to look far: the Audi 80 GLE is, at the higher performance end of the smaller engined traditional cars, quite exceptional in many ways. Its power to weight ratio is very high and not surprisingly it performs accordingly. Furthermore, at least in E guise, its fuel economy for its weight is more than acceptable, if not good. This is a modern and good piece of machinery with equal style and more than reasonable handling.

But what about the Cortina? It seems impossible to get Ford to lie down. This car has, of course, been with us for rather a long time but as the Mark 4 with Ghia trim it is certainly not old fashioned to look at and is generally clean of limb. Furthermore, for its poor power to weight ratio it goes rather well and is equally good, at least unless flogged, in terms of its fuel efficiency. We prefer this car in its 2 litre form, but it is difficult to say a lot against it except that, to put it mildly, it just isn't all that innovatory!

Turning now to our man who likes his driving: he too wouldn't go far wrong with the Audi 80 GLE, but there are cars in the group which are certainly more fun and just as functional. We have already mentioned the Lancia Delta, a delightful car, and the Peugeot 305 SR, and suggested that they should be transplanted to Class 2 where they look more at home.

Examining the other cars in the class, the data for the Escort 1.6 Ghia stand out. Unfortunately it stands out considerably more than is imaginably possible or believable, and we accordingly fear that Ford's computed data were, to say the least, questionable. In a way it may be noted that the simple approach we have taken here to the data analysis demonstrates the point in as conclusive a manner as one could imagine. A pity though, we still like the car to drive and admire!

For the admirers of Italian style we have the Alfa Sud, good enough in many ways in standard form, but delightful as the Veloce: this, for once, is a really well mannered front-engined car with good handling and sufficient pace for most.

From the German stables we have the Golf Convertible and GTi, and the Scirocco GLi/Storm. All three are in their own ways exceptional motor cars. The convertible really is a practicable four seat small convertible and in this it is fairly remarkable. Its performance, too, is far from sedate, but perhaps it needs the sunshine. The GTi, on the other hand, is quite a car, small (if not extraordinarily so for its space usage) and yet with exceptional performance, performance dimension and handling. A jaunty and fine piece of engineering. We are generally surprised that the car manages in this bigger engined class so well.

The high performance Scirocco is rather smoother and handles in our opinion a little better, but it feels light for all that power. A point which is clearly demonstrated by the data is that once cars of this sort are expected to perform to this degree it is no longer practicable to expect good fuel efficiency figures. Absolutely, however, fuel economy will still be better than for the bigger cars though the latter might appear to be better balanced in having good Performance Dimensions and good fuel efficiency figures.

For our money it looks hard to go wrong with either the Golf GTi or the Audi 80 GLE.

Class 3   Data Summary

Datum Point		Perform-ance	Power Weight	PD	FE
A	Alfa Sud Sprint Veloce	10.9	95	11.5	1.38
B	Audi 80 GLE	11.8	106	11.1	1.44
C	Ford Cortina 1.6 Ghia	9.3	78	11.8	1.6
D	Ford Escort 1600 Ghia	11.4	81	14.1	1.52
E	Lancia Delta 1500	8.1	80	10.1	1.51
F	Peugeot 305 SR	7.2	71	10.2	1.69
G	VW Golf Convertible	10.4	101	10.3	1.48
H	VW Golf GTi	12.3	105	11.7	1.41
I	VW Scirocco	13.2	111	11.9	1.35

VW efficiency at all levels.

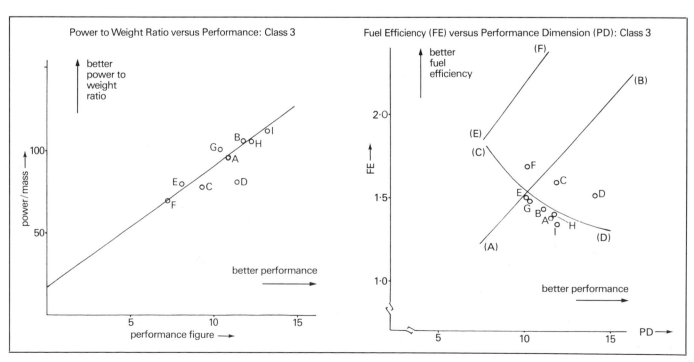

Power to Weight Ratio versus Performance: Class 3

better
power to
weight
ratio

power / mass →

better performance

performance figure →

Fuel Efficiency (FE) versus Performance Dimension (PD): Class 3

better
fuel
efficiency

FE →

better performance

PD →

3 Heat and Work in the Engine

We are all familiar with the meanings of words like 'energy' and 'work': when we are energetic, we have the capacity to do work. Similarly, everyday life shows us that bigger forces are required to give bigger masses the same acceleration, and that similarly different amounts of work are done in moving them the same distance. These ideas have already been discussed in The Measure of Performance (page 30). Here we are interested in the conversion of the chemical energy from the fuel into work. Why is it, for example, that engines cannot convert all the fuel's energy into work, and does this mean that electrically powered cars are more efficient than those with internal combustion engines?

Fortunately unlike subjects such as politics or economics there really are some rock solid ground rules to help our understanding. The first of these laws is that energy cannot be created or destroyed, just converted from one form to another. Slightly more formally: the change in internal energy of a body is equal to the sum of the heat and work energy given it. The second law is mainly about machines: it says that no machine can be made which does nothing other than transfer heat from a cooler to a hotter body. This effectively means that anyone who claims to have made a perpetual motion machine is deluding himself.

A quick overall look at how a car is moved from place to place will familiarize us with the basic concepts. The source of energy is the petrol. When this is burnt, chemical energy is converted into heat. This in turn causes the gases in the combustion chamber to expand and so to apply a force to the piston which moves, and in turn rotates the wheels of the car. The return stroke of the piston expels the now cooler but hot gases down the exhaust pipe; immediately we can tell that not all the energy released from the petrol has gone into the work of propelling the car – some went down the exhaust pipe, still in the form of heat. Again, we know that the gearbox and bearings get hot, so that tells us that some of the work done by the engine is converted back into heat energy even while the rest is used in getting the car going. Of course we could now stop the car, by putting on the brakes, so converting its kinetic energy into heat in the discs and brake pads.

The point is that none of the chemical energy from the fuel is ever destroyed: it's just successively converted from one form to another, the losses and gains always balancing up exactly; in the end, the whole chain of activity just serves to heat up the surroundings a bit. This is the first law in operation.

Where we see the second law with depressing clarity is that while any work in the end gets fully dissipated as heat, at no stage did we ever manage to convert heat energy fully into useful work. The realization that heat is itself a form of energy came first to Benjamin Thompson, an American who later became Count Rumford at the Bavarian court. At the end of the 18th century he got rather fed up about how when boring out cannon the work done got converted into heat. It took another fifty years before Joule fully established the equivalence of work and heat. This simply shows that it's never a bad idea to do a job properly: it is after all Joule rather than Rumford whose name was given to a unit of energy.

So far however it is not yet clear why we can't, with a bit more cunning, get all that heat energy in the exhaust gases of the engine converted into useful work. If we could, the engine would be 100 per cent efficient. Sadly we will see that, even in principle, the *ideal* efficiency of a combustion engine cannot be higher than about 65 per cent; and in reality it is nearer to about 35 per cent.

Heat is energy in motion. If we put two bodies with different temperatures in contact, heat flows spontaneously from the hotter to the colder until they have the same temperature. If we are going to use a source of heat, such as burning fuel, as a source of energy we have to get it out. We need some cooler body present, for the heat to flow to. Since this cooler body must heat up, it is retaining in itself a proportion of the heat energy which is supposed to be being converted into useful work.

It is no good insulating the cold body; even if this were remotely possible, the hot body wouldn't then be in contact, the flow of heat would not then occur, and neither work nor heat could be extracted. If, of course, we could take the heat which ended up in the colder body back, and put it into the original heat

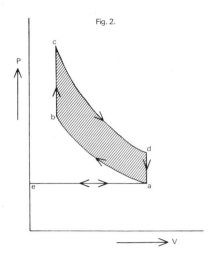

Fig. 2.

Figure 2 *The Otto cycle: an idealized approach to the work done in a petrol engine. The shaded area on the pressure (P) versus volume (V) chart is proportional to the work which is extracted. This is the area which should be maximized*

source, all would be well, but this is just what the second law stated was impossible – without doing some work: and that would defeat the object. Under the most ideal circumstances imaginable, exactly the same amount of work would be required in putting this heat back into the hot source as could ever be extracted when it flowed from the hot source into the cooler body.

This is set out in figure 1 below. The hot source is at some high temperature T_1 and the cold body or sink is at T_2. Heat flows in energy totals labelled Q_1 and Q_2 from one to the other. The flow of heat energy takes place in an engine, which at best diverts W of the flow into useful work. The first law of thermodynamics says that $W = Q_1 - Q_2$. The efficiency, E, of the engine is W/Q_1; which is of course the output divided by the input, or the fraction of the available heat converted into work.

$$E = 1 - \frac{Q_2}{Q_1}$$

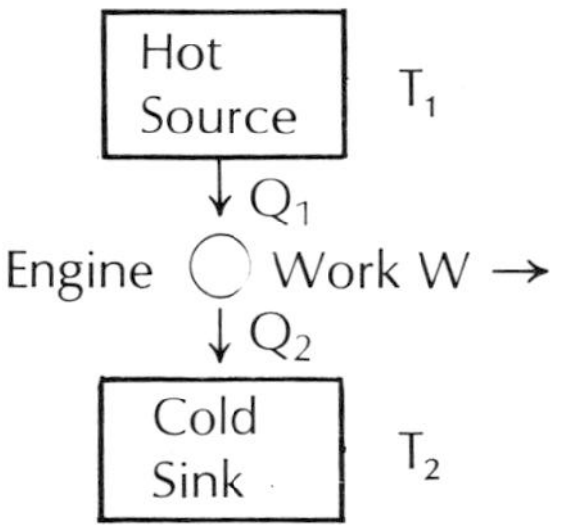

```
                    ┌────────┐
                    │  Hot   │  T₁
                    │ Source │
                    └────────┘
                        ↓ Q₁
        Engine       ◯  Work W →
                        ↓ Q₂
                    ┌────────┐
                    │  Cold  │  T₂
                    │  Sink  │
                    └────────┘
```

Fig. 1

But Q_2/Q_1 must be related to the temperature differences. After all if the source and sink are at the same temperature no heat flows. In fact a scale of temperature can be defined in this way so that

$$\frac{Q_2}{Q_1} = T_2/T_1 .$$

This is the Kelvin or absolute scale of temperature for which the units are the same as degrees Centigrade, but 0° Centigrade (C) is equal to 273.2° Kelvin (K) and 100°C = 373.2°K. The scale is absolute in the sense that whereas negative Centigrade temperatures are familiar, negative temperatures on the Kelvin scale do not occur.

O"K" is an absolute zero of temperature.

We can now put our relationship for the ideal engine for the conversion of heat into work into the more usable form:

$$E = 1 - \frac{T_2}{T_1}$$

At best our cold sink is the surroundings at about 10°C or 283°K while it would be inadvisable to run an engine much above 600°C or 873°K because at high temperatures most materials, at least with time, would be mechanically unstable. Actually the temperature in the exploding gases in the combustion chamber can be as high as 2000°C for an extremely short period of time and this can help us a bit, as well as pointing to one of the fundamental limitations of a turbine where the moving rotor sees the hot burning gases more continuously. Anyway the temperatures given above suggest an efficiency (E) of about 68 per cent. However, in real combustion engines all the troublesome effects, such as acceleration, turbulence and heat conduction away from the working volume, make attainable efficiencies only about half this figure.

Another way of examining the efficiency of a petrol engine is to describe the cycle of processes involved in a simple idealized way and to work out the heat flows and work done during each stage. The idealized process is known as the Otto cycle, as shown in figure 2 above, where the state of the gases can be read off on the two scales: the vertical giving the value of the pressure and the horizontal the volume.

The piston sucks air and petrol vapour into the cylinder from e to a. In the compression stroke from a to b, all the work done is used to heat the mixture. In an idealization of the combustion process the temperature and thus pressure are raised still further, but at constant volume, to the point c, before the piston moves down. The hot gas itself now does work pushing down the piston, with no further intake of heat from the surroundings, and the gases reach the point d. The exhaust valve is now opened and, since at the end of the power stroke the gas is still hot, some will escape

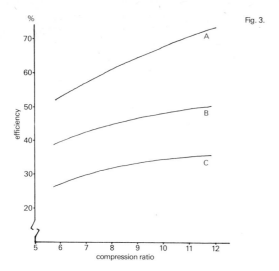

Fig. 3.

Figure 3   Curve A shows the totally idealized efficiencies as possible for the very simple model considered in the text. Curve B is a more realistic model for the thermal efficiency. Curve C is a typical real engine 'work out/heat of fuel in' efficiency and thus reflects the extra internal frictional losses. Note that pre-ignition limits the curves to compression ratios of about 10.5

between d and a, before exhaustion of the chamber from a to e.

The nature of the processes idealized in this way allows the magnitudes of pressure and volume at the points a, b, c and d to be related, and this in turn, with a little arithmetic, allows us to rewrite the efficiency statement as

$$E \simeq 1 - \frac{1}{\sqrt{r}}$$

where r is the compression ratio V_1/V_2.

This immediately points to the importance of the compression ratio of an engine. The higher this is, the greater the efficiency. Figure 3 above shows how the idealized efficiencies, and the actual attainable values for a typical engine, are related to the compression ratio.

Sadly, in real petrol engines the compression ratio cannot be made greater than about 10 because for much larger values the rise of temperature during the compression stroke would be sufficient to give ignition before the appointed time for the spark to be produced. This is preignition, an uncomfortable process in which an attempt is made to make the engine run backwards. We can now understand why lead additives are put into petrol, which raise the temperature of spontaneous ignition: they make higher compression ratios safe, and thus allow increased efficiency. In turn, we can understand the frustration of the engineers who seek to raise the efficiency of their engines in the face of anti-pollution laws, which will prohibit the use of these poisonous additives altogether.

Similar idealized cycles can be drawn for diesel engines, which on paper show that, at least as four-stroke engines, the former tend to have poorer efficiencies than the latter for similar compression ratios. This disadvantage of the diesel engine is more than compensated by the fact that in a diesel it is only air that is compressed during the compression stroke, the diesel fuel vapour being injected at the top of this stroke. Higher ratios of compression are therefore possible without any danger of preignition; and for this reason practical diesel engines can be considerably more efficient than petrol engines.

What then about the electric car? Electric power stored in a battery can be converted with extremely high efficiency, using an electric motor, into useful work for propulsion. Does this mean that being energy conscious we should take up the electric car seriously, despite the ghastly problems associated with the weight of the batteries needed to store sufficient energy for anything other than a gentle trip about town?

Unfortunately, when the batteries are charged the electrical energy that is put into them comes from a power station by the conversion, again, of some primary chemical energy fuel source such as coal or gas into heat energy which in turn, via turbines, produces the electricity. This primary process is, as for any engine, inefficient and overall the amounts of primary fuel required for a given amount of useful work in a car are pretty similar.

The main advantage of the electric car approach is that the heat loss in the power station is in one place and at least some attempt can be made to use the 'waste' heat. For cars with combustion engines this is impracticable.

Interestingly enough, some attempts have been made to harness the exhaust gases from the petrol engine, to run not only turbochargers but also, by exhausting at somewhat higher pressures, low temperature turbines from which power can be directly channelled to the road wheels.

Class 4   1700-2200cc

INTRODUCTION

Cars in this group should cater for the keen motorist: the driver who both enjoys going from place to place quickly and efficiently, and needs a reasonable amount of space. In this class he expects to go quickly, while keeping his passengers relaxed.

In a sense perhaps here we see rather easier and more traditional problems for the manufacturers than were faced by him with the rather more diverse requirements of the car buyer in either Class 2 or 3. The engineer has more room and weight to do a good job, and in general the products show this. At the same time the very lack of challenge, coupled with the demands of the marketplace, have meant that at least in recent years the more startling advances have been made in the newer requirement areas such as Class 3.

Engine design and development cost millions of pounds in the 1980s. Ford have found that the research and development for the new Escort cost £500 million, and several firms rather than face up to this have continued to develop their old engines, or added a turbo. The third possibility is to accept a Japanese power unit, as Lotus with Toyota and BL with Honda. The other answer is to create a combine and within it an engine development centre. This has been done by Citroën, Renault and Volvo – the Douvrin plant providing engines for all three firms. We thus discover that in the selection of cars which we have included in this category, of 1700–2200 cc, the Douvrin 2-litre all-alloy engine is found both in the Citroën CX Athena and the Peugeot 505.

The cars which have been chosen for this category initially on the basis of their good PD and fuel efficiency figures include examples from VW/Audi, Alfa Romeo, Ford, Peugeot and BMW. The Ford Cortina is deservedly one of the most popular cars for company fleets. Although the current example is first rate, we look forward to the new model which should prove to be a beautiful design. This is a bonus because Cortinas have made a name for their practicality and no-nonsense grit, but beauty as well?

Fuego GTX 2 litres – a remarkably well designed car

71

The bodyshells are by Giugiaro and similar in design. The 1.6, 1.8 and 2.0 litre engines, with their chain-driven oh camshafts, and the admirable suspension system, transaxle and Watt linkage are more important than a bodyshell could ever be

ALFA ROMEO GIULIETTA 2.0

This is not the place to go into the history of the Alfa Romeo marque although the current road cars owe so much to the traditions of dedicated racing car designers such as Satta Puglia that a thought at least should be spared for the two stage super-charged Tipo 159, which ruled the early postwar Grand Prix circuit.

While Puglia's four-cylinder '1900' touring car founded the commercial success of the company, its engine's twin chain driven overhead camshaft and 90 degree oriented valves looks, in its alloy head, remarkably like the current Giulietta engine. Many improvements have, of course, been made, but the basic concept went through the early Giuliettas of over twenty years ago, emerged in the seventies in the Alfettas, and has returned to the new Giulietta series.

For Alfa Romeo the Giuliettas with 1.6, 1.8 and 2.0 litre engines and before them the closely related Alfettas show their racing antecedents. The concept taken from the track is simple: it is to get the weight distribution right by putting the engine at the front and the gearbox at the back, together with the differential.

One might think that this should have the secondary advantage of making clutch replacement less of the disaster it can be if the engine has to be moved, but from personal if perhaps untutored experience on a mechanically similar Alfetta, this turns out not to be so: the rear suspension has to be moved out of the way instead.

However, the car is not an underweight overstrung racing machine. Far from it, it has large power reserves with peak, but then only slowly falling, torque from relatively low rpm compared with that for maximum power, and the engine approaches indestructability. Similarly the suspension and basic frame of both the Alfettas and the Giuliettas are fairly massive by comparison with their competitors.

We see in the Giulietta the right way of using race track experience in making a family saloon (and this *is* all it is). Alfa Romeo's approach has clearly been to detune their superb engine sufficiently to give it added flexibility and improved economy, to develop systematically and

Alfa Romeo Giulietta 2.0

Engine: 4 cylinders in line, double overhead camshaft, chain driven
Capacity: 1962 cc
Bore; stroke: 84 mm   88.5 mm
Carburation: 2 horizontal Dellorto
Max. power at 5400 rpm: 130 bhp   95.6 kW
Max. torque at 4000 rpm: 131 ft/lb   177.5 Nm

Transmission: Rear wheel drive via de Dion back-axle with 5 speed manual gearbox mounted with clutch ahead of the differential

Suspension:
Front: independent coil springs with wishbones and anti-roll bar.
Rear: de Dion axle tube with longitudinal struts connected by spherical joint side anchorage by Watts parallelogram axle assembly with gearbox connected to body by hypoid bevel pinion

Steering: Rack and pinion

Brakes: Servo assisted dual circuit front/rear with brake power regulator for rear wheels. All discs, rear mounted inboard

Dimensions:
Length: 13 ft 10 in   4.21 m
Kerb weight: 2428 lb   1100 kg

Performance:
Maximum speed: 112 mph   180 km/h
0–60 mph: 9.3 sec
Fuel consumption
   at 56 mph: 40.9 mpg   6.9 litres/100 km
   urban: 21.9 mpg   12.8 litres/100 km

Insurance Rating: 7

Derived Data:
bhp/litre (kW/litre): 66.2   48.7
bhp/ton (kW/tonne): 109.8   79.5
Speed × acceleration: 12.0
Performance Dimension: 11.0
Petrol consumption/ton at 56 mph (10/F): 5.8   (1.71)

---

make more stable and safe their highly advanced (for a road car) rear suspension, and then to call in the best designers to make the masterful engineering not just look good but be still more functional. As might be expected, when the search for compactness and efficient use of space goes hand in hand with a requirement for aerodynamic efficiency, the Italians naturally come up with a solution which is also elegant.

Having driven many thousands of miles in our own less beautiful but mechanically similar Alfetta 1.8, which is perhaps even more of a wolf in sheep's clothing, we can authoritatively state that the overall concept works. Certainly the Giulietta is great fun to drive, but not perhaps as much fun as one might have hoped given the Alfetta's behaviour.

The Giulietta's road holding is good, but not as good as it should be. Despite having set off to get the weight distribution right, in fact it ends up in this car being relatively poor. The result is fairly bad understeer particularly at low speeds. Of course this can be countered with the appropriate torque but the driver's attention is required and demanded.

While both the Giulietta and older Alfetta will do virtually anything asked of them, neither is particularly forgiving. They respond graciously to being driven, but feel distinctly ordinary if left alone. There are generally strong differences in the feel of whole ranges of one marque from another and in this it is interesting to compare the performance saloons of Germany, the BMWs, with those of Italy – arguably the Giuliettas and more recent GTVs. The BMWs are smooth almost to the point of lacking soul, with a terribly solid surefootedness: the Alfas are by comparison postively light of foot.

The Giulietta, even with its tendency to understeer, is a highly desirable family motor car. Given Alfa's reputation, and the proven ability of the suspension with a properly distributed weight above it, one hopes that appropriate modifications will be made. One can also only hope that Alfa have in fact, as they claim, learnt from past mistakes on corrosion protection.

73

A roomy five-door car with excellent roadholding

AUDI 100

The Audi 100 has a 5-cylinder in line, single overhead camshaft engine with a power of 136 bhp, a top speed of 117 mph, and 0–60 acceleration of 9.5 seconds. It also has a rather conservative image, in the same way that most Mercedes are conservative, which is no bad thing.

The suspension follows the established VW norm – MacPherson struts and lower wishbones with anti-roll bar front, and torsion beam axle with Panhard rod, at the rear. Brakes are disc front, drums rear, and need to be discs all round due to the performance.

The new facia has speedometer, tachometer drive and clock, plus improved ventilation and a padded steering wheel. There is nothing luxurious about it, but nor is there anything lacking. VW and Audi have added an economy, or vacuum gauge, to advise drivers when they should drive more economically – a small arrow on the instrument panel which lights up when a computer believes it is time to change up.

Although it does this very well, following its advice has a depressing effect, like cribbing at school. We find it

more satisfying to try to achieve better fuel consumption figures by using every economical driving device in the business.

Handling and roadholding are first rate, but not so satisfying as the 80 GLE. The bigger shell is heavier and more difficult to throw about, but still immensely satisfying. There is a lot of room inside the car. It has a low centre of gravity and at the end of long journeys no one grumbled. The electric door lifts and centre locking, heating and ventilation, are all fine, but the steerwheel is too large and ugly with it, safety pad or no.

We, the co-authors, have cars of our own, plus cars to road test, and if the Audi 100 was available it was always used – a compliment. The car's performance figures are clearly very good. We felt that it is in the first three we would choose in the 1700–2200 cc category, together with the Alfa Romeo Giulietta and the Renault Fuego. The Fuego is the most visually attractive, the Alfa is first choice for drivers and the Audi 100 has more going for it in several directions – simultaneously.

The safety pad protects the driver

Audi 100 Saloon GL5E and CD5E manual
(The CD5E includes extra features such as central locking and electrically operated windows)

Engine: 5 cylinders in line single overhead camshaft, belt driven
Capacity: 2144 cc
Bore; stroke: 79.5 mm   86.4 mm
Compression ratio: 9.3 to 1
Injection: Bosch K-Jetronic
Max. power at 5700 rpm: 136 bhp   100 kW
Max. torque at 4200 rpm: 136 ft/lb   185 Nm

Transmission: Front wheel drive by 4 speed (or extra: 5 speed) manual gearbox via differential and double joint semi-axles. 3 speed, automatic standard on CD model can be optionally discarded

Suspension: Coil springs all round.
Front: independent MacPherson struts and lower wishbones and anti-roll bar.
Rear: torsion crank axle with Panhard rod

Steering: Power assisted rack and pinion
Turning circle: 37 ft 8.5 in   11.3 m

Brakes: Dual diagonal servo assisted. Front discs and rear drums

Dimensions:
Length: 15 ft 4 in   4.68 m
Weight unladen: 2649 lb   1204 kg

Performance:
Maximum speed: 117 mph   188 km/h
0–60 mph: 9.5 sec
Fuel consumption
    at 56 mph: 31.4 mpg   9 litres/100 km
    at 75 mph: 25.7 mpg   11 litres/100 km
    urban: 18.5 mpg   15.3 litres/100 km

Insurance Rating: 7

Derived Data:
bhp/litre (kW/litre): 63.4   46.6
bhp/ton (kW/tonne): 106   76.7
Speed × acceleration: 12.3
Performance Dimension: 11.6
Petrol consumption/ton at 56 mph (10/F): 7.02   (1.42)
Change in petrol consumption between 56 & 75 mph: 22%

BMW 316 and 320

The smallest of the BMW cars, the 316 has a four-cylinder engine with a solex carburettor, producing 90 bhp at 5500 rpm, 105 ft/lb of torque at 4000 rpm, 103 mph and 0–60 in 11.6 seconds. Steering is by ZF rack and pinion, brakes are disc front, drums rear, and the unladen weight is a ton.

The price puts it in competition with the VW Golf GTi, the Alfa Romeo Giulietta 1.6, the Lancia Beta 1600 Coupé and the Ford Escort XRS. The BMW 316 is a quality car made small and less expensive, which is something almost everyone is looking for, for it is a well known fact that you cannot make a volume production car into a quality car by adding expensive extras.

As a matter of fact in standard form the 316 is rather stark. Its quality is indisputably there, but it is bereft of the 5 speed box, rev counter, alloy wheels, competition suspension and sliding roof, all of which we should love to put straight back again. As against the élite exotic rockets for two, this is more of a family car with sporting characteristics, and excellent in that category.

The 1766 cc engine is the only four cylinder now made by BMW, and the unit from which the superb F2 engine is derived. It therefore comes as a depressing shock to find that the top speed of 103 is inferior to the Golf GTi's 110, and the acceleration 0–60 of 11.6 is slower than the Golf's 8.2. But wait, the 316 can progress at near its top speed all day long, with complete refinement, engine and transmission sweetness, and a quietness which the Golf GTi never achieves. The precision of handling and total response from power unit and chassis, helped by putting back the Bilstein dampers, puts the car in a high category.

The pilot has been taken care of in seating, controls and visibility, and the rear passengers have sufficient room and well designed seats. The heating and ventilation are satisfactory, and the suspension first rate.

For an 800 mile road test including the mountains of the West Coast of Scotland, and motorways to and from, the 316 produced an overall fuel consumption of 26.5 mpg and no problems or criticisms. Made aware of

Opposite: *BMW 316*

Right: *BMW 320*

BMW 316 and (320)

Engine: 4 cylinders (6 cylinders) inclined
Capacity: 1766 (1990) cc
Bore; stroke: 89 (80) mm 71 (66) mm
Compression ratio: 8.3 (9.2) to 1
Carburation: Compound Solex DIDTA 32/33 (Compound Solex 4A)
Max. power at 6000 rpm: 98 (122) bhp 72 (90) kW
Max. torque at 4000 rpm: 104.9 (117.9) ft/lb 142 (160) Nm

Transmission: 4 speed Getrag manual (Automatic: ZF 3HP22)

Suspension:
Front: independent struts with coil springs. Torsion bar stabilizer acts as tension strut.
Rear: independent coil spring struts and trailing arms and swing bracket on differential. Axle/gearbox unit 3 point suspended. (Anti-roll bar)

Steering: ZF rack and pinion, lock to lock 4.05 turns
Turning circle: 31 ft 6 in 9.6 m

Brakes: Dual circuit front/rear, servo assisted. 10.1 in (25.7 cm) front discs, 9.9 in (25.2 cm) rear drums

Dimensions:
Length: 14 ft 3½ in 4.35 m
Kerb weight: 2249 (2459) lb 1020 (1115) kg

Performance:
Maximum speed: 103 (113) mph 165 (181) km/h
0–60 mph: 11.6 (10.4) sec
Fuel consumption
at 56 mph: 32.6 (31.3) mpg 7.2 (7.5) litres/100 km
at 75 mph: 24.2 (23.3) mpg 9.7 (10.1) litres/100 km
urban: 19.8 (18.1) mpg 11.9 (13.0) litres/100 km

Insurance Rating: 7

Derived Data:
bhp/litre (kW/litre): 55.5 (61.3) 40.8 (45.2)
bhp/ton (kW/tonne): 88.8 (101.9) 64.2 (74)
Speed × acceleration: 8.9 (10.9)
Performance Dimension: 10 (10.7)
Petrol consumption/ton at 56 mph (10/F): 6.5 (6.3)
1.54 (1.59)
Change in petrol consumption between 56 & 75 mph: 35% (35%)

---

the ultimate by the experience of driving the 635 CSi, we anticipated disappointments, but there were none. It rained with a real frenzy in the Highlands, but the 316 positively refused to skid about or oversteer and the fact that there was a very slight whine from first gear was not, we felt, reprehensible.

The highest levels of motoring technology are being realized, increasingly, in more compact motor cars, and the BMW 320 is a prime example. The six cylinder engine has a crankshaft with twelve counter-weights and is therefore free from vibration. An unobtrusive front spoiler lowers wind resistance and diminishes front-axle lift, and this is necessary because the 1990 cc engine has an output of 90 kW (122 bhp) producing a maximum speed of 113 mph (181 km/h) and acceleration from 0–60 mph in 10.4 seconds (the automatic box taking 13.6 seconds). There is an optional overdrive fifth gear on the Getrag gearbox which one imagines will soon be made standard as it is invaluable. The steering is by ZF rack

and pinion and the brakes are disc front, drum rear. The petrol consumption of 29 mpg is considerably improved due to the overdrive fifth gear.

As always, the BMW seats are so well shaped, carefully sprung, and capable of such fine adjustment that anyone of any size or shape can be made comfortable. The three rotary controls for heating (temperature, distribution and fan) together with the overall volume slide for ventilation are among the best and most effective we have seen. One of the outstanding features of the 3 series is that the overall finish bears a relationship only to the BMW standard and not the price.

CITROËN CX ATHENA

While new to the Citroën, the Douvrin engine, made by Française de Mécanique and known as the 829 unit, is fitted to both the Renault 20 and the Peugeot 505. In the CX Athena it has a twin choke Weber DMTR 46/250 carburettor and gives the car a maximum power output/tonne of 59.4 kW, only about 9 per cent less than the fuel injected, bigger but older 2397 cc engine, for example in the rather heavier GTi. Like that of the GTi, the Athena's power to weight ratio is well above average, and its performance dimension of 11.8 equals that of the GSA Pallas; indeed, in the whole of the Citroën range it is bettered only by the GTi.

Interestingly, it is not the engine alone which makes the Athena economic, nor is it entirely the aerodynamic bodyshell, a common feature of the CX range. A comparison of the fuel consumption for the Reflex and Athena is informative. The essential difference between the two cars, both of which have the Douvrin engine, is the improvement in power usage facilitated by the 5 speed gearbox of the Athena.

The Athena thus has a slightly better performance than the Reflex and markedly improved fuel consumption. At 90 km/h the petrol consumption is 7.1 litres/100 km; some 10 per cent better than the Reflex. In terms of fuel usage/ton at this speed the figure of 5.4 litres/100 km/ton is nearly 20 per cent better than that of any of the GS or Visa range except for the specially economical GS Special, which it betters by a mere 10 per cent!

Like the CX GTi, the Athena is a car with both good performance and good fuel consumption. Comparison of petrol consumption with performance dimension for both cars suggests that the Athena has the better combination, but this is not the only reason why we prefer it to the GTi. We have noted (Citroën GTi page 104) the general problems for the uninitiated driver in a CX, though given familiarization, our only retained dislike concerned the Varipower steering. Essentially perhaps the basic problem with the GTi is that its potential performance somewhat outstrips its *comfor-*

Opposite: *Most Citroëns look as though they could wear wings to advantage*

Right: *The 2 litre Douvrin engine with twin-choke Weber carburettor*

Citroën CX Athena

Engine: Single ohc belt driven. 4 in line, transverse. Head and block light alloy.
Capacity: 1995 cc
Bore; stroke: 88 mm   82 mm
Compression ratio: 9.2 to 1
Carburettor: Weber twin choke 46/250
Max. power at 5500 rpm: 106 bhp   79.1 kW
Max. torque at 3250 rpm: 122 lb/ft   165 Nm

Transmission: 5 speed all synchromesh gearbox. Front wheel with constant velocity drive shafts

Suspension: Hydropneumatic, self-levelling

Steering: Fully powered VariPower rack and pinion
Turning circle: 35 ft 9 in   10.9 m

Brakes: Power operated hydraulic dual circuit front and rear discs (front ventilated)

Dimensions:
Length: 15 ft 2½ in   4.64 m
Kerb weight: 2712 lb   1230 kg

Performance:
Maximum speed: 109 mph   175 km/h
0–60 mph: 11.4 sec
Fuel consumption
  at 56 mph: 34.8 mpg   7.1 litres/100 km
  at 75 mph: 31.4 mpg   9.0 litres/100 km
  urban: 23.3 mpg   12.1 litres/100 km

Insurance Rating: 6

Derived Data:
bhp/litre (kW/litre): 53.1   39.6
bhp/ton (kW/tonne): 80.9   59.4
Speed × acceleration: 9.6
Performance Dimension: 11.8
Petrol consumption/ton at 56 mph (10/F): 5.4 (1.85)
Change in petrol consumption between 56 & 75 mph: 27%

---

table, though not its *safe*, handling capability. This is less true for the Athena, though it too is far from sluggardly. We feel perhaps that the Athena can be enjoyed by passengers and driver alike rather more than the GTi, in that the admittedly totally safe roll and pitch on being steered hard are a bit less apparent. In our opinion, the Athena's marginally lower power gives the car the best balance of performance, comfort and economy.

The Athena is generally well equipped, the seats superbly comfortable and supportive, and the leg room for the rear passengers more than adequate. The heating system is now efficient and easy to generate despite the proximity of the controls, effectively out of sight at the driver's side, to the height change lever. The car is naturally quiet. All the CX range are well soundproofed and relaxing at high speed, partially because of the smooth body lines and low drag factor. The Douvrin engine is however naturally quieter than either its predecessor or the 2.4 litre unit, and adds a note of refinement with singular lack of fuss.

The driver's instrumentation is generally adequate, the battery of warning lights readily visible through the steering wheel. While many dislike the rotating drum rev counter and speedometer, they are clear and their relatively small size compared with more conventional instrumentation make it the more surprising that an oil pressure gauge is not included on the facia. Warning lights tend to be signals of disaster! The control pods for indicators, lights, windscreen wipers and horn are accessible to the driver's finger tips and excellent, though why the indicators are not self-cancelling seems a bit Gallic.

FIAT MIRAFIORI SPORT

The Fiat Abarth 131 Rally car, which won the World Rally Championships in 1977, 78 and 80, is closely related to the Fiat Mirafiori Sport. Seventy-five per cent related. Sceptical about this fact, and feeling certain that the other twenty-five per cent might be the parts which really mattered, we drove the test car.

After a hundred miles, covering the hideous mishmash of cross country roads from the South East to Wales, we found that it was a better car than most; sober and almost unfaultable. For another hundred miles, it persuaded us that it was better than that, because the smaller roads around the Snowdonia range suited it to perfection. It was flexible enough and strong enough, and made like a sporting rifle, all the controls working well.

Except for that hideous stylist's job of a facia (stylists should be shown a Bugatti facia and told 'this is the latest and best, copy it carefully'), they have been kept out of this car in the main, and it is simple and beautiful because of it, inside and out.

The seats are supportive in all directions, and the driver's position is perfect – commanding. The passengers did not object to anything and were not thrown about, even on the Welsh whirligig minor roads. Then on the return journey, another 250 miles, now with a navigator who found the motorway, when the engine showed that it was a master of high speed cruising, and the suspension having a well earned rest from the mountains and the sudden irregularities of sliding slates and rocks.

As we got out, and looking at it with different eyes and a feeling of complete respect, we discovered that it is *the* most unostentatious, modest, but extremely virile sports car – a wolf dressed rather like a mole. With rally gruelling and regular modifications it has learned the hard, pragmatic way to a kind of perfection.

With world success since 1977, it might well have had a few appalling go faster stripes like the Starsky and Hutch car, but its disarming simplicity is one of the other good things about it. No high jinks, no operatics, just a

Fiat Mirafiori 131 Sport

Engine: 4 cylinders in line, belt driven double overhead camshaft. Alloy head.
Capacity: 1995 cc
Bore; stroke: 84 mm   90 mm
Compression ratio: 8.9 to 1
Carburation: Twin choke Weber 34 ADF 15/250
Max. power at 5800 rpm: 115 bhp   85.8 kW
Max. torque at 3600 rpm: 123 ft/lb   167 Nm

Transmission: 5 speed manual

Suspension:
Front: independent by MacPherson struts, coil springs, lower transverse links and trailing links and anti-roll bar.
Rear: live axle located by four trailing arms and a Panhard rod

Steering: Rack and pinion
Turning circle: 33 ft 9 in   10.3 m

Brakes: Dual, split front/rear, servo assisted. 8.9 in (22.6 cm) discs on front, 9 in (22.9 cm) drums on rear

Dimensions:
Length: 14 ft   4.27 m
Kerb weight: 2374 lb   1076 kg

Performance:
Maximum speed: 109 mph   170 km/h
0–60 mph: 10.3 secs
Fuel consumption
   at 56 mph: 33.2 mpg   8.5 litres/100 km
   at 75 mph: 26.3 mpg   10.7 litres/100 km
   urban: 21.9 mpg   12.9 litres/100 km

Insurance Rating: 6

Derived Data:
bhp/litre (kW/litre): 57.6   43
bhp/ton (kW/tonne): 99.1   72.8
Speed × acceleration: 10.6
Performance Dimension: 10.7
Petrol consumption/ton at 56 mph (10/F): 7.3   (1.36)
Change in petrol consumption between 56 & 75 mph: 26%

hard to beat driving machine. The twin cam engine transmits its 112 bhp smoothly through the 5 speed gearbox with its well placed ratios to give a 0–60 mph acceleration time of 10.3 seconds, and an average fuel consumption of 30 mpg. The rally car develops 140 bhp, and the racing version 215 bhp. If you look carefully at those figures you will notice that the rally car has 28 more bhp, while the ultimate version has 103 more bhp. Both also have very much better power/weight ratios, but at the expense of comfort.

Left: *An unassuming appearance concealing power and efficiency*

Above: *The Fiat Abarth 131 rally car, world champion 1977, 78 and 80*

Right: *This one is classically simple with twin-choke Weber and double oh camshafts*

FORD CORTINA 2.0 GL

A word or two more on the Mk 4 Cortinas would appear to be necessary. Admittedly one of us at least must admit to a fair amount of bias, both for many of the Ford range and for several of the Alfas, having owned a number of them. While it is true that the two marques are very different in their approach to mechanical innovation, they do in fact have common attributes.

They go rather well, and are interesting to drive. This, amazingly, is nearly as true of the 2 litre Cortina as it is of the Giulietta. In fact in terms of performance alone, as we describe it, the ancient 1993 cc belt driven overhead camshaft Ford engine comes out quite extraordinarily well.

An interesting comparison can be made on the Cortina with the use of the 2.3 litre, more modern V6 engine. The car with the latter power unit is marginally quicker, but has a bhp 14 per cent better and is only slightly heavier. Thus, while the 2.0 litre car has the exceptional Performance Dimension of 12.3, the 2.3 litre Cortina manages only a laudable, but essentially unremarkable, figure of 11.6.

Equally, if we compare the cars on fuel efficiency, the bigger engined V6 uses a fair amount more fuel, and has a fuel efficiency figure of only 1.44 to compare with 1.55 for the 2 litre car. The comparison brings out the point that, at least in this instance, the smaller engined car can have both better performance and better economy: a fairly unusual feat.

Interestingly enough, however, in the heavier Granada the position is reversed; the fuel consumption figures of the two engines are almost identical, but the more powerful V6 engine gives the better performance and Performance Dimension. Examples of this type, showing reversed performance behaviour for a given pair of engines in two different bodies are necessarily rare but serve to demonstrate rather neatly the way in which performance is a function of the whole car, not just the engine.

The curves, brightware and extravaganza of the old Ford bodyshell have all been honed away. The shape now has a classical simplicity which puts it in the top rank. (It is also a relief to see bodyshells which are not influenced by Giugiaro or Bertone)

Ford Cortina 2.0 L and GL Manual

Engine: 4 cylinders, single overhead camshaft, belt driven
Capacity: 1993 cc
Bore; stroke: 90.8 mm   77 mm
Compression ratio: 9.2 to 1
Carburation: Ford
Max. power at 5200 rpm: 101 bhp   75.3 kW
Max. torque at 4000 rpm: 112.8 ft/lb   153 Nm

Transmission: Four speed manual rear wheel drive

Suspension:
Front: independent short and long arms, coil springs and anti-roll bar.
Rear: four bar link variable rate coil springs and anti-roll bar

Steering: Rack and pinion 3.7 turns lock to lock
Turning circle: 32 ft 9.5 in   10.1 m

Brakes: Dual line, servo assisted 9.75 in (24.8 cm) discs on front and 9 in (22.9 cm) drums on rear

Dimensions:
Length: 14 ft 3 in   4.34 m
Kerb weight: 2376 lb   1080 kg

Performance:
Maximum speed: 105 mph   169 km/h
0–60 mph: 9.8 secs
Fuel consumption
   at 56 mph: 37.7 mpg   7.5 litres/100 km
   at 75 mph: 28.8 mpg   9.8 litres/100 km
   urban: 25.5 mpg   11.1 litres/100 km

Insurance Rating: 5

Derived Data:
bhp/litre (kW/litre): 50.7   37.8
bhp/ton (kW/tonne): 87   63.9
Speed × acceleration: 10.7
Performance Dimension: 12.3
Petrol consumption/ton at 56 mph (10/F): 6.46   (1.55)
Change in petrol consumption between 56 & 75 mph: 31%

PEUGEOT 504 GR

It will undoubtedly surprise the fashion conscious to see this fairly ancient car listed here rather than, say, the much newer 505 GR. After all the 504 was launched in 1968, and the 505, at least in TL and STL form, is fairly hot off the development track with the 2 litre Douvrin of the Renault 20 and the Citroën CX.

In a sense we should perhaps more fairly compare the 505 TL with the old 504 GR, and then certainly the 505 TL would win hands down. The 505 TL has, in fact, a performance dimension of 11.6, rather similar to that of the smaller engined 504 GR, but it is also more economic. The PD of the 505 GR with the more familiar older Peugeot 2 litre engine is about 10.5, which puts the car just about exactly on our average behavioural line.

One can take these things too far, however, and it's certainly worth noting (see summary, page 90) that the 505 GR is considerably more energy conscious than its predecessor. In a sense we can thus understand why the 505, although faster and more accelerative than the 504, does not do still better for its increased power to

weight ratio. The car's behavioural characteristics must follow the trend CD in fuel economy versus PD (*Fuel Efficiency*, page 92) and it has simply been guided into an overall position in which it doesn't look as good as the 504 on PD alone.

Really we have chosen the 504 GR here to make precisely this point. While the PD alone is a good guide to engineering quality (and the 504 GR is a well designed car) examining the relative behaviour in terms of fuel usage and PD gives just the added information needed to form a sensible impression. In fact the 505 is based fairly heavily on the 504, both having essentially the same overall layout with front mounted engine and rear wheel drive, and both sharing the same suspension geometry.

It is fundamentally for us the return to a rear wheel drive, an increasing rarity in modern medium sized saloons, which brings home the essential difficulties of making any front wheel drive car handle as responsively. While everyone admired the 504 for its

In theory we are concerned with the relative merits of the 504 and 505 when put into the mathematical melting pot, but visually the 505 wins with ease, both inside and out

Peugeot 504 (505) GR

Engine: 4 cylinders in line, 45° inclined. (Aluminium alloy head, side camshaft)
Capacity: 1796 (1971) cc
Bore; stroke: 84 (88) mm   81 (81) mm
Compression ratio: 8.8 to 1
Carburation: single (twin) choke
Max. power at 5100 (5200) rpm: 79 (96) bhp   58.9 (71.6) kW
Max. torque at 2500 (3000) rpm: 105 (118) ft/lb   142.4 (160) Nm

Transmission: 4 speed manual (optional automatic)

Suspension:
Front: independent struts, coil springs, anti-roll bar.
Rear: independent semi-trailing arms, coil springs, anti-roll bar

Steering: Rack and pinion (powered, 3¼ turns lock to lock)
Turning circle: 35 ft 9 in (34 ft 9 in)   10.9 (10.6) m

Brakes: Dual circuit servo assisted. Front discs, rear drums

Dimensions:
Length: 14 ft 9 in (15 ft)   4.49 (4.58) m
Weight unladen: 2557 (2645) lb   1160 (1200) kg

Performance:
Maximum speed: 96 (102) mph   154 (164) km/h
0–60 mph: 12.9 (13) sec
Fuel consumption
   at 56 mph: 35.7 (39.8) mpg   7.9 (7.1) litres/100 km
   at 75 mph: 26.9 (29.1) mpg   10.5 (9.7) litres/100 km
   urban: 22 (24.8) mpg   12.8 (11.4) litres/100 km

Insurance Rating: 4 (6)

Derived Data:
bhp/litre (kW/litre): 44 (48.7)   32.8 (36.3)
bhp/ton (kW/tonne): 63.6 (74.9)   46.7 (55)
Speed × acceleration: 7.44 (7.85)
Performance Dimension: 11.7 (10.5)
Petrol consumption/ton at 56 mph (10/F): 6.36 (5.54)   1.57 (1.8)
Change in petrol consumption between 56 & 75 mph: 33% (37%)

handling capabilities the 505, with its slight revisions of springs and dampers and more importantly wider track, is a definite improvement. Actually, although the power steering on the 505 TL is good, relatively small cars like the 504 don't need it, and this again is a basic reason we could give for preferring the 504. It is, though, fairly nonsensical to suggest that one should prefer a car with slightly less good cornering ability just because one can feel more sensitively its limitations!

By now the cat should be out of the bag. The 504 GR is here, rather than say the 505 TL, partly because for its time the 504 was remarkable and partly to make the point that one needs to examine the performance and fuel efficiency, as well as the Performance Dimension, before deciding what is best. We would still like to see the 505 GR pushed a little bit further down the track from economy to improved performance, however, to make it a better balanced car.

But the point is that given the presence of as good a performer as the 505 TL, the other car should be the slow drinker, and this is clearly the way Peugeot have taken their development from the old 504, with its remarkably high torque (at low rpm) engine. The 505 TL will undoubtedly, and rightly, do well, but at the lower power end of the scale we think one can fairly decide that the 504 GR is a better balanced car than the 505 GR.

Above and opposite below: *One of the most original and attractive bodies of 1981 as an aerodynamic shape, and an interior with great variety of use*

Opposite above: *The cutaway shows the Douvrin 4-cylinder all-alloy engine with electronic ignition and Weber carburettor*

RENAULT FUEGO GTX

The Renault Fuego has a drag coefficient of 0.34 per cent recorded at the St Cyr wind tunnel, which is 29 per cent better than the quite pretty but distinctly middle-aged Ford Capri, measured in the same tunnel at the same time.

The GTX uses the Douvrin 2 litre all alloy 4-cylinder engine developing 110 bhp and 119 ft/lb torque, which is also the power unit of the Renault 20TS, Citroën Athena and Peugeot 505. A sophisticated computer-controlled electronic ignition system improves the combustion process, and carburation is by Weber. The engine is placed longitudinally and ahead of the front axle line, the power coming through a five speed box to the front wheels.

The front suspension is of pressed wishbones with coil springs, damper units and anti-roll bar, together with newly designed steering with negative offset geometry, and power assisted rack and pinion. Rear suspension consists of a dead rear axle, located by trailing arms, central A bracket, and anti-roll bar.

The good aerodynamics mean not only that there is little wind noise but also both that the top speed is high and the high speed acceleration is good. But the weight at 2377 lb (1080 kg) (due to the luxurious interior), together with high intermediate gearing, make acceleration lower down disappointing. Handling is excellent. The power steering, negative offset geometry, Pirelli P6s and the only very slight and predictable understeer make it much more satisfactory in this respect than other Renaults. The brakes are very good indeed.

The interior is spacious, the boot is enormous, and the folding rear seats make it more so. Ventilation and heating is newly designed and first rate.

The pilot has a superb facia layout, with 14 warning lights, excellent dials, and large press panel switches beside the binnacle. The passengers are well looked after also with ergonomically well designed seats, together with real four seater space and habitability. The interior in fact is so well designed and luxurious that passengers feel aware and proud of it and keep it so.

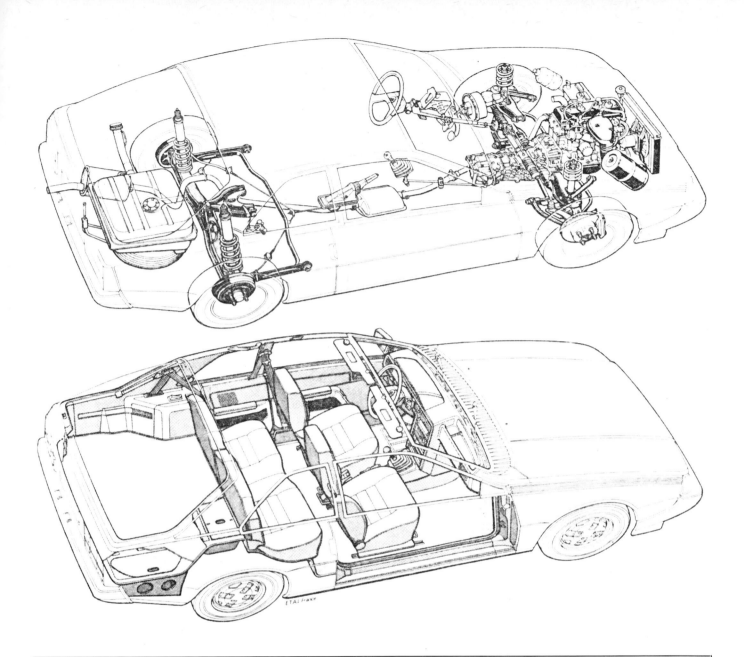

ETAI France

Renault Fuego TX and GTX

Engine: '829' all alloy, ohc, 4 cylinders in line
Capacity: 1995 cc
Bore; stroke: 88 mm 82 mm
Max. power at 5500 rpm: 110 bhp 82 kW
Max. torque at 3000 rpm: 120 ft/lb 163 Nm

Transmission: 4 speed manual

Suspension: Anti-roll bars front and rear.
Front: independent, transverse 4 bar linkage, double
wishbones and coil springs.
Rear: rigid axle and coil springs

Steering: Rack and pinion (negative offset geometry)

Brakes: Double, servo assisted 9.4 in (23.9 cm) discs at front
and 9 in (22.9 cm) drums on rear

Dimensions:
Length: 14 ft 3½ in 4.36 m
Kerb weight: 2377 lb 1080 kg

Performance:
Maximum speed: 115 mph 185 km/h
0–60 mph: 10.1 sec
Fuel consumption
  at 56 mph: 43.5 mpg 6.5 litres/100 km
  at 75 mph: 34.4 mpg 8.2 litres/100 km
  urban: 24.4 mpg 11.6 litres/100 km

Insurance Rating: 6

Derived Data:
bhp/litre (kW/litre): 55.1 41.1
bhp/ton (kW/tonne): 94.7 69.5
Speed × acceleration: 11.4
Performance Dimension: 12.0
Petrol consumption/ton at 56 mph (10/F): 5.6 (1.79)
Change in petrol consumption between 56 & 75 mph: 26%

TALBOT SUNBEAM LOTUS

This car is genuinely intriguing. Before we get down to why, it must be said from the outset that in terms at least of its acceleration it is outstanding. It accelerates to 60 mph in a time rather less than that taken by a Lotus Elite or Eclat, which have an improved engine and are of similar weight, and equally outstrips 'super cars' such as the Maserati Kyalami. It takes a Ferrari 308 GTB to knock a mere 3 per cent off the relevant time, though a car like the Lotus Esprit does the job rather more effectively.

Essentially the Talbot Sunbeam is a rather light weight and graceful looking car, particularly from the rear with its large glass tail gate. In most forms it is far from slow if generally not all that adventurous. It thus comes as somewhat of a shock to feel one's apprehension rising on first acquaintance with Lotus variant. The black and silver paintwork and alloy wheels together with high backed grey driving seat (actually giving rather little lateral support) are all aggression. This car is an adrenalin raiser.

The engine at least is a very pleasing sight. The unit was designed by Lotus specifically for Talbot and much effort has clearly gone into the collaboration to ensure that the car be sufficiently flexible for road use as well as being a base for competition development. The '911' engine (do Porsche mind?) is essentially a mid way house in terms of both power and refinement between the old '907' and the '912' used by Lotus in their own 2.2 series cars (see Lotus Esprit 2.2 p. 162).

With the capacity of the 912 it lacks, despite its sixteen valves, the higher rpm, torque or power of the latter engine. It it were not however for Lotus' development to the 912 stage one would say that the 911 was superb, and even in the presence of the 912 the 911 remains exceptional. Of course without the engine Talbot would not have an appropriately glamorous package to advertise the rest of the range, though this is unfair to the extent that the car clearly is an important part of Talbot's own competition programme and thus a lot more than a billboard.

In this context it's perhaps surprising that more has

Talbot Sunbeam Lotus

Engine: '911' Lotus engine, slant 4 cylinders in line, alloy block and head with dohc belt driven for 4 valves per cylinder
Capacity: 2172 cc
Bore; stroke: 95.2 mm   76.2 mm
Compression ratio: 9.4 to 1
Carburation: 2 Dellorto DHLA 45E twin choke (downdraught)
Max. power at 6500 rpm: 150 bhp   118.8 kW
Max. torque at 5000 rpm: 150 ft/lb   203.5 Nm

Transmission: Manual 5 speed ZF box

Suspension: Coil springs all round with live rear axle and MacPherson struts, lower transverse arms and drag links and an anti-roll bar at the front

Steering: Rack and pinion

Brakes: Servo assisted dual circuit front/rear for 9.5 in (24.1 cm) discs at front and 8 in (20.3 cm) drums at rear

Dimensions:
Length: 12 ft 6.5 in   3.83 m
Kerb weight: 2116 lb   960 kg

Performance:
Maximum speed: 118 mph   190 km/h
0–60 mph: 6.8 secs
Fuel consumption
   at 56 mph: 30.1 mpg   9.38 litres/100 km
   at 75 mph: 22.4 mpg   12.6 litres/100 km
   urban: 13.8 mpg   20.5 litres/100 km

Insurance Rating: 6

Derived Data:
bhp/litre (kW/litre): 69.1   51.5
bhp/ton (kW/tonne): 143.6   105.3
Speed × acceleration: 17.3
Performance Dimension: 12.1
Petrol consumption/ton at 56 mph: 9.0
Change in petrol consumption between 56 & 75 mph: 34%

not been done to match the engine to the rest of the car. While the Ti handles well with its much less powerful engine, the suspension has essentially just been stiffened up a little while the front discs have been thickened. Other modifications include the incorporation of the ZF gearbox originally designed to handle the power from really brutal engines.

Though the car is to say the least not cheap, do we thus see the signs of the relatively inexpensive incomplete development of an existing model? Depressingly, while a performance dimension of 12.1 looks good at first sight, for the car's power to weight ratio this figure is in fact just about on the 'average behavioural line'.

Again, the petrol consumption figures are horrifying. The car drinks more petrol for what it does than it should, and that by a very unhealthy margin. That this is not the fault of the engine is clearly demonstrated by comparison with the performance figures and petrol consumptions of the four seat Lotus, which is actually of very similar weight, with either the lower powered old 907 engine or the newer 912 unit. The Elite 2.2 has for example a Performance Dimension of 13.9, and petrol consumptions at 56 and 75 mph which are respectively 17 and 24 per cent better than those for the Sunbeam Lotus.

An unfair comparison? Certainly, at least to the extent that the Lotus is a fully engineered and developed piece of machinery. It also undoubtedly costs even more, but perhaps on the above basis one can see why this had to be so.

The Sunbeam Lotus is not a bad car, and it doesn't after all pretend to be anything other than what it is: an extremely exhilarating and aggressively styled modification of a good basic family saloon.

1700–2200 cc: SUMMARY

Few could really logically argue that they have a genuine need for bigger cars than we see in this group, and still fewer could claim that they regularly needed the performance that can be obtained with at least the more highly stressed engines of this size. At the same time, while the high speeds attainable are of use now legally only on the *Autobahns*, good acceleration in the 50–70 mph speed range can do a lot for the sanity of even the average driver, as well as get him out of trouble if his driving skills turn out not to be as good as he or his passengers would wish them to be.

Cars of this engine size can show a surprising range of performance: for some the manufacturer has been more concerned with quality of finish, for others he goes all out for the highest performance possible. As usual, one could argue that it is with the better balanced car that we should be concerned, though there are adherents to both extremes who do need to be catered for.

Somewhat surprisingly, at the low end of the performance scale we have the smaller engined, and conventionally aspirated, BMWs both of the 3 and 5 series. These are, however, undoubtedly beautifully finished motor cars, and for their power to weight ratio none perform badly, and equally for their weight they are rather economic, demonstrating their superior engineering. We see however that not all BMWs are particularly performance conscious!

At the other end of the scale we have the Lotus engined Talbot Sunbeam: all engine, but for its performance a rather poor performance dimension and fuel efficiency figure. This is not a sports car, in the sense that it doesn't appear to be engineered as such, more a very fast toy.

The two Peugeots were included really as a demonstration of how the old 504 can hold its head up quite well, but it should be remembered that the 505 with the 2 litre Douvrin engine matches the old car's PD with much better performance; the 505 GR is really strictly the economy car and this shows in its data.

The 2 litre Mirafiori is certainly not slow. Even if it appears to be more of a scaled up small car than a detuned sports car our experiences left us with a very favourable impression. We then have a group of cars which in their own individual ways are all exceptional. That fifth cylinder of the Audi 100 G5E certainly does give it smoothness as well as good performance. The old Capri 2.0S is for its power to weight ratio very quick and again surprisingly economic for its weight, though if driven hard it gets a lot more thirsty. In the Cortina we have the extraordinary ability of Ford to come up with a desirable product which is undoubtedly awfully good value for money. With the old 2 litre four-cylinder ohc engine it has really quite reasonable performance and economy and will rightly go on selling well.

For the individualist with a penchant for styling, the Athena is a very desirable motor car, and though in the lower end of the performance bracket clearly well engineered as well as handsome.

For us, however, the two cars of real interest here are the Giulietta and the Fuego. Perhaps in the Giulietta we are a bit biased but that old double overhead camshaft engine is worth a fraction of understeer any day. The Renault Fuego, though by no means the car of highest performance in the group, looks as if it could well be a winner. While we, however, will stick to our Alfa we know that for the still more traditionally minded the Audi 100 GL5E takes an awful lot of beating.

Class 4 Data Summary

Datum Point		Perform-ance	Power Weight	PD	FE
A	Alfa Romeo Giulietta 2.0	12	110	11	1.71
B	Audi 100 GL5E	12.3	106	11.6	1.42
C	BMW 318	8.9	89	10	1.54
D	BMW 320	10.9	111	10.7	1.59
E	Citroën CX Athena	9.6	81	11.8	1.85
F	Fiat Mirafiori 131	10.6	99	10.7	1.36
G	Ford Cortina 2.0	10.7	87	12.3	1.55
H	Peugeot 504 GR	7.4	64	11.7	1.57
I	Peugeot 505 GR	7.8	75	10.5	1.8
J	Renault Fuego GTX	11.4	95	12	1.79
K	Talbot Sunbeam Lotus	17.3	144	12.1	1.11

Alfa Romeo 2 litre Giulietta

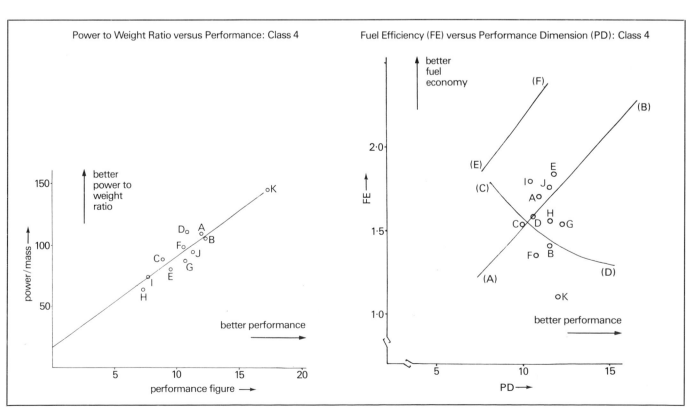

4 Fuel Efficiency

We think perhaps both too little and too much about a car's fuel consumption. On the one hand there is a tendency to feel that improved performance must surely demand increased fuel usage, and on the other manufacturers advertise, and governments demand, better figures coupled with decreased pollution. In the following paragraphs we will see that neither attitude is wholly justifiable.

ENERGY IN THE MARKET ECONOMY

A first approach might be to consider the fraction of a car's running costs which might be saved by, say, a 30 per cent improvement in fuel consumption. For the average driver of a 2 litre car, the potential monetary saving would be a little more than his comprehensive insurance costs (if he hasn't made any claims recently) and perhaps a quarter or less of his yearly depreciation loss. The proud owner of an aluminium bodied prewar 4 1/4 litre Bentley can laugh his head off while pouring in the petrol. He has an asset which has made, and will continue to make the average company stock look pretty stupid. Furthermore, like the owner of an Afghan carpet or Georgian writing desk he has an aesthetically pleasing and useful possession.

Unfortunately in this age of the consumer undurable, the likelihood of many modern cars attaining the same position in years to come is fairly remote. One has to look for the rare and the beautiful in engineering and form, with more than a touch of craftsmanship.

It is not only the demands of mass production which make such cars unusual. Pressed steel body panels and chassisless production techniques aid the manufacturer in producing relatively light (and thus improved in performance) cars at lower costs. They aid *him* further in demanding replacement when rust takes its natural toll. Clearly we should not however blame the manufacturer: it could be argued that he simply supplies what is demanded, and in the competitive market place will go out of business if he doesn't do it efficiently. In a sense, however, the manufacturer both creates the demand by his advertising technique, and ensures that the new car buyer will sell and buy again relatively quickly because of the increased depreciation rate which tends to accompany the onset of the inevitable deterioration.

Equally depressingly, in an economy where the standard of living is not rising, it would require government legislation to make a manufacturer think more than casually (and with a slight shudder) about increasing the life expectancy of his product. Like it or not we are in a situation where replacement, ruled essentially by fashion, governs his approach. Perhaps the essential point is that energy is not yet priced highly enough. The costs of double glazing one's house are not met for many years in fuel cost savings. Equally, in a throw-away society, to replace one's car, and concomitant costs, with one that has only marginally improved fuel consumption figures, cannot be monetarily sensible.

Interestingly an apparently different answer appears if we consider the 'costs' in terms of the amount of energy used. The chemical energy stored in a gallon of petrol is thermally equivalent to about 45 kilowatt hours (kW/h) (though less than 35 per cent of this energy is used by an engine in doing useful work). A typical motorist will thus use about 15,000 kW/h in a year.

A reasonable estimate of the primary energy required to make a car is about 30,000 kW/h, so a 30 per cent saving in petrol consumption would provide enough energy to make a new car about once every six years. The implications are obvious: in an energy conscious society, the use of primary energy resources to power motor cars is flagrantly wasteful.

It is true that the car buyer can put some pressure on the manufacturer both to make his car more economical to run and to give it a bigger life expectancy. But in the end the manufacturer's need to produce to show a profit must come to the fore, whatever his advertisements might imply. Without economic expansion, there would have to be government legislation, and probably subsidy, to put all manufacturers into the same position before any substantial improvement in the situation might be expected.

THE EFFECTS OF LEGISLATION

Governmental demands can be dangerous things, and they can often be counter-productive. At the risk of oversimplifying, we currently have intense encouragement, if not laws, to reduce pollution, to save energy by reducing fuel consumption and to make transport safer. Part at least of the safety attitudes involve requirements for lack of damage to specific parts of the car frame for given speeds of impact. These requirements essentially mean added weight to increase strength; but this then means added fuel consumption, at least for an equivalent performance.

Again, at first sight, decreased pollution implies efficient burning of fuel and reduced fuel consumption, but in general the legislatures of the consumer societies are incensed by the dangers of lead pollution. Lead additives are used in high octane fuels to increase the compression ratio which can be used in an engine, since this in turn increases its efficiency.

Lead is undoubtedly dangerous as a poison, however, and particularly so since it is cumulative. Since recent studies have shown that up to 20 per cent of the lead intake, small though this is, by people in some urban communities can be from the air, and since it is clear that it is difficult to define a 'safe dose', many countries are determined to ban the material's use. Such a ban is expected, for example, in Australia by 1985; since no suitable alternative additive is known, octane levels of petrol will have to be reduced to about 91.

Without major engine design philosophy changes the price that will be paid is an increase in petrol consumption of arguably about 5 per cent. One can only hope that the family with old lead water pipes appreciate such a world energy sacrifice sufficiently to replace them. On this sort of topic one can but sympathize with the engineers striving for already generally mutually incompatible goals in the design of the ideal motor car.

THE MEASURE OF FUEL EFFICIENCY

There is clearly, however, no harm in encouraging the engine and car designer by the enforced publication of a car's fuel consumption figures for specific types of road test. Figures are currently demanded in the UK for a specific type of urban cycle and for a constant speed of 90 km/h (56 mph). Figures are normally also given for a speed of 120 km/h (75 mph), and in our view it is a pity that these results too are not legally required since comparisons of the constant speed fuel consumption at two speeds can tell one a lot about how good a car is.

A first somewhat simplistic attitude might be to say that the lower the petrol consumption the 'better' the car. But we have to find ways of making realistic comparisons, bearing in mind a car's performance and load-bearing capabilities. As usual, given enough computer time and sufficient data, a phenomenological treatment at least could be taken to a level at which really useful information could be obtained. Here, however, we are more interested in providing the potential car buyer with a simple means of making realistic comparisons, and of understanding the implications, using data generally available. The question we must also seek to answer is whether or not petrol consumption figures can give us added information on a car's quality. We will see that they can.

The first thing we must understand is that it is much simpler to compare fuel consumption figures at different speeds on the basis of a requirement to cover a given distance at a given speed rather than in terms of the distance that can be covered with a given amount of fuel. This is because, if a speed dependent force is to be overcome by doing work and burning fuel, it's easier to find out about the force if we hold the distance covered constant.

With this fairly trivial point out of the way we can go forward on the basis of a consideration of fuel usage in terms of litres required/100 km travelled. For the uninitiated, this figure is obtained by taking a fuel consumption in terms of miles per gallon and dividing it into the number 282.5. Thus a car which will go say 28.25 miles on a gallon of petrol needs 10 litres to cover 100 km.

FRICTION LOSS AND DRAG

The next, more difficult thing to sort out, is what the fuel is used for. Alright: to make the car move! But what are the forces against which work must be done, and can we take a simplified approach to them? Once get a car with ideal bearings going at a constant speed on a flat surface in a vacuum, or in air going along at the same speed, and no work is required to keep it going. A real car, with less than ideal bearings, would not slow down, even without an engine, except for the fact that a braking effect would occur because of frictional losses in these bearings. Put an engine in the car and drive it with a geared transmission and life becomes a bit more complicated.

While the work done against the frictional losses in, for example, wheel bearings, remains constant in going a given distance and is independent of the speed, the more major trouble is that the car has to be forced through the air. Furthermore the bigger the engine torque and power required to keep the car going, the bigger the forces in the gear trains where work also has to be done against correspondingly increased frictional forces. It is for this reason that only a roughly constant fraction of the engine power is available to do useful work. Beware, incidentally, of reduction in oil pressure with an over-hot engine: it isn't only more petrol that will be required as the frictional forces in the bearings increase!

What then of the work required to push the car through the air? Rather a lot is said by manufacturers in general about the relative aerodynamic form and 'drag factors' of the models they and their competitors produce. Just how important is the wind resistance of a car? At the speeds of interest to us, the approximation normally employed is that the force exerted by the air on a car moving through it, at a given speed, is proportional to the frontal area, the square of the speed, the air density and a constant for a given car: its 'drag factor'. This number is roughly 0.2 for an 'ideally' shaped and totally unusable vehicle, and for well designed cars lies between about 0.3 and 0.4.

For the most lamentable shapes of body which could loosely be described as being in the form of a car, it is difficult to imagine the drag factor being bigger than about 0.5. Taking a realistic attitude to good and average figures as 0.32 and 0.4 respectively, and holding everything else constant, the resultant difference in wind resistance between our paragon and sinner would thus be 25 per cent. But such an increase would also be obtained for either with a speed increase of only about 10 km/h at 90 km/h. Clearly in relative terms speed matters more than shape so far as economy is concerned.

In fact shape is probably more important in determining the safety of a car, particularly with respect to its susceptibility to cross winds at high speed. The forces due to wind resistance are high and it is also important that both the relative and absolute loading on front and rear tyres should remain relatively constant as the speed is increased. The average motorist has no particular wish to get a pilot's licence, and it is for this reason as much as for a reduction in drag that modern cars tend to look a bit like a wing upside down. For a number of reasons however, not least the lack of a skirt and the impracticability of the correct underbody shape, it would appear to be difficult to make the effect really useful.

FUEL USAGE AND CHANGE OF SPEED

Returning to the topic of fuel consumption we may summarize, with some simplification, by saying that if a car's engine is working at a rate P, a roughly constant fraction of this power, $P(1-A)$, survives to do work against the wind resistance and constant frictional forces. Thus in going a given distance d, in a time, t, and at a speed v $(=d/t)$ the engine will do an amount of work Pt of which $P(1-A)t$ will be required to do work $B \cdot d$ against the constant frictional forces and CV^2d against the forces due to the wind.

While A, B and C are constants, C being proportional to the drag factor, we can therefore see that on changing the speed from V_1 to V_2 the change in the work required to do this, in going a fixed distance using a given gear, is equal to

$$\frac{C(V_2{}^2 - V_1{}^2)d}{(1 - A)}$$

More importantly for our purposes, we can also see that the rate at which the work required increases with speed is proportional to the speed. Now if an engine works at a roughly constant efficiency at speeds of interest, we may reasonably expect the rate of increase in petrol consumption to be similarly proportional to the speed.

So how do the rates of increase in petrol consumption of real cars on changing their speed compare with this simple approach? This is where the reader can get out his calculator: the generally published figures for a car are for speeds of 90 km/h and 120 km/h and typically the fractional differences in consumption between these speeds vary between about 40 and 25 per cent; our simple model suggests 33 per cent.

Generally larger cars tend to show smaller fractional changes than the lower powered. This would certainly be explained if in the gear used the small car's power output was approaching or had gone beyond its peak as the engine speed was increased. The low figures, generally for cars with high maximum speeds, suggest that the overall efficiency increases over the relevant speed range.

This is actually in any simple terms rather surprising: an important and basic fact about engine design is that the brake specific fuel consumption (the ratio of the fuel used to the work done) should not be strongly dependent on engine revs. Increases of less than about 25 per cent are better explained if it is assumed that a constant amount, rather than a constant fraction, of the power is used in gear train losses. This would certainly tend to be a better approximation when the engine is very under-stressed, as is the case when constant speed consumption figures are obtained for high speed cars.

In general it would appear that high fractional increases of petrol consumption, above about 40 per cent, on increasing the speed from 90 to 120 km/h,

suggest that the relevant vehicle is more efficiently run at lower speeds. Similarly, while in absolute terms clearly more petrol is still required to go faster when the relevant fractional change is less than 33 per cent, as it tends to be for the more high powered vehicles, low figures are generally indicative of the car's having been designed to run at higher speeds.

We may take as an arbitrary example the Ford range of manual saloon cars. The maximum speeds and fractional changes in fuel consumption for these cars are shown in table I, while in figure 1 the fractional change in consumption is plotted as a function of the fraction of the maximum speed which the lower testing speed (56 mph, 90 km/h) represents. We see a clearly

Table I Ford Manual Saloons S = maximum speed			
	S mph (km/h)	90/S (km/h)	% change in fuel/100 km for speed change from 90 to 120 km/h
Fiesta			
950	80 (129)	0.7	46.5
1100	90 (145)	0.62	40.2
L950	85 (137)	0.66	40.9
1300	98 (158)	0.57	31.2
Escort			
1117	90 (145)	0.62	37
1.3 CVM	98 (158)	0.57	28.4
1.6 CVM	104 (167)	0.54	28.2
XR3	113 (182)	0.49	28.9
Cortina			
1.3 ohv	87 (140)	0.64	36.1
1.6 ohc	94 (151)	0.6	34
2.0 ohc	105 (169)	0.53	30.9
2.3 V6	109 (175)	0.51	27.7
Capri			
1.3 ohv	92 (148)	0.61	30.3
S1.6 ohc	119 (191)	0.51	38.6
S2.0 ohc 2V	113 (182)	0.49	31
3.0 V6 2V	124 (199)	0.45	24.3
Granada			
2.0 ohc 2V	102 (164)	0.55	32.5
2.3 V6 2V	107 (172)	0.52	25.8
2.8 V6 2V	114 (183)	0.49	27.2
2.8 V6 i	120 (193)	0.46	26.6

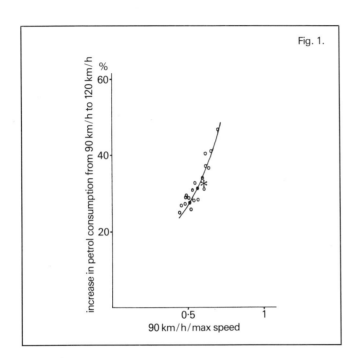

Fig. 1.

(y-axis label) increase in petrol consumption from 90 km/h to 120 km/h   %

(x-axis label) 90 km/h / max speed

this book we have taken the 90 km/h figures which, given current UK legislation, is the figure most manufacturers try to improve. Generally of course we are used to the idea that the bigger the car the more fuel is required to drive it along, and consumptions range from as low as 5 litres/100 km to as high as 15 litres/100 km at 90 km/h.

Actually it's not all that easy to explain why this is so. Of course the lighter the car the smaller the frictional losses, but the force due to wind resistance is proportional to the frontal area rather than the weight. While a direct proportionality between frontal area and weight would not be expected, a marked and clear rationalization of the figures is in fact obtained by normalizing them with respect to weight (as with the performance dimension the figure used is the kerb weight + 0.1 ton). Petrol consumptions/ton at 90 km/h are very rarely less than about 5.5 litres/100 km/ton or more than 7 litres/100 km/ton.

Again examining a broad range of cars is informative, and for this purpose we show data for some seventeen

uniform behaviour to the extent that in a rough and ready way the change in petrol consumption figure plotted in this way might almost be used to predict the maximum speed!

More interestingly, we see that our simple model's prediction of a 33 per cent change occurs when 56 mph is about 0.6 of the maximum speed. 75 mph (120 km/h) would then be about 80 per cent of the maximum speed. The general trend is thus pointing to the simplistically expected importance of not running an engine much beyond the revs at which the torque or brake mean effective pressure peak.

FUEL USAGE AND PERFORMANCE

What about petrol consumption in absolute terms? Again it's simpler to consider consumptions for a constant speed though whether one examines the figures for 90 or 120 km/h is fairly arbitrary. Throughout

Table II	British Leyland Manual Saloons			
	A l/100 km at 90 km/h	B l/100 km /ton	Performance Dimension	10/B
Mini Metro				
1000 ohv	5.8	8.2	6.5	1.22
L	5.3	6.4	9.9	1.56
HLE	4.8	5.8	8.6	1.72
1.3 HLS	5.5	6.6	10.5	1.52
Allegro				
1.1	6.1	6.8	8.7	1.48
1.3 S	6.1	6.6	10	1.52
1.5 S	6.5	6.9	9.3	1.45
1.7	6.5	6.9	10.1	1.45
Ital				
1.3 S	6.3	6.1	9	1.63
1.7 S	7	6.7	11	1.49
Rover				
2300	8.6	6.1	12	1.63
2600 S	7.1	5.0	13.8	2
3500 SE	7.8	5.4	11.9	1.85
Jaguar				
3.4	9.5	5.0	11.6	1.98
4.2	10.0	5.3	11.3	1.89
5.3	14.6	7.3	13.4	1.36
XJS	14.3	7.6	15.5	1.33

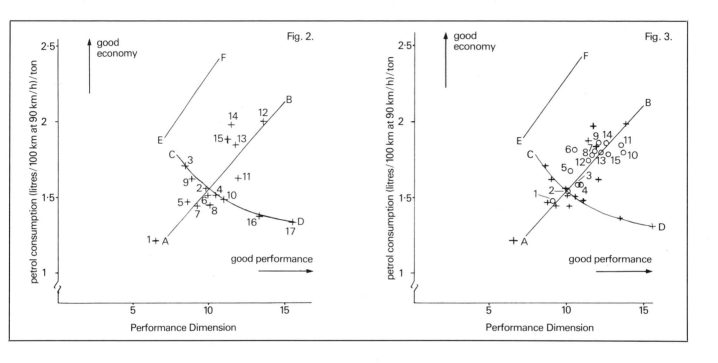

Fig. 2.

Fig. 3.

of the more different cars in the British Leyland range in table II. At first sight it would appear that the normalization procedure has overestimated the effect of weight: the Mini has a fuel consumption/ton 60 per cent larger than that of a Rover 2600S! We have however included in the table the cars' performance dimensions (calculated as described on page 30) and it will be remembered that roughly speaking the better the car the bigger the performance dimension. We now see that the Rover has a PD nearly twice that of the Mini.

Admittedly the examples chosen are extreme, but they point to a possible relationship between the petrol consumption and the performance dimension. We have thus plotted the reciprocal of the petrol consumption/ton against the performance dimension for the cars in table II (see figure 2). In a sense a high PD value is indicative, as the ratio of performance to power/ton, of 'something for nothing' and we have argued that high values are associated with good engineering design.

Would we then expect that high or low fuel consumption figures should correlate with the PD? Good performance in such terms should generally relate to lower demands on fuel. This is the general trend shown by the limited data represented here, and is emphasized by the inclusion of data for fifteen of the BMW range, see table III and figure 3.

The general behavioural line for cars that correlate good performance with decreased fuel consumption is thus represented for this data by the line AB. We see however that there are some cars which tend to show improved performance dimensions only with increased petrol consumption. Marked examples in figure 2 are cars 16 and 17, the admittedly excellent fuel injected Jaguar 5.3 and XJS respectively.

Similarly a comparison of the Metro HE and HLS, the economy and super, follows the same latter trend but with the opposite emphasis. Now economy is achieved at the expense of a reduced PD, the same being apparently true for cars 9 and 10, the ITAL 1.3S and 1.7S.

Table III	BMW			
	A l/100 km at 90 km/h	B l/100 km /ton	Performance Dimension	10/B
316	7.4	6.7	9.1	1.49
318	7.2	6.5	10	1.54
320	7.5	6.3	10.7	1.59
323i	7.7	6.3	10.9	1.59
518	7.8	5.9	10.2	1.69
520	7.6	5.5	10.5	1.83
525	7.9	5.5	11.7	1.82
528i	8.3	5.6	11.6	1.79
628 CSi	8.2	5.4	12.1	1.86
633 CSi	8.6	5.6	13.7	1.8
635 CSi	8.5	5.4	13.5	1.85
728i	8.9	5.7	11.3	1.75
732i	8.9	5.5	12.7	1.8
735i	8.6	5.4	12.5	1.87
735i	8.5	5.6	12.6	1.79

It would thus seem that the data also point to a second type of behaviour shown by a different 'family' of cars from that represented by the line AB. This second family gives reduced performance with added economy and vice versa, and follows the trend CD in figure 3.

It is clearly far too easy to read rather too much into comparisons of the type we have undertaken here. However it would generally seem to be fair to suggest that it should be better to have improved PD with lower fuel consumption (AB) than the converse (CD). There are admittedly occasions in which this sort of approach is far too wearing on the driver's natural animal demands: the XJS is a superb motor car!

Again, there is a current trend to design a car around the 90 km/h petrol consumption figures and there are certainly now whole ranges made by some manufac-turers which follow the AB trend but lie up to perhaps 5 or 10 per cent above this line. Any argument of improved petrol consumption with no loss of perfor-mance needs to be examined carefully however, and it is often the case that while the 90 km/h figures for an 'economy' car might appear to manage this, com-parison of figures for higher speeds shows reverse behaviour.

Perhaps however this misses the point: if you want an economy car you drive it slowly and under such circumstances win. Some of the newer VW economy range give petrol consumption figures rivalling the general trend for diesel engined cars. This incidentally is a line parallel to AB some 40 to 50 per cent above it, as might generally be expected. Similarly some of the latest diesels, notably the new VW Golf diesel achieve astonishingly low fuel consumptions/ton for their performance.

To summarize: fuel consumption is not necessarily the most important feature in the average motorist's costs: depreciation, particularly given inflation, will normally be the most ugly contender. More interest-ingly, we have seen that fractional changes in fuel consumption with speed follow predictable trends and suggest, as might be expected, appropriate speeds at which a given car should be driven. We also find three distinct families of behaviour when comparing fuel consumption with performance dimension. On com-mon sense grounds the cars that manage to attain high values of PD with low consumptions (trends AB and EF for the diesels) would appear to be better than those that can only manage one at the expense of the other (trend CD).

Class 5 2200-3000cc

INTRODUCTION

The economy-conscious world is trying hard to banish cars of anything over 2 litres in capacity, so this category is in trouble. This is a shame because it is the power available from engines of this size which takes everything in its stride – space, comfort and performance with silence. But try to sell one of these 2 to 3 litre cars and you will instantly find that depreciation has taken a longer slide than in the smaller sizes. Depreciation also relates, of course, to technological improvements, so that if the latest model has an improved fuel consumption and goes faster, and they usually do, the older model will be more undesirable than ever.

It has not always been the case that small means good and large means ostentation. During the depression of the 1930s, with rising unemployment and falling car sales, more than half of the new cars were quite enormous. The Austin 7 and the Morris Minor were introduced as bait to ensnare a whole new section of the population by showing them that motoring could be enjoyed on a shoestring, and they succeeded, while the already entrenched motorists continued with cars like the 7 litre Rolls-Royce Phantom II, the V12, sleeve-valve Daimler with Wilson pre-selector gearbox and fluid flywheel, Roesch Talbot, Daimler-Benz type 770s and V16 Cadillacs. There was also a remarkable interest in straight-eights – never notable for their fuel economy. An article in the *Autocar* of 1930 listed sixty-six different models with these engines, of which seven were British, all showing a commendable absorption in engineering and an almost total disinterest in the economics of it all.

The demise of so many estimable manufacturers at that time should, we suppose, be a terrible warning to us all, but it still goes on. Lamborghini, in the far-out élite area, are walking a tightrope. The business of car making has become a 'whole earth' concept. Car manufacture, with its initially simple slow transformation from manual to machine production has turned, with the aid of robots and computers, into a weird, complex interrelationship of capital, trades unions, multiple interrelated research, advertising and geophysics, and the economic balance of whole countries can be swayed by it. Late entrants to this whirligig, such as the Japanese,

had the advantage initially of being unencumbered by obsolete machinery, retrogressive ideas, and trades union shibboleths.

The next stage of development may conceivably be for the car to be unencumbered by the reciprocating engine. We know what the ultimate development of the piston engine is, because it was achieved with the two-stage supercharged Rolls-Royce Merlin aero-engine, and other engines designed for use in aircraft. The car is slowly following, and borrowing, from that encyclopaedia of ideas within it. Then aircraft adopted jet engines which are very much simpler. There must surely be a new means of propulsion for the car also? It is obvious that fifty years from now reciprocating engines will only be found in science museums, but what simple power unit will succeed it? The fact that the Rover turbine did not start a trek towards a new propulsion, and only Mazda are still making the Wankel engine, does not mean that a new power unit is still not just round the corner which will make those nitrided and exquisitely well balanced crankshafts, which no longer throw their connecting rods or run their bearings like they used to, very old hat. Enough of dreaming, but it *will* happen. Earlier this century the Japanese were looking inscrutably at a camera because they had never seen one before.

Nevertheless, with this category we haven't yet quite left the realms of the car which at least some people might reasonably expect to be able to purchase. The emphasis is now increasingly on the comfort which can come with the bigger body of the higher powered car.

But this does not mean that our comfortable driver need forego performance. The cars in this group were chosen because their Performance Dimension and fuel efficiency figures were noticeably good. In fact here the design engineer has the room and the spare weight carrying capacity to get the suspension and handling that bit better and to get adequate performance at a reasonable fuel efficiency figure, even if good values in this latter area disguise a thirst which in absolute terms has to be much worse than that of less heavy cars.

ALFA ROMEO GTV6 2.5

Two other Alfa Romeo cars are described in this book; the Sprint Veloce and the Giulietta. Both in their own way depart from the Alfa traditions, to a greater or lesser extent. The traditions of interest to us are the application of ideas from racing experience to the family motorist's car. We saw with the Giulietta that while the superb double overhead camshaft four cylinder engine of the Alfettas was retained, as was the concept of a rear mounted gearbox, the weight distribution ultimately was not as good as it should have been. The result in the current Giuliettas is understeer, without astute driver care, the like of which would have ashamed Puglia!

The GTV, whether the older 2.0 litre retaining the trusted engine, or the new GTV6 with its V6, keeps the same suspension concept as the earlier car and manages the weight distribution much better. Furthermore the GTV has a lower centre of gravity, so the handling behaviour is necessarily much better than in the more mundane saloons, of which we have considerable experience, such as the Alfetta.

In a way, rather sadly, we see in the GTV6 2.5 perhaps the final departure from the better Alfas of the superb old Alfa 4-cylinder engine, though the traditional suspension is retained with a vengeance. The GTV 2.0 always handled well, and with a performance figure of 12.9, a top speed of 120 mph and 0–60 mph in 9.3 seconds, giving a PD of 11.5, it is no pussyfoot.

In the GTV6 we see the natural progression of a good car. Given that in this case the suspension can handle it, further power is supplied. In this instance we are presented with a transplantation of the Alfa 6 engine, though we never felt that car capable of using the engine to its best advantage, despite a barrage of six downdraught Solex carburettors.

In the GTV6 2.5 the engine looks better. Furthermore, the carburettors are now discarded in favour of a Bosch fuel injection system, and even with the only moderate compression ratio of 9 to 1 we now see the development of a very usable 160 bhp, some 30 bhp more than given by the 2 litre engine.

Opposite: *Here is running sculpture of the highest order*

Right: *An inspired power unit, now fuel-injected*

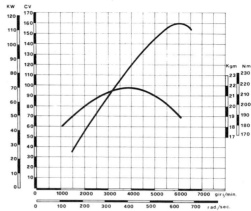

Bhp and torque curves

Alfa Romeo GTV 6 2.5

Engine: 60° V6 sohc belt driven/back. Longitudinally front mounted. Block and head light alloy
Capacity: 2492 cc
Bore; stroke: 88 mm   68.3 mm
Compression ratio: 9 to 1
Injection: Indirect electronic
Max. power at 6000 rpm: 157.5 bhp   117.6 kW
Max. torque at 4000 rpm   156.9 ft/lb   212.9 Nm

Transmission: 5 speeds manual to rear wheels

Suspension:
Front: independent 4 link mounting with twin bars.
Rear: de Dion axle with converging side members and Watts parallelogram. Anti-roll bar

Steering: Rack and pinion 3.5 turns lock to lock
Turning circle: 30 ft 10 in   10.1 m

Brakes: Dual circuit servo assisted. 10.5 in (26.7 cm) front ventilated discs, 9.8 in (24.9 cm) rear discs

Dimensions:
Length: 14 ft   4.26 m
Kerb weight: 2675 lb   1210 kg
Performance:
Maximum speed: 127 mph   205 km/h
0–60 mph: 8.5 sec*
Fuel consumption
   at 56 mph: 36.7 mpg   7.7 litres/100 km
   at 75 mph: 28.5 mpg   9.9 litres/100 km
   urban: 19.1 mpg   14.8 litres/100 km
*estimated from standing 400 m time

Insurance Rating: 7

Derived Data:
bhp/litre (kW/litre): 63.2   47.2
bhp/ton (kW/tonne): 121.8   89.4
Speed × acceleration: 14.9
Performance Dimension: 12.3
Petrol consumption/ton at 56 mph (10/F): 5.95   1.68
Change in petrol consumption between 56 & 75 mph: 28%

Early reports of the GTV6 suggest that it has lost none of the handling capabilities of the 2 litre GTV, and that the added power from the handsome looking engine is used to its best advantage. Certainly the car also looks better, with its moulded front spoiler capping the front bumper and containing the inset indicators, while the general decrease in the chrome level does nothing but enhance its already lean look.

Sadly we gather that the drag coefficient of the car is not improved, but at 0.39 it is certainly not bad. However, the instrumentation and facia design has been improved, but this is trivial compared with the impression that here we really do have a car that combines the pleasure of high speed long distance travelling with a jaunty suppleness that is just as at home in the high street as in country back lanes.

We have had some difficulty in assessing the car's performance dimension, in that times are only available for standing start 400 m and 1 km distances. However if our estimate of a time for 0–60 mph of 8.5 seconds (from these figures) is correct (and we certainly cannot see how it can be too wrong) the car should live up to all our expectations. On figures which we know more reliably we can also see that, with a fuel efficiency figure of 1.68 and the approximate PD of 12.3, the car too is in the clearly exciting family of those cars which combine performance with a reasonably sober attitude to the fuel pump.

We have not driven the car but our experience with the GTV 2.0 makes us surprised at the choice of such low gear ratios in 1st and 2nd for the GTV6. We would feel that with the added power they must surely lead to an over fussy approach to getting under way with no visible improvement in acceleration. This apart, it is clear that Alfa Romeo have a car which should give pleasure to all.

BMW 323i

Quality of this order is rare. A small car beyond criticism with an august pedigree, capable of 24 mpg and 118 mph, and in the habit of being mechanically superb at all times, come rain or shine, it has a price which relates to its undeniable qualities. The car is the result of superb engineering, tested and proved in competition. It is a product distilled from Formula two. The refinement is still very much in evidence at the low rev end when the peak revs have desisted, and there is time to be aware of the atmosphere of quality in the interior.

A special innovation is the use of a new double-joint spring-strut front suspension, used for the first time. In the case of BMW automatic transmissions are fitted as optional extras, but we found the five speed manual, which has an overdrive fifth, provided more satisfactory performance together with economy. Recaro seats with adjustable thigh support are available as an extra and we found them to be the best we have ever used, although the standard seats are completely supportive. The brake pad wear sensors on front left and rear right

wheels are more reassuring than listening for that nerve-disturbing screech when the pads really *do* wear out.

Many motoring journalists who have probably had a moment of forgetfulness and lack of concentration, say that this, and other BMWs, are tail happy in the wet. This is nonsense. They must go back and practice more driving in the wet.

The driver has no steering adjustment, but the driving position is so fortunate that it is unnecessary, and the throttle, clutch and brake pedals are all perfectly placed. The side support on the seat keeps him steady, and his passenger does not fall about either. Typical of BMW thoroughness is that after surveying the impeccable facia, one finds that the door mirror is electrically adjustable, and indeed the left-hand mirror.

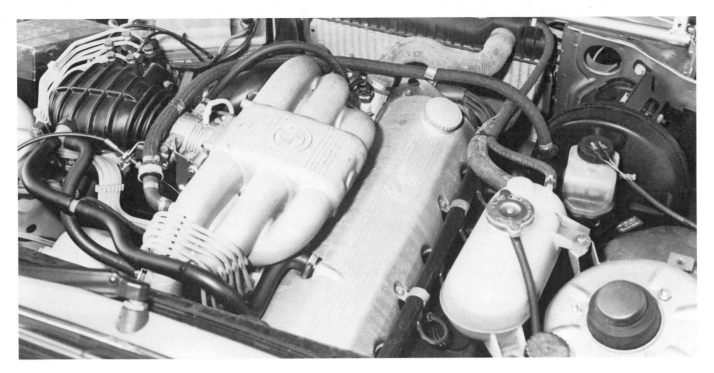

Above: *Top levels of engineering and design are immediately apparent in this engine*

Right: *Functional beauty*

Opposite: *BMW believe more in technological developments than frequent body styling changes*

BMW 323i

Engine: 6 cylinders inclined
Capacity: 2315 cc
Bore; stroke: 80 mm 76.8 mm
Compression ratio: 9.5 to 1
Injection: Bosch K-Jetronic
Max. power at 5800 rpm: 143 bhp 105 kW
Max. torque at 4500 rpm: 140.3 ft/lb 190 Nm

Transmission: 4 speed Getrag Manual (Automatic: ZF 3HP22)

Suspension:
Front: independent struts with coil springs. Torsion bar stabilizer acts as tension strut.
Rear: independent coil spring struts and trailing arms and swing bracket on differential. Axle/gearbox unit 3 point suspended. Anti-roll bar

Steering: ZF rack and pinion, lock to lock 4.05 turns
Turning circle: 31 ft 6 in 9.6 m

Brakes: Dual circuit front/rear. Servo assisted. Inner vented 10.1 in (25.7 cm) front discs, 10.2 in (25.9 cm) rear discs

Dimensions:
Length: 14 ft 3½ in 4.35 m
Weight unladen: 2503 lb 1135 kg

Performance:
Maximum speed: 118 mph 190 km/h
0–60 mph: 9.2 sec
Fuel consumption
  at 56 mph: 30.5 mpg 7.7 litres/100 km
  at 75 mph: 22.4 mpg 10.5 litres/100 km
  urban: 16.4 mpg 14.3 litres/100 km

Insurance Rating: 7

Derived Data:
bhp/litre (kW/litre): 61.8 45.4
bhp/ton (kW/tonne): 117.4 84.9
Speed × acceleration: 12.8
Performance Dimension: 10.9
Petrol consumption/ton at 56 mph (10/F): 6.3 (1.59)
Change in petrol consumption between 56 & 75 mph: 36%

CITROËN CX GTi

There are numerous versions of the CX, ranging from the basic 4 speed Reflex with the 2 litre Douvrin engine to the Prestige, with air conditioning as standard. The CX GTi cannot be excluded from the 2.2–3 litre class. At first, one might think that a 2.4 litre engine would leave this car underpowered. The power output per litre of fuel is not particularly high and the output/tonne at 64.7 kW is rather on the low side for what is clearly a relatively high performance car. An interesting comparison is provided by the BL 2200 Princess which has a power output only 4 per cent less but a performance dimension of only 10.5 to compare with the excellent figure of 13.1 for the CX GTi.

The difference is even more apparent when we look at fuel consumption: at 90 km/h the Princess uses 8.3 litres/100 km and the CX GTi 8.1 litres. The Citroën is however, markedly heavier and, when weight is included in the calculation, uses 14 per cent less petrol per ton; it thus belongs to the interesting class of cars that have both a high value of performance dimension and

low petrol consumption for their weight. While none of the CX 2400 saloons has poor performance figures, the GTi has both the lowest fuel consumption per ton and highest PD in the group, and this is mainly because of the combination of fuel injection with a good and well ratioed manual gear box.

What then of the GTi as a car to drive? On a motorway, however loaded, the combination of the self-levelling system with a good aerodynamic shape makes the car unsusceptible to cross winds and smooth and comfortable for the passenger; but does the car's handling and safety match its performance? We began this book by saying that a car can have instant feel and soul and will either drive well or badly from the moment one first gets into it. Perhaps the GTi is an exception: while all round visibility is excellent, one would need a periscope to see where the car's corners are. The first-time driver can be mildly nervous on first standing on the brakes, which will stop the car almost before he has noticed moving his foot: were this unexpected jolt to

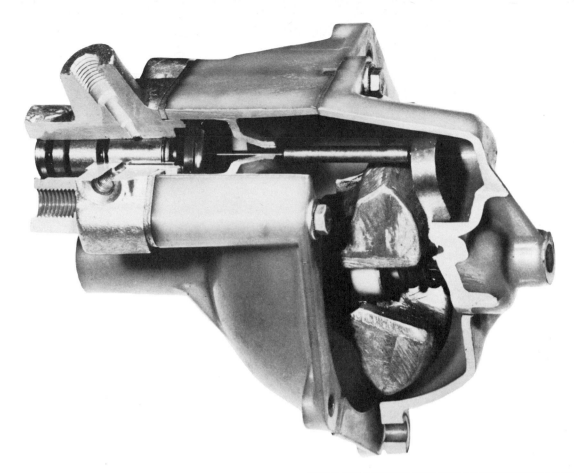

Above: *The steering governor of the Citroën CX varipower steering. No other steering system is so alarmingly Napoleonic and utterly purposeful*

Opposite: *The GTi gives total aesthetic satisfaction. Note the rear spoiler*

make him loosen his grip on the steering wheel, he might not live to drive a Citroën again. The VariPower steering, while delightfully light in town, self-centres with alarming quickness for the uninitiated.

The CX is worth getting to know however, and we are surprised that the professional testers tend to retain a wariness for the braking system. We very soon found the brakes positively reassuring, and they have an extremely low tendency to fade, presumably because of the rather cunning ventilation of the front discs. Again, no driver remains too worried about not being able to see his bumpers after a mile or two.

Further, the handling is such that the car goes where it's steered, but in the end it is essentially steered rather than driven. It can be driven hard but in the end one has the impression that at least on winding country lanes, and despite a beautifully responsive engine and gearbox, the roll and pitch might make the less interested passenger search his map for a bigger road.

Citroën CX GTi

Engine: Ohv 4 in line transverse
Capacity: 2347 cc
Bore; stroke: 93.5 mm   85.5 mm
Compression ratio: 8.75 to 1
Injection: Bosch L-Jetronic
Max. power at 4800 rpm: 128 bhp   95.5 kW
Max. torque at 3600 rpm: 145 ft/lb   197 Nm

Transmission: 5 speed all synchromesh gearbox. Front wheel with constant velocity driveshafts

Suspension: Hydropneumatic, self-levelling

Steering: Fully powered VariPower rack and pinion
Turning circle: 35 ft 9 in   10.9 m

Brakes: Power operated hydraulic dual circuit. Front and rear discs (front ventilated)

Dimensions:
Length: 15 ft 2.5 in   4.64 m
Kerb weight: 3031 lb   1375 kg
Payload: 1047 lb   475 kg

Performance:
Maximum speed: 117 mph   188 km/h
0–60 mph: 10.1 sec
Fuel consumption
   at 56 mph: 34.9 mpg   8.09 litres/100 km
   at 75 mph: 28.0 mpg   10.1 litres/100 km
   urban: 18.6 mpg   15.2 litres/100 km

Insurance Rating: 6

Derived Data:
bhp/litre (kW/litre): 54.5   40.6
bhp/ton (kW/tonne): 88.1   64.7
Speed × acceleration: 11.5
Performance Dimension: 13.1
Petrol consumption/ton at 56 mph (10/F): 5.6   (1.78)
Change in petrol consumption between 56 & 75 mph: 24.7%

FORD CAPRI 3.0 S and 2.0 S

Subjectively, we tried hard to keep the Capri out. After all it has been around for a very long time: the current Mk 2 appeared in 1974. Again, the car's styling is perhaps a little rakish, though if anything recent minor changes have cleaned it up somewhat. The car's inclusion however serves a number of purposes, and given that, by any standards, its performance is well above average for all cars sold today, there seems to be no way we can avoid giving you the data.

However, here we have a difficulty and this is the second reason for including it. The point is that the cars have been tested at different times over a number of years and the figures, particularly for acceleration, are not in agreement. While Ford currently claim a time for 0–60 mph of 8 sec, *Motor* reported in 1977 a time of 8.9 seconds, though more recently suggest that newer cars may be quicker. Our own rather less well controlled testing of a car about two years old suggested that it would be difficult to get the acceleration time as poor as 8.9 seconds – but nor could we match 8.0 seconds.

Unfortunately, errors and uncertainties in the basic data become increasingly important the higher the performance of the car. To make the point we include in the summary the position of the 3.0 S on Ford's figures and *Motor*'s 1977 data. Quite probably the correct value lies nearer to the position that Ford's figures currently suggest rather than the older value.

Perhaps the major trouble is that it requires a fairly careful assessment of a car to decide the optimum rpm to change from 1st to 2nd gear. It certainly isn't with the rev counter needle wrapped round the end stop. Even then the precise tune of a car can affect figures of this type more than the driver's skill or the state of the road.

Couple this with some uncertainty about the appropriate weight to use in the PD relationship as a function of the car weight when tested, often unknown, and an individual car's position on a power/weight versus speed × acceleration graph has an uncertainty for mid range performance figures around about 3 per cent. In the upper range this figure rises to about 5 per

Opposite: *The Ford men call the Capri 'Ford in drag' – and they don't mean coefficient! However, they are all proud of the 3 litre version's ability to really shift*

Right: *Businesslike and with a well designed binnacle full of the right instruments*

Ford Capri 3.0S (2.0S)

Engine: V6 2V
Capacity: 2994 (1998) cc
Bore; stroke: 93.7 (90.8) mm   72.4 (76.9) mm
Compression ratio: 9.0 (9.2) to 1
Carburation: twin venturi downdraught
Max. power at 5000 (5200) rpm: 138 (101) bhp   103 (75.3) kW
Max. torque at 3000 (4000) rpm: 173.6 (112.8) ft/lb
235 (153) Nm

Transmission: Four speed manual gearbox, rear wheel drive. Automatic: optional

Suspension:
Front: independent MacPherson struts with anti-roll bar.
Rear: semi-elliptic leaf springs and anti-roll bar

Steering: Rack and pinion, 3.3 turns lock to lock
Turning circle (kerb): 33 ft   10 m

Brakes: Dual circuit, servo assisted. 9.8 in (24.9 cm) front discs, 8 in (20.3 cm) rear drums

Dimensions:
Length: 14 ft 7 in   4.44 m
Kerb weight: 2541 (2268) lb   1155 (1031) kg

Performance: [ ] *Motor figures for 3 litre*
Maximum speed: 124 [119] (113) mph   119 (182) km/h
0–60 mph: 8 [8.9] (9.6) sec
Fuel consumption
    at 56 mph: 31.7 (42.2) mpg   8.9 (6.7) litres/100 km
    at 75 mph: 25.5 (32.2) mpg   11.1 (8.8) litres/100 km
    urban: 20.0 (23.7) mpg   14.1 (11.9) litres/100 km

Insurance Rating: 6 (5)

Derived Data:
bhp/litre (kW/litre): 46.1 (50.5)   34.4 (37.7)
bhp/ton (kW/tonne): 111.8 (90.8)   82.1 (66.6)
Speed × acceleration: 15.5 [13.3] (11.77)
Performance Dimension: 13.9 [11.8] (13.0)
Petrol consumption/ton at 56 mph (10/F): 7.2 (6.01)   1.38 (1.66)
Change in petrol consumption between 56 & 75 mph: 25% (31%)

---

cent, then almost entirely determined by uncertainties in the acceleration.

Fortunately, the spread of the test figures for the Capri 3.0 S is in fact at least partially explicable, and anyway exceptional: the two data points are the extremes. If we took the best 3.0 S figure we would have to conclude that the car has the same performance figure as the BMW 528i for a power to weight ratio just about 10 per cent poorer. In fact most of the BMW figures used are a little pessimistic, and our best estimate of the Capri's position would give it a performance figure of about 14.8 rather than 15.5. Fascinatingly, this would still leave the Capris with a PD rather better, but now only marginally better, than that of the 528i, though with somewhat poorer absolute performance.

Clearly, whatever the extent of our uncertainty, the Capri 3.0 S is a car to be reckoned with: we are comparing it with arguably the best (as a function of their relative PD values) of the 3, 5 and 7 series BMWs. It is only when we have examined the fuel efficiency figures

for the 528i and 3.0 S that we can form a complete picture. We now see that, while both cars have exceptional performance, that of the 528i is coupled with reasonable if not good fuel efficiency, while the 3.0 S, for its weight, drinks rather a lot of fuel.

Furthermore, the 528i handling is like silk while the Capri with conventional suspension (if now more modern gas fitted dampers to go with the former springing) has a ride which is jaunty and a tendency to oversteer which, though readily correctible, is a bit more exciting than it need be.

So we don't have a miracle: all in all the 3.0 S is not as good a car as the 528i, but then isn't it surprising that the much more advanced, fuel injected 528i is not a lot better?

The Capri 2.0 S figures are also given here because this, too, is a good car and an equally interesting comparison can be made with the data for the BMW 320. The reader can familiarize himself with our technique and come to his own conclusions.

FORD GRANADA 2.8i

So now the big Ford. The Mk 2 Granadas were introduced in 1977, and have made a deserved and heavy impression on the market. They come in a variety of engine sizes, and this makes them as interesting to analyze as to drive. For example, it will be remembered that on the Cortina the ohc 2 litre engine performed better than the V6 2293 engine. Now in the bigger Granada we see the reverse.

As may be seen from the data, both cars have good absolute performance, and perform well for their power to weight ratio, with very high PD values.

The V6 2.8i engined car, at least with a manual gearbox, is in a league of its own, however, with fuel injection raising the bhp of the engine from 136 to 160. The power is readily usable too: the car handles with its well developed but simple suspension firmly and positively, and is a genuine pleasure to drive. A noteworthy point for all the Granadas so far described is that for their power to weight ratio they give much better performance than the average.

Although we have not driven the Broadspeed, we include here a brief summary of some of the data from a *Motor* test of this adaptation of the 2.8i with a Garret T03 turbocharger. The car was praised not only for its increased performance (relative to the *automatic* 2.8i, though fair since the Broadspeed is an automatic too) but also for improvements in handling. Be that as it may, glance at our performance graph in this section's summary and you will see that the modifications don't seem to have given the performance they should have done for the power increase. Is this all the fault of the automatic transmission?

Opposite: *The new Ford international style*

Above: *The 2.8 litre fuel-injected engine brings the Ford almost into the same company as Mercedes and BMW regarding power and torque, but does not have the same overall perfection of engineering. This is the carburettor version*

Ford Granada 2.8i Ghia (Broadspeed Turbo)

Engine: V6 2V (+ Garrett Airesearch T03 twin turbocharger)
Capacity: 2792 cc
Bore; stroke: 93 mm   68.5 mm
Compression ratio: 9.2 to 1   (7.5 to 1)
Carburation: Bosch K-Jetronic
Max. power at 5700 (5600) rpm: 160 (232) bhp
119.3 (173) kW
Max. torque at 4300 (3200) rpm: 162 (270) ft/lb   220 (366) Nm

Transmission: Four speed manual, rear wheel drive
(3 speed automatic)

Suspension:
Front: independent short and long arms, coil springs and anti-roll bar.
Rear: independent, semi-trailing arms and coil springs

Steering: Rack and pinion 4.3 turns (power assisted: 3.5 turns) lock to lock. Power assistance standard on GL
Turning circle: 34 ft 5 in   10.5 m

Brakes: Dual line, servo assisted. 10.3 in (26.2 cm) discs on front and 9 in (22.9 cm) drums on rear

Dimensions:
Length: 15 ft 2½ in   4.63 m
Kerb weight: 3032 (3102) lb   1378 (1407) kg

Performance:
Maximum speed: 120 (130) mph   193 (209) km/h
0–60 mph: 8.6 (8.6) sec   (Broadspeed has lower relative times for higher speeds)
Fuel consumption (2.8i only)
    at 56 mph: 32.8 mpg   8.6 litres/100 km
    at 75 mph: 25.9 mpg   10.9 litres/100 km
    urban: 19.2 mpg   14.7 litres/100 km

Insurance Rating: 6 (7)

Derived Data:
bhp/litre (kW/litre): 57.3 (83)   42.7 (62)
bhp/ton (kW/tonne): 110.1 (156.2)   80.8 (114.7)
Speed × acceleration: 13.95 (15.1)
Performance Dimension: 12.7 (9.7)
Petrol consumption/ton at 56 mph: 6.25   1.60
Change in petrol consumption between 56 & 75 mph: 27%

MERCEDES-BENZ 230 E, CE and TE

The Mercedes-Benz models 230 E, 230 CE and 230 TE are now driven by a new 4-cylinder engine with fuel injection. The E stands for *Einspritzer* which means fuel injection. The 230 E is a four door saloon, the CE a two door coupé, and the TE an estate car.

The new 2299 cc engine develops 136 bhp (100 kW) at 5100 rpm compared with 108 bhp of the previous 230, and 148 ft/lb of torque at 3500 rpm compared with 137 at 3000. This has been achieved by a new crossflow cylinder head with hemispherical combustion chambers, an increased compression ratio of 9.0:1 and Bosch K-Jetronic fuel injection together with breakerless transistorized ignition.

The body is almost identical to that of the car it replaces, as are the suspension and steering. The new four speed automatic gearbox determines the general behaviour of the car to a large extent, and it is smooth, refined and unruffled at all times. The roadholding is excellent, on roads of all types and surfaces with a completely satisfactory ride quality. Noise suppression

is outstanding, and the ventilation and heating systems first rate, and consequently the passengers were totally at peace on the test ride. The driver's position is ideal, behind the large steering wheel, with well placed air ducts, businesslike pedals and instruments but minus a rev counter.

The 230 CE with fuel-injected engine has a claimed top speed of 112 mph (180 km/h) which is easily exceeded, in manual form, the new synchromesh box being a delight; it always was, of course, but now it is also lighter in weight. The one sad fact is that it has only four speeds, and the engine could so easily and to advantage use a long-legged fifth gear. No doubt Mercedes have already designed a five speed gearbox and it will be announced shortly.

The difference in ride and handling between the 230 CE with the four speed manual gearbox and the 280 SE with the four speed automatic transmission is very noticeable. The 230 CE is crisp and very alive, and the 280 SE smooth, powerful and relaxed to the point of

Above: *The new 2.3 litre engine and gearbox with Bosch K-jetronic fuel injection. The ram pipes are very much in evidence curving into the engine*

Opposite: *All Mercedes have the highest qualities at all levels. It shows here in the exterior design of these three 230 models, saloon, coupé and estate*

somnolence. In our chapter on automatics versus manuals (page 126), we mention this relaxing effect of the automatic. For nine years we have been driving the older 280 SE with the earlier three speed automatic box. It was obviously satisfactory to the point of perfection, but it did have this one Achilles heel; one felt that it would have been so much more vital with a five speed gearbox as well as more efficient and economical. It would appear to us that the lack of a five speed gearbox is the main element which has stopped Mercedes from total success in the World Rally Competitions.

The other factor, of course, is the power/weight ratio. While other manufacturers have won this event with special rally cars designed and developed with more power and less weight than the basic production models, Mercedes have, with pride in their engineering, fielded normal production models, showing absolute integrity.

Mercedes-Benz 230 CE Manual (Automatic)

Engine: 4 cylinders in line
Capacity: 2299 cc
Bore; stroke: 95.5 mm   80.2 mm
Compression ratio: 9 to 1
Injection: fuel injection mechanical
Max. power at 5100 rpm: 136 bhp   100 kW
Max. torque at 3500 rpm: 151 ft/lb   205 Nm

Transmission: Rear drive via 4 speed gear box or 4 speed torque converter

Suspension:
Front: coil springs, stabilizer and double control arms.
Rear: MB diagonal swing with brake torque compensation coil springs, stabilizer

Steering: MB power steering, 4.3 turns lock to lock

Brakes: Dual circuit servo assisted. Discs on all wheels

Dimensions:
Length: 15 ft 6 in   4.72 m
Kerb weight: 3065 lb   1390 kg

Performance:
Maximum speed: 112 (109) mph   180 (175) km/h
0–60 mph: 11.2 (12) sec
Fuel consumption
    at 56 mph: 35.3 (32.8) mpg   8.0 (8.6) litres/100 km
    at 75 mph: 27.2 (25.7) mpg   10.4 (11.0) litres/100 km
    urban: 20.8 (20.9) mpg   13.6 (13.5) litres/100 km

Insurance Rating: 7

Derived Data:
bhp/litre (kW/litre): 59.2   43.5
bhp/ton (kW/tonne): 92.6   67
Speed × acceleration: 10 (9.08)
Performance Dimension: 10.8 (9.8)
Petrol consumption/ton at 56 mph (10/F): 5.44 (5.85)   1.84 (1.71)
Change in petrol consumption between 56 & 75 mph: 30% (28%)

MERCEDES-BENZ 280 SE and CE

The first Benz was a three wheel vehicle because Carl Benz had not completed his research on the steering system for a four wheeler. This he did, in 1893, with Patent No. DRP 73515 for rack and pinion steering, this being installed in his four wheel Victoria of the same year, which had a claimed top speed of 30 km/h and a hair raising centre of gravity.

Daimler-Benz have been concerned with research and development ever since and to some purpose. Seven years have been spent in developing the new S class, which provides increased performance but with reduced fuel consumption from the three new engines. The 2.8 litre now performs like the former 3.5 litre, the 3.8 litre V8 like the old 4.5 litre engine, and the new 500 SE is similar in performance to the 6.9 litre engine.

The new bodyshells have 14 per cent less drag and are considerably lighter in weight than their forerunners. The new four speed automatic transmission has an improved torque converter of smaller diameter, which reduces mechanical losses in the transmission and

consequently works smoothly, efficiently, and over a wide range.

In addition there is a completely new, electronically controlled ventilation and heating system. The seats have an electric seat adjustment controlled by a seat-shaped switch on the door. Moving the shape in the desired direction automatically moves the seat itself, to achieve total comfort. A hydro-pneumatic suspension system, available previously on the 450 SEL 6.9 flagship, is now available on the V8 powered cars and the estates.

The ABS braking system, developed jointly by Bosch and Daimler-Benz, makes its debut on the new 500 SE and SEL models, and is available on the new 280 SE and 380 SE models, as an optional extra. The ABS system is so good that it should be a legally compulsory item of equipment on all cars, in the best of all possible worlds, and the number of accidents would fall very dramatically. (See page 231.)

Mercedes, always noted for quality control, inspection and operation testing at all levels, have

Opposite: *The new S-class saloon in the wind-tunnel*

Right: *The compact, straight six engine with overhead camshafts and fuel injection fills the engine bay*

Mercedes-Benz 280 CE Manual (Automatic)

Engine: 6 cylinders in line
Capacity: 2746 cc
Bore; stroke: 86 mm   78.8 mm
Compression ratio: 9 to 1
Injection: fuel injection mechanical
Max. power at 5800 rpm: 185 bhp   136 kW
Max. torque at 4500 rpm: 176.8 ft/lb   240 Nm

Transmission: Rear drive via 4 speed manual gear box or 4 speed automatic with torque converter

Suspension:
Front: coil springs, stabilizer and double control arms.
Rear: MB diagonal swing with brake torque compensation coil springs, stabilizer

Steering: MB power steering. 4.3 turns lock to lock

Brakes: Dual circuit servo assisted. Discs on all wheels

Dimensions:
Length: 15 ft 6 in   4.72 m
Kerb weight: 3195 lb   1450 kg

Performance:
Maximum speed: 124 (121) mph   200 (195) km/h
0–60 mph: 9.6 (10.5) sec
Fuel consumption
   at 56 mph: 30.4 (27.4) mpg   9.3 (10.3) litres/100 km
   at 75 mph: 23.9 (21.4) mpg   11.8 (13.2) litres/100 km
   urban: 15.4 (16.5) mpg   18.3 (17.1) litres/100 km

Insurance Rating: 7

Derived Data:
bhp/litre (kW/litre): 67.4   49.5
bhp/ton (kW/tonne): 118.7   87.2
Speed × acceleration: 12.9 (11.5)
Performance Dimension: 10.9 (9.7)
Petrol consumption/ton at 56 mph: 6.09 (6.25)   (1.64 (1.48))
Change in petrol consumption between 56 & 75 mph: 27% (28%)

introduced electronic testing equipment for the automatic monitoring of bolted connections in areas vital to safety; from chassis, steering and brakes to the precise adjustment of the steering geometry.

Also, anti-corrosion processes have been stepped up. The steel sheet for body shells is coated immediately, at the rolling mill, with zinc-dust paint, and the cathaphoretic dip painting increases anti-corrosion. Body cavities are waxed, and the underside of the body is sealed with a specially bonded PVC. Figures given recently by the head of research and development at Daimler-Benz, Professor Hubertus Christ, indicate that the new S class will be in active service after the turn of the century.

Manufacturers normally loan their vehicle for road testing for seven days, but this is a car to which we can add the personal experience of owning and driving a 280 SE since 1972, covering a distance of 98,500 miles. During that time it was exemplary at all times, demanding only one new exhaust valve and an exhaust system.

It refused to work on only one occasion, which it

chose carefully. Invited to be an external assessor at a university in Paris, I had it serviced, checked, wax-polished, and then drove it to a hotel in the Faubourg St Germain. It then refused to budge. A transporter came and swept it off to the Panthéon, where the Mercedes star shines. There was nothing wrong with him really, all he needed was a new alternator.

One of the main achievements of the designers in developing the new S class was to reduce fuel consumption over the previous cars by 10 per cent, but losing none of the normal Mercedes characteristics. So the 280 SE has impeccable road holding, neutral handling, powerful brakes (which need no ABS system yet), total bump absorption, low noise level, minimum body roll and a superb driving position related to vision, facia, pedals and steering wheel. It has a total functioning practicability combined with an aura of real quality. Safety, dependability, serenity and durability are all qualities which have been considered, designed and then built into it.

113

OPEL MONZA

The Monza has balance and integrity. It handles well, with ride comfort and complete controllability at speed and in really adverse conditions. Unlike some of the faster exotica it does not need hair-trigger reactions and professional drivers' reflexes.

Herbert Oberhaus, Opel's chief engineer, is to be congratulated on producing a coupé up to the same high standards as cars which cost almost twice as much. Again this is a company which participates in and learns from, competition. The Opel Ascona 400 is a car which is going from strength to strength, and some of the expertise has found its way into the Monza.

The Monza has been rightly criticized for several reasons since its launch in the second half of 1976, but everyone realized its enormous potential. Opel have doggedly faced up to getting it right, and they have. The suspension refinement was there in the first place, together with the remarkably well designed coupé body by Henry Haga, but the build quality and finish have been improved. In addition, the continued criticisms of

the lack of what can only be called good taste in choice of colours and materials, which always sadly differentiated it from the more expensive marques, has been taken care of. By comparison with issues like engineering, this matter of minor aesthetics is trivial, but it is still pleasing to see the improvement.

The driving position is right, helped by a seat which is supportive and adjustable. The pedals are well placed and progressive, the wheel small and the instruments sensible. All switches are well placed and logical. The 5 speed ZF gearbox is a total pleasure, with well spaced ratios. The top speed of 130 mph and acceleration from 0–60 in 8.5 seconds are facts which put Monza, together with its other qualities, in the same class as BMW and Mercedes. Driving with total gusto, we had a fuel consumption of just over 22 mpg; normal touring gave 27, and with conscious economy – driving using fifth a great deal, it was 32 mpg. So the Monza is a safe, fast, dependable, well-engineered coupé which is also economical for its size.

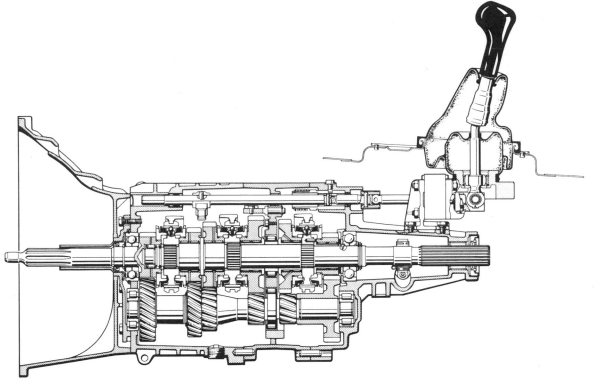

Above: *The manual gearbox, showing strength and simplicity*

Opposite above: *The Monza coupé, designed by Henry Haga, has had a great deal of influence*

Opposite below: *The massive three litre, six-cylinder in line engine with Bosch L-jetronic injection*

Right: *Final drive and differential*

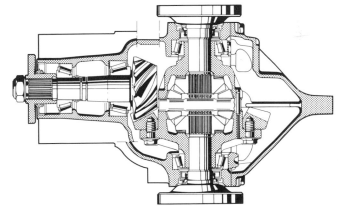

Opel Monza S 2-door hatchback coupé

Engine: Six cylinders in line. Camshaft in head with dual roller chain drive. Cast iron head and block
Capacity: 2968 cc
Bore; stroke: 95 mm   70 mm
Compression ratio: 9.4 to 1
Injection: Bosch L-Jetronic
Max. power at 5800 rpm: 180 bhp   132 kW
Max. torque at 4600 rpm: 183 ft/lb   248 Nm

Transmission: Five speed manual (Opel automatic on Monza E)

Suspension:
Front: independent with MacPherson strut, control arm with tension rod, torsion bar stabilizer.
Rear: independent, with semi-trailing arms, and progressive rate conical miniblock coil springs; torsion bar stabilizer

Steering: Circulating ball power steering
Turning circle: 32 ft 4 in   9.3 m

Brakes: Dual circuit power assisted with ventilated discs at front and solid discs at rear

Dimensions:
Length: 15 ft 5 in   4.70 m
Kerb weight: 3030 lb   1374 kg

Performance:
Maximum speed: 135 mph   217 km/h
0–60 mph: 8.5 secs
Fuel consumption
   at 56 mph: 31.4 mpg   9.0 litres/100 km
   at 75 mph: 25.2 mpg   11.2 litres/100 km
   urban: 18.1 mpg   15.6 litres/100 km

Insurance Rating: 7

Derived Data:
bhp/litre (kW/litre): 60.6   44.5
bhp/ton (kW/tonne): 124   89.5
Speed × acceleration: 15.9
Performance Dimension: 12.8
Petrol consumption/ton at 56 mph (10/F): 6.19   (1.61)
Change in petrol consumption between 56 & 75 mph: 24%

OPEL SENATOR 3.0 S and CD

The 3.0 S Senator has a solid build quality, high equipment levels, and it is impressively refined as a piece of engineering, at all times.

The engines in the 3.0 S and the CD are identical, except for a difference in compression ratio (9.25:1 for the 3.0 S and 9.4:1 for the CD). The CD, due to its Bosch L-Jetronic fuel injection however, gives a power output of 180 bhp against the carburettor version's 150, and a torque of 182 ft/lb against 170 ft/lb.

The fuel consumption of 21 mpg for the carburettor version and 17 for the fuel injected model is *not* caused by this change, as fuel injection invariably gives an improved fuel consumption, but by the reduction in weight and the change from automatic to manual gearbox. Top speed drops from 125 to 116 mph.

The manual gearbox has well judged ratios, and with 60 mph in second, provides controlled and safe overtaking ability. The ZF power assisted steering is the right choice for this vehicle, and the handling balance is right at all times and one of the most satisfying of the Senator's noticeably good characteristics, due to the classic basic suspension system plus mini-bloc springs.

The change in character from the CD to the 3.0 S is remarkable. The CD is serene, self-confident, unruffled and dignified. The 3.0 S is a different Senator altogether, a well dressed spartan trimmed down in weight and consequently more economical. The bhp/litre figure of 50 is good without being outstanding. It is the balance of dynamic qualities which make it a good car. The power unit and the suspension make a well engineered unity which is efficient and practical.

In a four hundred mile drive up the West Coast of Scotland, most of it in rain which was washing the Highlands to a pure cobalt blue, and on many roads which were more picturesque than easy, it never put a wheel wrong and gave a fuel consumption of 26 mpg. Returning by a shorter and faster route on the motorways, showed the big six-cylinder engine using its 150 bhp and its MacPherson struts plus special GM springs in the suspension to advantage, the discs front

Opposite: Opel have been simplifying: staying with the essentials and removing unnecessary decoration

Right: The massive three litre, six-cylinder in line engine with Bosch L-jetronic injection

---

Opel Senator CD (3.0 S Manual)

Engine: Six cylinders in line, camshaft in head with dual roller chain drive
Capacity: 2968 cc
Bore; stroke: 95 mm 70 mm
Compression ratio: 9.4 (9.25) to 1
Carburation: Bosch L-Jetronic (1 DVG Solex 4 choke downdraught)
Max. power at 5800 (5200) rpm: 180 (150) bhp 132 (110) kW
Max. torque at 4600 (3400) rpm: 183 (170) ft/lb 248 (230) Nm

Transmission: Opel hydraulic three-element torque converter with automatically shifting three-speed planetary gear set (Four-speed manual gearbox)

Suspension:
Front: independent with MacPherson strut, control arm with tension rod torsion bar stabilizer.
Rear: independent with semi-trailing arms, double conical progressive rate coil springs

Steering: Circulating ball power steering
Turning circle: 32 ft 4 in 9.3 m

Brakes: Dual circuit power assisted discs all round, ventilated at front

Dimensions:
Length: 15 ft 9.5 in 4.81 m
Kerb weight: 3027 lb 1373 kg

Performance:
Maximum speed: 128 (120) mph 206 (193) km/h
0–60 mph: 10.5 sec
Fuel consumption
    at 56 mph: 29.1 (28.5) mpg 9.7 (9.9) litres/100 km
    at 75 mph: 23 (22.8) mpg 12.3 (12.4) litres/100 km
    urban: 19.3 (17.7) mpg 14.6 (16) litres/100 km

Insurance Rating: 7

Derived Data:
bhp/litre (kW/litre): 60.6 (50.5) 44.5 (37)
bhp/ton (kW/tonne): 124 (103.3) 89.5 (74.6)
Speed × acceleration: 12.2 (11.4)
Performance Dimension: 9.8 (11.1)
Petrol consumption/ton at 56 mph (10/F): 6.69 (6.83) 1.49 (1.46)
Change in petrol consumption between 56 & 75 mph: 26% (25%)

---

and rear being used with need due to a dangerous situation, and proving themselves.

The Senator in both forms – fuel injected with automatic transmission or carburettor with manual gearbox, is a well made powerful car, ideal for long distance cruising. The body shell is marked by an aesthetically satisfactory shape, its wedge-shaped nose particularly. The design of the body structure, using the finite element method, has achieved a relatively low kerb weight, and a power/weight ratio of 131.9 bhp/ton.

The boot is large enough and the engine strong enough for any family. There is also built-in safety

Above: *The engine while being overhauled shows more complexity than when stowed away in the engine bay*

Left: *The enormous 604 looks trim from above*

Right: *A simple and undatable facia*

PEUGEOT 604 Ti

The Peugeot Ti uses the Douvrin PSA V6 engine with aluminium alloy block and heads, and hemispherical combustion chambers, which is also used by Volvo in the 264 and 265 GLE. Bosch injected, the engine gives 144 bhp at 5500 rpm and 159.8 lb/ft of torque at 3000 rpm. Acceleration from 0–60 mph takes 10.4 seconds. The fuel consumption overall was 24 mpg over a 500 mile test drive which included motorway, city and country B roads.

The 604 Ti impressed us. It is an honest and unassumingly swift long distance cruiser, with good visibility due to the large glass areas and thin pillars. The passengers felt that they enjoyed very high standards of comfort, space, and an outstanding ride. This latter was partly due to the excellent Peugeot double-acting dampers, but they were all certain that it was due to the well designed and comfortably sprung velour upholstery.

The power assisted rack and pinion steering, large pedals, sensible facia and instrumentation, together with the flexible engine and smooth automatic transmission, make driving this quite large Lion of Belfort an undisturbed pleasure, including the night drive, enjoying the four Marchal lamps.

While the design of the bodyshell breaks no new ground, it has a restrained simple elegance that should last without modifications for some years; and the technology of the contents is not likely to get out of date for some time either – a highly advanced Douvrin engine, with Bosch K-Jetronic fuel injection, transistorized ignition, power assisted steering, GM automatic gearbox, all round disc brakes, electrically lifted windows and sun roof.

A friend who accompanied us on the test drive bought one the following week, which surprised us because he has been driving Rovers since they had that shining radiator with the Viking's head on it.

118

Peugeot 604 Ti

Engine: V6 sohc/bank aluminium alloy block and head
Capacity: 2664 cc
Bore; stroke: 88 mm   73 mm
Compression ratio: 8.65 to 1
Injection: Bosch K-Jetronic
Max. power at 5500 rpm: 144 bhp   107.4 kW
Max. torque at 3500 rpm: 159.8 ft/lb   216.8 Nm

Transmission: 5 speed manual gearbox (GM automatic gearbox with torque converter optional)

Suspension:
Front: independent by MacPherson struts, coil springs and anti-roll bar.
Rear: independent by semi trailing arms, coil springs and anti-roll bar

Steering: Rack and pinion
Turning circle: 37 ft 9 in   11.5 m

Brakes: Dual split front/rear servo assisted. 10.7 in (27.2 cm) front and rear discs

Dimensions:
Length: 15 ft 6 in   4.72 m
Weight unladen: 3109 lb   1410 kg

Performance:
Maximum speed: 119 mph
0–60 mph: 9.7 sec
Fuel consumption
   at 56 mph: 33.2 mpg   8.5 litres/100 km
   at 75 mph: 26.1 mpg   10.8 litres/100 km
   urban: 16.8 mpg   16.8 litres/100 km

Insurance Rating: 7

Derived Data:
bhp/litre (kW/litre): 54   40.3
bhp/ton (kW/tonne): 96.8   71.1
Speed × acceleration: 12.3
Performance Dimension: 12.7
Petrol consumption/ton at 56 mph (10/F): 5.71   (1.75)
Change in petrol consumption between 56 & 75 mph: 27%

Above: *A compact, well designed body with good build quality and integrity*

Right: *Modern design relying upon practicality plus pure form rather than expensive materials*

RENAULT 30 TX

This book, concerned with the best cars, contains four cars made by the Régie Nationale des Usines Renault. Of these, the 30 TX is the largest and indeed the Régie flagship. The 30 TX is fuel injected and powered by the Douvrin 2664 cc V6 engine, shared by Peugeot and Volvo. This is a lot of power for a front wheel drive, and it is noticeable when starting quickly, but otherwise it provides well balanced performance, with effortless cruising speeds up to its maximum of 114 mph (184 km/h).

The suspension is set up for an executive's comfort and allows some lateral float rather than the harder and more controlled suspension of a GT. The seats are all comfortable and the whole car has a noticeably luxurious feeling to it, with sufficient space, but the whole car seen from the outside is most compact.

The car is fully equipped ánd well appointed with commendable good taste, and yet has remarkably versatile load and passenger carrying abilities, which comes as a surprise. It has the full inventory of the luxury car – fuel injection, transistorized ignition, five speed gearbox, splendid adjustable controlled beam Cibié headlamps with washers, central door locking, electric window lifts and sunroof, rear window wash/wipe, rear fog lamp, well designed facia and switches, and an aura of quiet elegance.

The 5 speed gearbox gives ratios of 3.36, 2.06, 1.38, 1.06 and 0.82 to 1, with a final drive of 3.889 to 1. Acceleration from 0–60 takes 10.2 seconds. The Douvrin engine has remarkable power, flexibility and engineering integrity. One expects this standard of engineering from a manufacturer who has won recently at Le Mans (1978) and in Formula One also, with their Turbo. This is in fact a well designed, well engineered car with integrity, all the appurtenances of luxury, and of all things, modesty.

Above: *The competent Douvrin V6 2.6 litre engine with Bosch K-jetronic injection*

Renault 30 TX automatic

Engine: 90° V6 all alloy with chain driven sohc per bank
Capacity: 2664 cc
Bore; stroke: 88 mm   73 mm
Compression ratio: 9.2 to 1
Injection: Bosch K-Jetronic
Max. power at 5500 rpm: 142 bhp   106 kW
Max. torque at 3000 rpm: 161 ft/lb   218 Nm

Transmission: 3 speed automatic with torque converter. A 5 speed manual gearbox comes cheaper and gives improved performance and better economy (see *Automatic v. Manual*)

Suspension:
Front: independent by upper transverse link, forward reaction arm, lower wishbone coil springs and anti-roll bar.
Rear: independent by MacPherson struts with wide based lower links and anti-roll bar

Steering: Power assisted rack and pinion

Brakes: Dual circuit in all four and front. 9.9 in (25.2 cm) ventilated front discs, 10 in (25.4 cm) rear discs

Dimensions:
Length: 14 ft 10 in   4.52 m
Weight unladen: 2822 lb   1285 kg

Performance:
Maximum speed: 114 mph   184 km/h
0–60 mph: 10.5 secs
Fuel consumption
   at 56 mph: 31.7 mpg   8.9 litres/100 km
   at 75 mph: 24.4 mpg   11.6 litres/100 km
   urban: 18.5 mpg   15.3 litres/100 km

Insurance Rating: 6

Derived Data:
bhp/litre (kW/litre): 53.3   39.8
bhp/ton (kW/tonne): 104.4   76.7
Speed × acceleration: 10.5
Performance Dimension: 10.4
Petrol consumption/ton at 56 mph (10/F): 6.5   (1.52)
Change in petrol consumption between 56 & 75 mph: 30.3%

Above: *The enormous hatchback*   Opposite: *Elegant porpoise*

ROVER 2600 S

The natural development of this car was to produce a new engine. This is precisely what has happened, and now the car in its more natural habitat of the 'under 3 litres' outperforms most of its rivals.

When the 3500 SD1 was first launched, although we were surprised by its performance, we found its shape a bit hard to get used to. With more effort, and the passing of a few years, the car still tends to remind us, with its somewhat bulbous and rounded lines, of a porpoise a bit low in the water. But then they too had a good designer to help them travel with a low drag coefficient. One's only criticism on these grounds, perhaps, remains that the external form has made accommodation in the rear, though perfectly comfortable, a little on the sparse side.

The straight six engine was designed specifically for the car. It has an aluminium alloy head and a belt driven single overhead camshaft. With twin SU carburettors it develops 123 bhp in the 2300 and 136 bhp in the 2600. It is an essentially simple but clearly efficient engine and

while excluding the delights of such complications as desmodronic valves has a rather cunning air temperature control unit. This, using a bimetallic self-adjusting valve, ensures the optimum air petrol mix at any given running temperature, and aids the fuel efficiency figures.

For the car's performance, its frugality is astounding. The petrol consumption/ton at 56 mph is in fact better than that for many of the older diesels with half the performance dimension. It is the combination of the car's performance dimension, 13.8 (derived from a speed of 118 mph and a 0–60 mph time of only 9 seconds) and the high fuel efficiency figure of 2.01 which shows that the car is particularly well engineered. This is a true and natural successor to the 3500 and the new six-cylinder engine will form a valuable platform for a considerable amount of further development.

Enough has been said about the car's handling and ride in the many articles which have appeared on the 3500. The suspension is unchanged in the 2600 S. The five speed manual gearbox drives a live rear axle located

Rover 2600 S

Engine: 6 cylinders in line, aluminium alloy head. Single belt driven ohc
Capacity: 2597 cc
Bore; stroke: 81 mm   84 mm
Compression ratio: 9.25 to 1
Carburation: Twin SU HS6
Max. power at 5000 rpm: 136 bhp   101.4 kW
Max. torque at 3750 rpm: 152 ft/lb   206.2 Nm

Transmission: 5 speed manual gearbox

Suspension:
Front: independent coil sprung, MacPherson struts. Lower wishbones formed by transverse arm and anti-roll bar.
Rear: live axle held by torque tube, Watts linkage and radius arms. Coil springs with self-energizing, self-levelling damper struts

Steering: Rack and pinion power assisted. 2.7 turns lock to lock
Turning circle: 34 ft 3 in   11.5 m

Brakes: Servo assisted dual circuit split front/rear. 10.1 in (25.7 cm) front discs, 9 in (22.9 cm) rear drums

Dimensions:
Length: 15 ft 5 in   4.70 m
Kerb weight: 2978 lb   1351 kg

Performance:
Maximum speed: 118 mph   190 km/h
0–60 mph: 9 sec
Fuel consumption
    at 56 mph: 39.6 mpg   7.1 litres/100 km
    at 75 mph: 31.5 mpg   9 litres/100 km
    urban: 18.5 mpg   15.3 litres/100 km

Insurance Rating: 6

Derived Data:
bhp/litre (kW/litre): 52.4   39
bhp/ton (kW/tonne): 95.1   69.8
Speed × acceleration: 13.1
Performance Dimension: 13.8
Petrol consumption/ton at 56 mph (10/F): 4.97   (2.01)
Change in petrol consumption between 56 & 75 mph: 27%

by a torque tube, longitudinal radius arms and a Watts linkage. While MacPherson struts are used at the front, self-levelling damper struts at the rear undoubtedly improve the ride with variable loads. One expects rather than finds that the ride is inferior to that for fully independent suspension – even if this is so the car's handling, poise and quick smoothness at speed make it a great pleasure to drive.

We have owned several Rovers going back to a freewheel 12 and including that unfaultable car – the 3 litre prior to the Buick-engined 3.5. As BL were unable to loan us a car for road testing (although we offered a time within a six month period) we remembered a friend who has bought *only* Rovers for thirty years or more. He likes the 2600 for the same reasons that we do, but dislikes it for its lack of quality control: the facia box is falling apart, the interior upholstery bad and serious blisters on the exterior paintwork, despite all the new technology. The older Rovers never had such faults, he assured us.

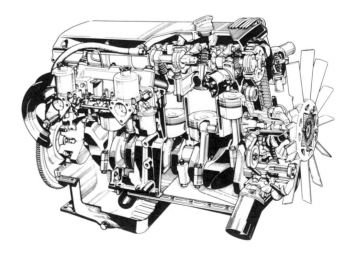

Belt driven ohc, with inclined valves, together with the classic English use of twin SV carburettors

2200–3000 cc: SUMMARY

No car in the class is exactly sluggish, but in a sense we here have the smaller Mercedes taking the role the BMWs did in Class 4. Those big Mercedes bodies need a lot of power, and clearly the emphasis for even the 2 door sleeker looking cars, the 'CEs', is more on comfort than shattering acceleration. The 280 CE has however a very respectable performance, at least as a manual, though many still prefer the automatic.

For some reason Mercedes have stayed with the K level of fuel injection, whereas other manufacturers tend to use the more advanced versions such as the L or M electronic systems. Mercedes, with their general attitudes to perfection, argue that they prefer a system which they, at least, consider to be more reliable.

In sharp contrast, we now have the BMWs reaching respectability. All four cars listed have very healthy performance which in our opinion reaches its pleasurable best in cars like the 528i, though we gather that the emphasis in the future is to be on the 3 and 7 series, at least at this range of engine size.

Two points are worth noting here: firstly that the 525, as a conventionally aspirated car, though marginally the poorest performer in the group of four, in fact manages a very respectable Performance Dimension and a good fuel efficiency figure. Secondly, the PD and fuel efficiency for the 528i and 535i are identical, though the latter car is of course the real performer. The BMW 728i is however quite a car whether on small roads or motorways!

Another big car, where we have an interesting example of fuel injection being squandered on an automatic transmission, is the Opel Senator. The performance is poorer for the manual, conventionally aspirated, car than for the fuel injected automatic but the fuel efficiency figures are similar and the Performance Dimension is markedly worse with the automatic transmission. The Monza is a different car altogether, clearly well engineered and balanced. We find it very desirable as the high performer here.

Again it seems impossible to keep Fords out of the listings: the newer Granadas are, we feel, good looking cars and in 2.8i Ghia form both well equipped, efficient and of good performance. The 2.3 and 2.8 conventionally aspirated cars are included solely for comparison, as is the Broadspeed turbo modified car. While this car certainly has much improved performance, it needs an awful lot more power to manage it, as can be seen from the poor PD figure. The older Capri 3.0 S is perhaps more sporty and certainly even on *Motor*'s old figures has both good performance and a good PD, though notably without injection. This only seems to be achieved with a poorish fuel efficiency figure.

The French offerings, though not in the main exactly new, are not bad at all. The Citroën CX GTi manages extremely well with its lower powered engine and we would find it fantastic with just a fraction less roll and less quirkily self-centering steering. A friend with a Renault 30 TX swears by it, though he now says he is going to trade it in for a manual version which has much better figures (we've left them for you to work out). Similarly, the Peugeot 604 Ti, if it doesn't stand alone in the group, is certainly not an embarrassment.

The two cars which excite us here are the new Alfa GTV6 and the Rover 2600 S. While the latter car still looks awfully rounded to us, its performance is above average but its PD and fuel efficiency figures are both exceptional: a major achievement. Couple this with the car's renowned handling ability and we have a car which could be anyone's choice. Our interest in the Alfa is more biased, though if anything we suspect that this has led us to underestimate its acceleration figures. We look forward with rather twitching fingers to an opportunity to drive the car in this country.

While none of the cars discussed could possibly be described as unpleasant we have mutual difficulty in picking the best. One of us will always settle for the BMW, and in particular the 528i, the other for the Rover 2600 S. When will we see the latter car fuel injected please?

Above: *Opel Monza – speed and comfort with complete reliability*

Below: *Alfa Romeo GTV6 2.5 litre fuel injection model – a fast executive express*

Class 5 Data Summary

Datum Point		Performance	Power Weight	PD	FE
A	Alfa Romeo GTV 6 2.5	14.9	122	12.3	1.68
B	BMW 323i	12.8	118	10.9	1.59
C	BMW 525	12.2	104	11.7	1.82
D	BMW 528i	15.5	124	12.6	1.79
E	BMW 728i	13.3	117	11.3	1.75
F	Citroën CX GTi	11.5	88	13.1	1.78
G	Ford Capri 3.0 S	15.5	112	13.9	1.38
Ga	(Motor)	13.3	112	11.8	1.38
H	Ford Granada 2.3 V6 (2V)	10.5	83	12.6	1.63
I	Ford Granada 2.8 V6 (2V)	11.9	94	12.7	1.6
J	Ford Granada 2.8i	13.9	110	12.7	1.69
K	Ford Granada 2.8 Broadspeed	15.1	156	9.7	
L	Mercedes-Benz 230 CE	10	93	10.8	1.84
La		9.1	93	9.8	1.71
M	Mercedes-Benz 280 CE	12.9	119	10.9	1.64
Ma		11.5	119	9.7	1.48
N	Opel Monza S	15.9	124	12.8	1.61
O	Opel Senator	11.4	103	11.1	1.46
P	Opel Senator CD	12.2	124	9.8	1.49
Q	Peugeot 604 Ti	12.3	97	12.7	1.75
R	Renault 30 TX	10.5	104	10.4	1.52
S	Rover 2600 S	13.1	95	13.8	2.01

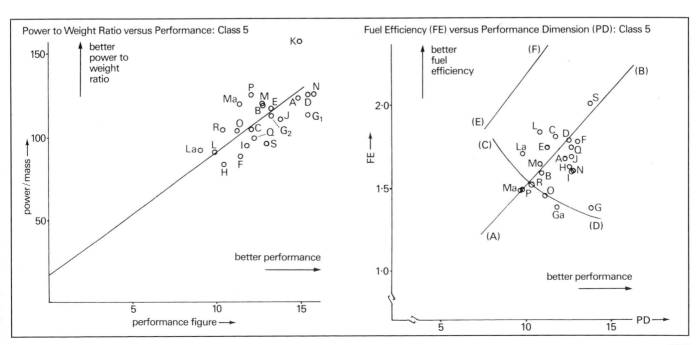

Power to Weight Ratio versus Performance: Class 5

better power to weight ratio

power / mass →

better performance

performance figure →

Fuel Efficiency (FE) versus Performance Dimension (PD): Class 5

better fuel efficiency

FE →

better performance

PD →

5 Automatic versus Manual

Cars with automatic gearboxes make driving more relaxed. Those people who use the car as a hermit his cell, a place to think, make decisions and meditate, invariably have automatic transmissions together with air conditioning, so that with windows closed, the serene, moving cell can even assist in problem solving. Almost all American cars use them, and most manufacturers duplicate many of their models in both manual and automatic form.

While in general it is the larger and more powerful cars that tend to have automatic transmissions there is some demand for smaller vehicles with only two pedals. Such cars are partially for the disabled and presumably also for those who have generally found driving a manual confusing with only two feet. Given the average driver's competence at managing the extra clutch pedal it's usually worrying to change over to only two. The average Buick or Cadillac responds alarmingly to having both feet firmly smashed down on the wide pedal of the power assisted brakes.

At the heart of the automatic box are two sets of epicyclic gears. An epicycle is a circular path the centre of which moves along the circumference of a larger circle. Ptolemy used them to describe the motion of the planets and the word has its origins in Greek: 'epi' means upon and 'kuklos' is a circle. It is thus fairly easy to visualize the ring gear in the gearbox being internally toothed and meshing with the not surprisingly named sun gear and planetary gears. When the sun and ring gears are locked together, it makes direct drive. The other ratios are obtainable by using the other gears in different relationships. There is nothing particularly *new* about epicyclic gears. Henry Ford's Model T of 1908–27 had an epicyclic gearbox. They were also used in the Rolls-Royce Merlin supercharger, and they are in fact an ideal way of changing gear ratios smoothly and effectively.

In automatics, the clutch is replaced by a fluid coupling or a torque converter. Fluid couplings consist of two bowl-shaped moving parts with rims close but

Mercedes new automatic four speed transmission

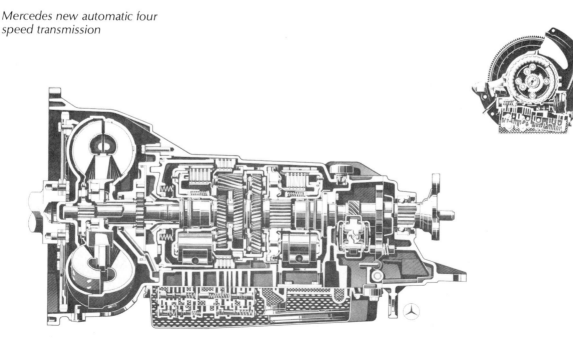

not touching. Inside the bowls are vanes. The impeller, which is the bowl nearest to and driven by the crankshaft, faces the other bowl called the turbine, and flings hydraulic fluid into its vanes. At idling speed the force is not sufficient to make the turbine rotate, but with more acceleration the force exerted by the hydraulic fluid turns the turbine and the car moves smoothly forward. With increased engine speed, the rpm of impeller and turbine rapidly become identical.

Torque converters are better than fluid couplings. In the torque converter there is a small vaned wheel between the impeller and the turbine, called the reactor or stator. This wheel turns at the same speed as the turbine. When extra power is needed, such as accelerating from rest, the reactor is locked and its vanes direct the hydraulic fluid back from the turbine into the impeller. By this means the impeller doubles the crankshaft torque at engine speeds of up to about 3000 rpm.

The automatic box selects gears in response to the speed or torque of the input shaft attached to the turbine.

Automatics have three or four ratios and work by a system of epicyclic gear trains, clutches, brake bands, relays and hydraulic clutches. It is the linked epicyclic gears which are the most crucial part of the system. Each of these consists of a geared sun wheel, which meshes with two planet wheels that orbit around it. The planet wheels also mesh with the teeth on the inner circumference of the annulus. In most automatics there are two epicyclic gears with a sun wheel which is common to both. The system is designed so that each of the main components can be braked while the unbraked ones turn the output shaft, and the gear ratio selected depends on which component is braked.

The appropriate selection is determined by sensors which respond to the speed of the output shaft, and the turning effort delivered by the torque converter. The sensors operate a hydraulic system which in turn activates clutches and brake bands.

Returning to the problem of efficiency, the description above makes it clear that the locking behaviour in the torque converter involves the rapid motion of liquids, the torque being carried ultimately by viscous shearing stresses. This involves the dissipation of energy, so already we have some gleam of hope for the enthusiastic gear shifter, all elbows, enjoying just the right gear for that particularly exhilarating corner.

We can however be a little more objective: tables I and II show comparative data for a variety of fairly arbitrarily chosen cars marketed in both manual and automatic form. Table I shows the basic published information and in table II the now familiar derived figures are collected for comparison. It will be remembered that our measure of performance is the maximum speed divided by the time to 60 mph: this is shown in column G and is compared with the power to weight ratio, H, to derive the performance dimension, I.

If comparison of the pairs of figures is not enough, a glance at figure I immediately demonstrates that all the manuals individually give more performance for their power to weight ratio than their automatic counterparts. The line in this graph is the average behavioural line for all cars as discussed in chapter 1, and we see that the clear tendency is for the manuals to behave in general better than this line while the automatics fall short of it.

Indeed the cars form into two families, separated by the statistical analysis of their behaviour. It is also evident that the automatics do not fall short of the manuals by a constant ratio as the performance is improved, but by a steadily increasing one. The two families have different gradients on the graph: in other words, the bigger and more high powered the car, the greater the power loss as a fairly constant fraction of the performance.

Not many people seem to have appreciated this fact, though given the mechanics of the torque converter it is obvious. The automatic has more justification in the small car, or lower powered diesel, than in the petrol drinking limousine.

Manufacturers do however clearly try in the face of one footed demand: a more careful examination of the figures shows how more recently developed automatic

Table I
Comparative data for manual and automatic cars (M = manual, A = automatic)

Model		A Speed (mph)	B 0–60 mph (secs)	C bhp	D Weight (lb)	E 56 mph (litres/100 km)	F 75 mph (litres/100 km)
Mercedes 240 TD	M	89	22.5	72	3315	7.8	11
	A	86	25.4	72	3315	8.1	11.6
200 T	M	104	14.8	109	3205	8.3	10.7
	A	101	15.9	109	3205	8.9	11.4
250 T	M	115	11.6	140	3295	9.8	12.1
	A	112	12.5	140	3295	10.1	12.9
280 TE	M	124	9.9	185	3405	9.9	12.2
	A	121	11.9	185	3405	10.9	13.4
280 SL	M	125	9.8	185	3305	9.3	11.8
	A	121	10.7	185	3305	10.1	12.6
VW Golf GLS	M	97	12.7	70	2254	6.6	9.7
	A	95	14.9	70	2254	7.2	10.6
Passat LS	M	101	13	75	2463	6.1	8.5
	A	98	14.6	75	2518	7.5	10.7
Renault Fuego GTS	M	112	11.8	96	2278	6.5	8.5
	A	108	12.6	96	2322	7.4	9.6
Citroën CX GTi	M	117	10.2	128	3031	8.1	10.1
CX 2400	A	112	12.1	128	3031	9.0	11.7
Ford Cortina 1600 ohc	M	94	12.7	73	2321	7.1	9.5
	A	90	15.8	73	2321	8.1	10.4
2000 ohc	M	105	9.8	101	2376	7.5	9.8
	A	101	12.1	101	2376	8.2	11.0
2.3 V6	M	109	9.6	114	2486	8.4	10.7
	A	105	11.3	114	2486	9.0	11.2
Granada 2.3 V6	M	107	10.2	114	2855	8.4	10.6
	A	101	12.1	114	2855	9.5	11.9
2.8i	M	120	8.6	160	3032	8.6	10.9
	A	117	11.2	160	3032	9.7	11.8

Table II
Comparative data for manual and automatic cars

	G Speed/time	H bhp/weight	I PD	J %	K Fuel consump. at 56 mph/ton	L % change 56–75	56/A	M 100/K	
M	3.95	45.6	8.7	} 17.6	4.94	48.7	0.62	2.02	1
A	3.38	45.6	7.4		5.13	43.2	0.65	1.95	◯
M	7.02	71.2	9.9	} 11.2	5.42	27.7	0.53	1.84	2
A	6.36	71.2	8.9		5.81	28	0.55	1.72	◯
M	9.91	89.1	11.1	} 9.9	6.24	23.4	0.49	1.6	3
A	8.96	89.1	10.1		6.43	27.7	0.5	1.55	◯
M	12.5	114.2	11.0	} 23.6	6.05	24.5	0.45	1.65	4
A	10.16	114.2	8.9		6.73	22.9	0.46	1.49	◯
M	12.75	117.4	10.9	} 13.5	5.9	26.8	0.46	1.56	5
A	11.31	117.4	9.6		6.41	24.7	0.46	1.56	◯
M	7.63	69.6	11.0	} 19.6	6.55	46.9	0.58	1.52	6
A	6.37	69.6	9.2		7.15	47.2	0.59	1.39	◯
M	7.76	68.2	11.4	} 12.9	5.55	37.7	0.55	1.8	7
A	6.71	66.7	10.1		6.67	47.6	0.57	1.5	◯
M	9.49	85.9	11	} 8.9	5.8	30.7	0.5	1.72	8
A	8.57	84.5	10.1		6.5	29.7	0.52	1.53	◯
M	11.5	88.1	13.1	} 26	5.6	24.7	0.48	1.8	9
A	9.2	88.1	10.4		6.2	30	0.5	1.6	◯
M	7.4	64.2	11.5	} 30.7	6.2	34	0.59	1.6	10
A	5.7	64.2	8.8		7.1	28.3	0.62	1.4	◯
M	10.7	87	12.3	} 28.1	6.45	30.9	0.53	1.55	11
A	8.3	87	9.6		7.05	34.2	0.55	1.42	◯
M	11.3	97.8	11.6	} 22.1	6.95	27.3	0.51	1.44	12
A	9.3	97.8	9.5		7.47	24.6	0.53	1.34	◯
M	10.5	82.9	12.6	} 26	6.12	25.8	0.52	1.63	13
A	8.4	82.9	10		6.92	25.3	0.55	1.45	◯
M	13.9	110.1	12.7	} 33.6	5.92	26.6	0.47	1.69	14
A	10.4	110.1	9.5		6.68	21.7	0.48	1.5	◯

systems show smaller fractional differences between the paired PD figures for similar powers. Bearing in mind its high power, the fractional improvement of the manual Mercedes 280 SL over its automatic version is, for example, relatively small.

Column J, showing the percentage improvement of PD for manual over automatic, should only of course be viewed as a function of the power to weight ratio since the differences are, as we have explained, for essentially different families.

Our second fundamental method of comparing cars is to plot the reciprocal of their petrol consumption per ton at 56 mph (90 km/h) against their performance dimension. The data in columns I and M of table II is thus shown in figure 2. The lines on the graph illustrate the different classes of behaviour which we found for *manual* cars in the chapter on fuel efficiency (page 92). Line AB was for cars that managed improved performance dimension with improved fuel efficiency while line CD was for those that could only manage the one at the expense of the other. Line EF referred to diesels. Again the contrast between manual and automatic shows very clearly. It is not that the use of the automatic results in a worsening of just either performance or efficiency. It is clear that both figures become worse together in a trend that approximates to the slope of the line AB. The situation is thus materially worse than might have been initially expected from figure 1. A car in automatic form doesn't just perform less well than its manual equivalent, it performs less well while drinking a proportionately *increased* amount of petrol!

To complete our comparison figure 3 shows the figures for the percentage increase in petrol consumption on changing the speed from 56 to 75 mph (90 to 120 km/h) as a function of the fraction 56 mph (90 km/h) is of each car's maximum speed. This may be used in a rough and ready way, for manual cars, to predict one figure when given the other. The situation in this instance, on comparing our two families, is far less clear. There is in fact no systematic behavioural difference

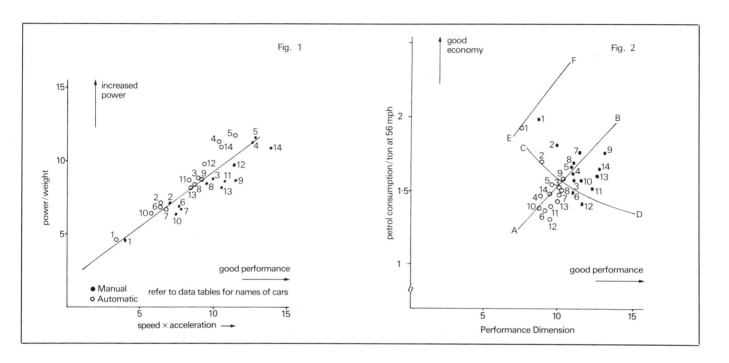

Fig. 1

increased power

power / weight

good performance

• Manual   refer to data tables for names of cars
○ Automatic

speed × acceleration ⟶

good economy

Fig. 2

petrol consumption / ton at 56 mph

good performance

Performance Dimension

between the classes. Generally the spread in the curve is markedly increased on including the automatics, and the reason for this perhaps lies in the greater difficulty of optimizing gear ratios for the automatics.

To summarize: in buying an automatic in preference to a manual you purchase, at added cost, a car which will have lower performance and give increased fuel bills. If you already have a chauffeur perhaps you should teach him how to use a gear lever while you meditate with more self satisfaction in the back seat.

Meanwhile perhaps racing gear-change fanatics might note that just one of those sporty changes out of a roundabout will knock the fuel bill for an average kilometre way over that of their more sedate colleague who lets the car do it. In this way the automatic is not just for the naturally meditative hermit, but will also do well for the defeatist, who knows he has no self discipline.

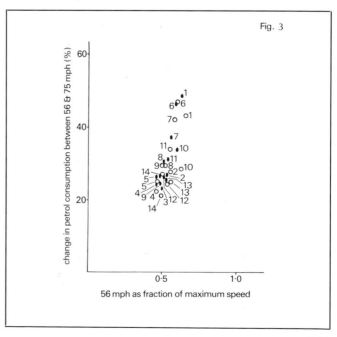

Fig. 3

change in petrol consumption between 56 & 75 mph (%)

56 mph as fraction of maximum speed

Class 6 Estate Cars

INTRODUCTION

The estate car of today started as the shooting brake or station wagon of the 1930s. In 1948 we designed a shooting brake on a Rolls-Royce Phantom II chassis, leaving the 7668 cc engine, the chassis and the whole beautiful front end up to and including the sliding partition, completely alone. The rear end, with speaking tube, Bedford cord seats and a great deal of expensive carpentry, were all removed and a deck of thin teak planks rather like a boat, laid to well beyond the original dimensions.

A simple structure of ash, marine ply and aluminium was erected above the deck, using rubber mounts cut from an enormous Avon tyre, and fastened by carriage bolts to the chassis. There were sliding windows: a must, because everyone without exception seemed to smoke Extra Strong Gold Flake cigarettes and there was no ventilation system.

Two doors at the back opened on large brass hinges, from a boat chandler who also provided other fittings which were adapted for different from their original functional uses inside, this being a genuine shooting brake. The people who wanted it were all as strong as horses and heavy with it. So, above all, it had to be strong, they might break things off without even thinking about it. There was no thought of power/weight ratio; in any case almost eight litres with a phenomenal amount of torque coped with it all.

The seats were redesigned from those folding wooden armchairs with canvas seats sometimes seen in the gardens of retired army officers. It had to be particularly watertight also, because it rains very hard in Northumberland, especially on the moors. The work was all carried out by two craftsmen who normally made sailing boats, so nothing was a problem. As they mentioned, it would not have to prove itself by floating evenly in the water.

Driving the thing about at various stages before completion was a great pleasure. Vandalism? Years later, it was being used as a delivery van for a smart dry cleaning firm, with the side windows covered in with painted metal. It still looked extraordinary, largely because of that Phantom II bonnet, and the surprising simplicity of the rest of it. Probably someone has removed all the vandalism and put a Hooper body back again.

Issigonis of course designed a small estate body for the Morris Minor which looked like a mini shooting brake. It was in no way comparable with grand shooting brakes really, but more economical to run and handier to park. The 1965 Renault 16 and then all the hatchbacks are a form of compromise solution, but this section is about proper estates, using the whole length of the vehicle behind the drivers seat.

Estate cars have been increasing in numbers and improving in design and construction since the 1950s when they started. It is a very sensible, functional vehicle which at its best can make the normal three box saloon look antiquated and pointless. Why not an aerodynamically designed *one* box vehicle tapered acutely towards the nose and mid-engined. What does the St Cyr wind tunnel say to that? The Citroën Safari was designed there, and it is the most beautiful of those which are shown here, but although desirable, still not breaking new ground.

What do we require of an estate car, without going off into fantasies?

(a) a vehicle to carry more than five people in comfort, together with an endless, unimaginable variety of loads.

(b) a power train capable of propelling it at reasonable speeds, with a cut-out for half the engine when travelling light, with no load or passengers.

(c) a suspension system to cope with the size, loads and possibility of awkward terrain.

Right: *Ford 2 litre estate car*

Below: *Volvo 265 Estate*

CITROËN CX SAFARI/FAMILIALE

The CX Safari is an exceptional vehicle, in that all the unique and well-known Citroën qualities – hydropneumatic suspension and self-levelling, aerodynamic shape, remarkable braking and economical cruising at high speeds, seem to be used to advantage to solve a number of awkward problems. Carrying eight people for example, could well have made the vehicle look like a bus, but the design and aerodynamics manage to make it look positively beautiful, despite its size. One of our families is the right size with precisely eight people, being six children and two adults and normally when in consort, we use a VW motor caravan because there is a Dalmatian as well. The Safari not only swallowed them all, but gave the whole ensemble an aura of well organized contented humans.

The fittings and appointments in the Safari are to the same high standards as the other cars in the CX range, and immediately dispel any idea that this is a utilitarian vehicle for carrying skis or hay, saddles and dirty boots. Nor is it a compromise – an unbalanced extension

added to a saloon. It has been designed specifically for its purpose, and the hydropneumatic suspension not only evens out road irregularities, it automatically self-levels under load. However much the load, the suspension compensates, and as a result, ground clearance remains constant, whether the car is fully laden or not. You can put half a ton into the Safari and it levels immediately. There are variations of seating and space, so that it can be turned into a five seater estate.

The Safari has VariPower rack and pinion steering which is precise but different from that of other cars. The four-wheel ventilated disc brakes are phenomenally powerful and have a much shorter travel than other brakes. The steering geometry gives undeviating straight-line stability despite the liner-like length of the vehicle, which is probably much longer than the other cars you have driven, and there is an emphasis on comfort in the ergonomically designed seats more reminiscent of a luxury saloon than an estate. The driver has a facia good enough for an astronaut, and a top

Left: *Citroëns, even at this size, have a tendency to make other cars look inexpressibly dowdy and demode*

Right: *Compact and accessible to a remarkable degree*

Citroën CX Safari and Familiale Manual

Engine: 4 cylinders in line, ohv, transverse
Capacity: 2347 cc
Bore; stroke: 93.5 mm   85.5 mm
Compression ratio: 8.75 to 1
Carburation: Dual choke
Max. power at 5500 rpm: 115 bhp   85.8 kW
Max. torque at 2750 rpm: 132.4 ft/lb   179.6 Nm

Transmission: Five speed gearbox to front wheels (C-Matic 3 speed torque converter optional)

Suspension: Independent self-levelling hydropneumatic. Front: equal length double wishbones. Rear: trailing arms and anti-roll bars

Steering: Fully power VariPower. 2.5 turns lock to lock
Turning circle: 35 ft 9 in   10.9 m

Brakes: Powered dual circuit. Ventilated front and rear discs

Dimensions:
Length: 16 ft 3 in   4.95 m
Kerb weight: 3097 lb   1405 kg

Performance:
Maximum speed: 108 mph   174 km/h
0–60 mph: 12.4 sec
Fuel consumption
   at 56 mph: 30.7 mpg   9.2 litres/100 km
   at 75 mph: 24.6 mpg   11.5 litres/100 km
   urban: 19.1 mpg   14.8 litres/100 km
French Government Tests

Insurance Rating: 6/7

Derived Data:
bhp/litre (kW/litre): 49   36.6
bhp/ton (kW/tonne): 77.5   57
Speed × acceleration: 8.7
Performance Dimension: 11.2
Petrol consumption/ton at 56 mph (10/F): 6.2   (1.61)
Change in petrol consumption between 56 & 75 mph: 25%

speed of 108 mph, but by driving nearer to a constant 60 mph and admiring the view of the east coast of Scotland, we achieved 27 mpg.

The CX Safari is a completely civilized and modern motor car. Everything is so advanced in technology in fact, that one expects to find some other radical and unique power unit when opening the bonnet. If this is asking too much, the dual choke carburettor (which is good) could be changed for fuel injection, which would bring the power unit more into line with the hydropneumatic suspension and increase the brake horse power.

Right: *Citroën have an obsession about the driver's outfit and the need for fingertips to reach everything. In the CX it succeeds completely*

FORD GRANADA GHIA ESTATE

Most Fords are very much improved by Ghia, and this is particularly true in respect to the Granada Estate. Of all the cars which we drove during the last two years, this car is memorable for its quiet, powerful efficiency and a sense of peace at all times, due to a fine balance of power and suspension.

We have had cars with more in the way of top speed, in this estate category, but the Granada achieves its 110 mph (177 km/h) without any noise or fluster. It also has good road holding, with no quirks or uncertainties and no sudden oversteers with its long but steady tail.

The Ghia improvements have quite a lot to do with the air of peace, because subsequently I borrowed a friend's Granada, but not Ghia, Estate, and found it quite different, more like just an estate car. The four speed manual box could be improved to five, but we can think of nothing else, no other improvements, which is rare. The seats are well designed ergonomically, the whole car is spacious and well bred with all the equipment anyone could need.

We took some quiet satisfaction driving to Cornwall and back in convoy with friends in a Range Rover, proving at every point and in every way that the Granada was faster, accelerated better, kept its inhabitants more steady, drank a lot less petrol; we changed over the passengers half way, in case ours were insensitive or half-witted, but the new passengers agreed too.

The Range Rover did tow us out of some loose sand in a gulley just off the road, but that is what makes Range Rovers so abominably snooty. They do have more traction.

Above: *This section shows the carburettor version of the V6 Ford engine with pushrods. It is noted for extreme simplicity and designed for easy access*

Ford Granada 2.8 Ghia Estate

Engine: 2.8 litre V6 2V
Capacity: 2792 cc
Bore; stroke: 93 mm   68.5 mm
Compression ratio: 9.2 to 1
Max. power at 5200 rpm: 135 bhp   100.7 kW
Max. torque at 3000 rpm: 159 ft/lb   216 Nm

Transmission: Four speed manual, rear wheel drive
(optional 3 speed automatic)

Suspension:
Front: independent short and long arms, coil springs and
anti-roll bar.
Rear: independent, semi-trailing arms, coil springs

Steering: Rack and pinion 4.3 turns (power assisted: 3.5
turns) lock to lock, power assistance standard on GL
Turning circle: 34 ft 5 in   10.5 m

Brakes: Dual line, servo assisted. 10.3 in (26.2 cm) discs on
front and 9 in (22.9 cm) drums on rear

Dimensions:
Length: 15 ft 7 in   4.74 m
Kerb weight: 3089 lb   1403 kg

Performance:
Maximum speed: 110 mph
0–60 mph: 10.3 sec
Fuel consumption
   at 56 mph: 31.4 mpg   9.0 litres/100 km
   at 75 mph: 24.8 mpg   11.4 litres/100 km
   urban: 18.9 mpg   14.9 litres/100 km

Insurance Rating: 6

Derived Data:
bhp/litre (kW/litre): 48.3   36.1
bhp/ton (kW/tonne): 91.3   67
Speed × acceleration: 10.68
Performance Dimension: 11.7
Petrol consumption/ton at 56 mph (10/F): 6.08   (1.64)
Change in petrol consumption between 56 & 75 mph: 26.7%

Brilliant, functional design with no stylistic exaggerations.

MERCEDES-BENZ 280 TE ESTATE

We have tested all the vehicles in this section thoroughly, and are convinced that this is the best engineered of them all though the Citroën Safari is also a magnificent estate car. The point about the Mercedes 280 TE is that it has all the properties of the saloon in power-steering, handling, braking and general standards of comfort. The estate section is simply a useful addition. An estate with 185 bhp and capable of 121 mph (we found that this figure was modest) and with a 700 kg payload, is quite a vehicle.

Our test drives included quite a lot of East Anglia in appalling weather conditions which the Mercedes disregarded, and the passengers enjoyed the silent efficiency of it, making favourable comparisons with the 280 SE which is our normal family car.

The self levelling device has actually been in existence for some time, as an optional extra, on the large saloons and it has been interesting to see it being steadily improved. It has now been put to hard and sensible work in the estate and helps to make it into a unique and highly desirable vehicle.

The mechanical specifications of the estate are identical to the saloon equivalent, except that an automatic hydraulic self-levelling control device is added to the rear suspension. A sensor monitors the overall load, together with the rear axle load. Self-supporting spring struts together with softer coil springs are used in place of the standard dampers and springs of the saloon model. An oil pump driven by the engine extracts oil from a reservoir and pumps it to a valve which is controlled by the anti-roll bar on the rear axle. The pressurized oil remains in the reservoir when the car is unladen.

When a load is put into the estate, oil is fed to the spring struts. The more oil is pumped into the struts, the greater the pressure in the gas compartments, thus keeping the car level. Braking has been redesigned for the greater weight carried at the rear of the vehicle, larger pistons being fitted in the rear brake calipers to adjust the braking effect.

136

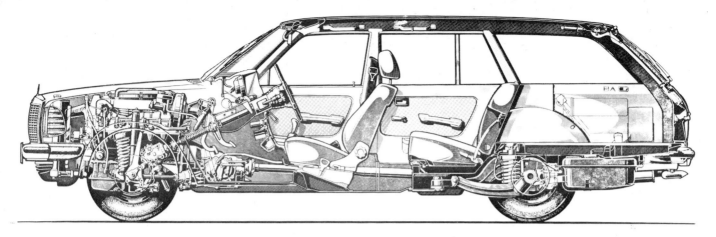

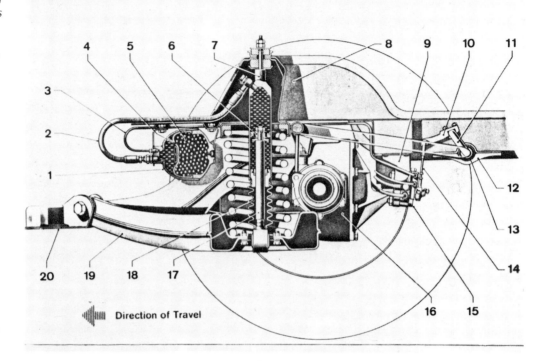

Above: *The best estate car in the world. This picture shows how the self-levelling device and the power train do not intrude on the interior space.*

Right: Self-levelling device
 1 *Gas-filled pressure reservoir*
 2 3 *Hydraulic fluid line*
 4 *Diaphragm*
 5 *Gas chamber*
 6 *Damper piston*
 7 *Hydropneumatic strut*
 8 *Side member*
 9 *Brackets*
10 *Torsion bar lever*
11 *Torsion bar*
12 *Brackets*
13 *Rubber mounting*
14 *Connecting rod*
15 *Level control valve*
16 *Rear axle housing*
17 *Piston rod*
18 *Rubber sleeve*
19 *Semi-trailing control arm*
20 *Rear axle carrier*

Direction of Travel

Mercedes-Benz 280 TE Manual (Automatic)

Engine: 6 cylinders in line
Capacity: 2746 cc
Bore; stroke: 86 mm   78.8 mm
Compression ratio: 9 to 1
Injection: Mechanical fuel injection
Max. power at 5800 rpm: 185 bhp   136 kW
Max. torque at 4500 rpm: 176.8 ft/lb   240 Nm

Transmission: Rear drive via 4 speed manual gear box or 4 speed automatic with torque converter

Suspension:
Front: coil springs, stabilizer and double control arms.
Rear: MB diagonal swing with brake torque compensation coil springs, stabilizer

Steering: MB power steering. 4.3 turns lock to lock

Brakes: Dual circuit servo assisted. Discs on all wheels

Dimensions:
Length: 15 ft 6 in   4.72 m
Kerb weight: 3405 lb   1545 kg

Performance:
Maximum speed: 124 (121) mph   200 (195) km/h
0–60 mph: 9.9 (11.9) sec
Fuel consumption
   at 56 mph: 28.8 (25.9) mpg   9.8 (10.9) litres/100 km
   at 75 mph: 23.1 (21.1) mpg   12.1 (13.4) litres/100 km
   urban: 16.4 (16.5) mpg   17.2 (17.1) litres/100 km

Insurance Rating: 7

Derived Data:
bhp/litre (kW/litre): 67.4   49.5
bhp/ton (kW/tonne): 114.2   82.6
Speed × acceleration: 12.5 (10.2)
Performance Dimension: 11.0 (8.9)
Petrol consumption/ton at 56 mph: 6.05 (6.73)   (1.65 (1.49))
Change in petrol consumption between 56 & 75 mph: 24.5% (23%)

RANGE ROVER

When the Range Rover was launched years ago, they made a spectacular drive from Alaska down the West Coast of North and South America, taking with them a few Land Rovers for equipment, fuel, food and extra personnel like camera-men. There were splendid pictures of the Range Rover traversing impossible land conditions, heroic in every spring and damper, brake horsepower and torque equal to everything.

There were dark stories, probably untrue, that actually the Land Rovers were forever pulling the Range Rovers out of trouble. At that time, having driven a Land Rover to Greece, and traversing it every which-way and negotiating the impossible every morning, afternoon and night for about two months to take photographs, with not a single problem, we felt that the stories might well be true.

Subsequently, however, living in Kent which is full of farmers, Range Rovers and Land Rovers, we find that the situation is often reversed. Range Rovers often do the pulling. Without knowing the exact circumstances

nothing can be learned from this, but the Range model's torque of 185 ft/lb plus enormous wheels equals a lot of traction. The Adwest Varamatic power steering is a positive advantage also, in dire situations, which is what these enormous vehicles are designed for, rather than frisky acceleration and tarmac driving.

Both Land Rovers and Range Rovers are not only well designed for their purpose, but have a phenomenal life span, like elephants and tortoises, so the rescuers could well be the newcomers, with only 80,000 miles on the clock, and those in the mud indomitable old rhinos which had achieved 150,000 with a few dubious services by small country garages interspersed over the years.

The Range Rover is one of the best four wheel drive estates in the world for difficult terrain. There are many four wheel drive vehicles being made now – but Land and Range Rovers have the advantage of enormous experience and no doubt there are developments for both of them impending. The performance dimension of this Rover is 8.3, using the ubiquitous 3.5 litre engine,

Opposite: *The Range Rover is at once an elegant car and a practical workhorse*

Right: *The all-alloy V8 ex-Buick, which has stood British Leyland in such good stead, fills the large engine bay, complete with its practical Zenith-Stromberg carburettors*

Range Rover

Engine: V8 aluminium alloy head and block ohv
Capacity: 3528 cc
Bore; stroke: 88.9 mm   71.1 mm
Compression ratio: 8.13 to 1
Carburation: 2 Zenith-Stromberg CD
Max. power at 5000 rpm: 132 bhp   98.5 kW
Max. torque at 2500 rpm: 185 ft/lb   251 Nm

Transmission: 4 speed main gearbox outputs to transfer 2 speed reduction unit. Front and rear drive permanently engaged via a third differential, which can be locked.

Suspension:
Front: coil sprung axle located by radius arms and Panhard rod.
Rear: coil sprung axle held by radius arms support rods and central wishbone assembly with a self energizing ride-level unit

Steering: Adwest Varamatic. 3.5 turns lock to lock. Manual worm and nut option
Turning circle: 37 ft   11.3 m

Brakes: Dual circuit servo assisted. Discs all round

Dimensions:
Length: 14 ft 8 in   4.47 m
Weight unladen: 3782 lb   1715 kg

Performance:
Maximum speed: 96 mph
0–60 mph: 15.7 sec

Insurance Rating: 6

Derived Data:
bhp/litre (kW/litre): 37.4   27.9
bhp/ton (kW/tonne): 73.8   54.2
Speed × acceleration: 6.1
Performance Dimension: 8.3

---

with bhp/litre of 37.4. Neither of these figures is outstanding, but the vehicle itself still is. It has practicality and overall quality of design and workmanship.

Range Rovers are designed for hard and difficult times when other vehicles have ground to a halt. Unless you put a Range Rover to the last test in a real way, you are using it as a grand estate vehicle for its spectacular looks. Drive it on the roads which have notices 'unsuitable for motor vehicles', through thick mud, up mountains, through streams. Subject it to merciless tasks and it will then show why it is in the top echelon of 4WD do-or-die vehicles – and handsome with it.

Again, BL were unable to provide a test car but several friends loaned us theirs, ranging over several years and they were all good.

A simple, strong and practical driver's outfit.

VOLVO 265 GLE ESTATE

For space, strength and practicability as a load carrier, the Volvo is in a class of its own. At point to point meetings, hunts, horse shows and pony clubs, they are predominant and provide a satisfactory service in this area of carrying saddles, tack, ponyriders, dogs and sacks of pony nuts. The whole car would appear to have been designed for big, strong no-nonsense people.

Contrast for example, many cars which, however technically excellent, are for rather smaller people with feet like mice. The pedals of the Volvo are ready for someone with a strong leather boot, size 10, and the leather seats for someone who has just been in the saddle. With an overall fuel consumption of 18.7 mpg they should not be penny-pinching either.

The engine is the Douvrin V6 which has been developed in common by Peugeot, Renault and Volvo. The same engine is used in the Peugeot 604 and the Renault 30, but producing variations in power and torque due to changes of carburation. This Douvrin engine has power, flexibility and complete integrity.

It has also proved itself by results in competition. For the 1980 Le Mans, mounted on WM cars, these engines fitted with double turbos gave an output of 450 bhp and gained 4th and 11th places. Therefore 1½ tons plus goods and passengers will be no problem for the engine for 150,000 miles or more.

The structure of the car will last a long car-lifetime as well, so it's just right for those who like to keep a car for ten years or longer. There are many cars which feel safe, but this one feels and probably is, *the* safest.

The Douvrin V6 is powerful, compact, fuel injected and designed for a long life

Volvo 265 GL and GLE

Engine: V6 'B28E' ohc block and head aluminium alloy
Capacity: 2849 cc
Bore; stroke: 91 mm   73 mm
Compression ratio: 9.5 to 1
Injection: Bosch K system
Max. power at 5500 rpm: 155 bhp   114 kW
Max. torque at 3000 rpm: 169.5 ft/lb   230 Nm

Transmission: 4 speed with overdrive (optional 3 stage torque converter)

Suspension: Sprung strut suspension with live rear axle

Steering: Power assisted rack and pinion
Turning circle (kerbs): 32 ft 2 in   9.8 m

Brakes: Servo assisted dual circuit. Front and rear discs

Dimensions:
Length: 15 ft 8½ in   4.78 m
Kerb weight: 3282 lb   1488 kg

Performance:
Maximum speed: 101 mph   162 km/h
0–60 mph: 10.6 sec
Fuel consumption
   at 56 mph: 32.8 mpg   8.6 litres/100 km
   urban: 15.3 mpg   18.5 litres/100 km

Insurance Rating: 7

Derived Data:
bhp/litre (kW/litre): 54.4   40
bhp/ton (kW/tonne): 99   71.7
Speed × acceleration: 9.52
Performance Dimension: 9.6
Petrol consumption/ton at 56 mph (10/F): 5.5   (1.81)

ESTATE CARS: SUMMARY

The role of the estate car has changed progressively over the last ten or fifteen years. This is mainly associated with the increasing popularity of the hatchback, which is now capable of fulfilling many of the tasks which could previously only be accomplished using an estate. Furthermore, the hatchbacks' generally versatile and variable internal format can mean that odd needs for lawnmower transportation or holiday camping can be met adequately without permanently dragging the elephant's cage. Now what advertisement does that remind you of?

There are however those who need a lot of carrying space fairly permanently: the traveller or antique dealer, the addictive camper or simply the large family. It would seem, in these circumstances, that there are no good arguments for a small estate car, if you really want one you want it big!

We have, however, considered one car which is in a sense more a large hatchback, mainly to satisfy those who really can't stand dragging their house behind them. This is the Lancia 2000 HPE. In fact it is no match in carrying capacity to its rivals in the group and is in this sense misnamed, but when put in the fraternity it has a good performance and seems more than adequately efficient. We like its shape, and suspect that it will go on being successful now the company has rid itself of corrosion problems. Essentially it has Italian style with a surprising touch of Germanic solidity. A satisfying but not an exciting car to drive.

The other successful odd man out in our group is of course the Range Rover. This is certainly not just a toy for shooting on the moors, though it fits that bill as well as it does motorway police work. Its weight, compared with a Land Rover, means that it copes with many rough ground chores that the latter vehicle can't manage, while its suspension is just about soft enough to cope with general road use. It is on this latter point that most of its American rivals fail. They are generally too comfortable on the road and thus far too soft for field work. In our view the Range Rover has no realistic competitor for the purchaser who genuinely needs all its abilities.

Turning now to the genuine estate cars, Ford manage to give us yet again a very functional and sensible version of the genre in the 2.8 Ghia, though even in this format it lives up to neither the style nor the performance of the Mercedes 280 TE. But then their prices are a little different!

The 280 TE is in our opinion a staggeringly satisfying car to drive; even when packed with children it handles with unruffled grace at speeds which totally belie the speedometer reading, which generally should be masked from otherwise ignorant but faint hearted passengers. The 280 TE certainly outperforms all the other cars in the group, though the figures for the Granada suggest that with rather lower power the latter car manages remarkably well. The Volvo, with that tremendous reputation for indestructability, will always have its admirers, but must it look quite so like a Sherman tank!

The French have one famous offering in the estates, the Safari or Familiale, as at home with the large family as in its job as the fast French motorway ambulance. It remains as idiosyncratic as one could wish, and while outperforming only the Range Rover and the diesels it is cursed by that French tax law on large engines. All the same, for those who like the Citroën, the Safari is a natural delight.

Logically the need for very high performance should not rank too highly here, though the power to cope with heavy loads is clearly important. On this basis there should be more good diesel estates. The coming of the Turbo diesel, long since well known to the lorry driver will, we think, given time sweep the board. We have included here the Mercedes 300 TD, and to whet the appetite the 300 TD Turbo, which it might be noted has improved fuel efficiency (at least at 56 mph) as well as improved performance.

Volvo 265 Estate – towing is no problem

Class 6   Data Summary

Datum Point		Perform-ance	Power Weight	PD	FE
A	Citroën CX Safari	8.7	78	11.2	1.61
B	Ford Granada 2.8 Ghia	10.7	91	11.7	1.64
C	Mercedes-Benz 280 TE	12.5	114	11	1.65
Ca	Mercedes-Benz 280 TE(A)	10.2	114	8.9	1.49
D	Mercedes-Benz 300 TD	5.2	54	9.8	2.05
Da	Mercedes-Benz 300 TD(A)	4.7	54	8.8	1.74
E	Mercedes-Benz 300 TD (turbo)	7.1	74	9.6	2.11
F	Range Rover	6.1	74	8.3	na
G	Volvo 265 GL and GLE	9.5	99	9.6	1.81

na = not available

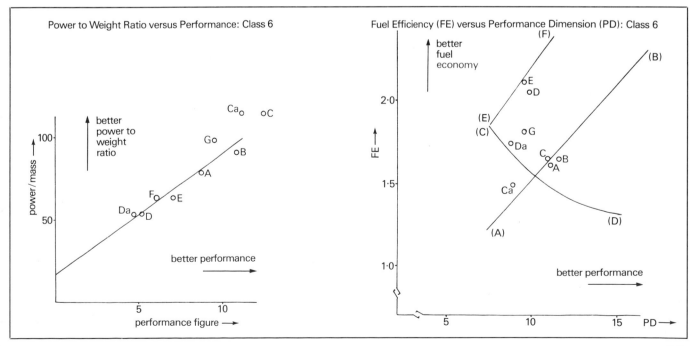

6 Fuel Injection versus Carburettor

Fuel injection is not a recent invention; it has been in existence right from the beginning of the internal combustion engine. Karl Benz began with a carburettor in 1885 but it was not a very satisfactory one, and for a few years injection pumps made by Deutz were the best system available, until 1892 when Wilhelm Maybach brought out a carburettor that took over the field.

The Wright Brothers' four-cylinder engine which made the first powered flight in 1903 used fuel injection, and so did two other early aircraft, those of Santos Dumont in 1906 and Eindecker in 1909.

In 1930 an intensive development programme for fuel injection was started by the Deutsche Versuchsanstalt für Luftfahrt, with the benefit of the research of Bosch, who had been working on injection pumps for diesels. The aircraft Germany produced in the thirties were to benefit from this in terms of very good performance, leading to an acknowledged German supremacy in the later prewar airshows.

After World War II the technology found a place in the Mercedes Silver Arrow racing car, with the added refinement of the ram effect. The ram effect is based on a splendid fluke of fluid dynamics, in which the air column in the intake pipe, at a particular range of engine speeds, will resonate in tune with the vibrations from the engine; the resonance produces a pulsating effect in the movement of the fuel in the intake pipe, assisting it on its way with an appreciable boost. The effect of this is a little bit like a mild form of supercharging – only free, gratis and for nothing.

With the engine arranged specially to take advantage of the ram effect, mainly by ensuring that the resonance takes place in the engine's maximum range of power, a gain in power of as much as ten per cent can be achieved. Mercedes began to harness this effect in commercial production with the 300 SL and the 300, and today it is used in all the Mercedes fuel injected engines.

In the middle fifties Bendix brought out an electronically controlled fuel injection system, followed by Bosch in 1958. It was the Bosch D-Jetronic system which first enabled petrol injection to reach a wider commercial market, by say 1960.

The basic principle of fuel injection is that while carburettors mix the fuel and air together some way before they reach the inside of the engine, which can be a rather rough-and-ready process by modern standards, the injection system achieves much greater precision and efficiency by delivering fuel much nearer to where it is needed. The fuel is sprayed rather than injected, either into the intake manifold or, as in large diesels, directly into the chamber. To take full advantage of the great precision this allows in administering the fuel, the intake of air too must be handled with equal precision.

Airflow sensor: as the air enters the system it encounters a hinged metal flap called a sensor which is mounted across the direction of the airstream and impedes its progress, until of course the air pushes the sensor back on its hinge, which it very quickly does. While the air which does pass increases its speed, there is an overall reduction of pressure on the flap and it settles back to its definitive position, which is an angle determined entirely by the rate of flow of the air. Therefore any change in the rate of flow is accurately registered by a change in the angle of the sensor, and the movements of the sensor provide the source of control for the fuel pressure.

Fuel distributor: control of the fuel pressure takes place in the fuel distributor, which is the junction in the fuel intake where the feed is divided out into separate pipes, one for each cylinder of the engine.

Each separate pipe has its own metering slit and pressure valve, and the flow of fuel is regulated by a plunger which dictates to the valves how much fuel they will permit to pass. A mechanical linkage reports any movement of the airflow sensor to the control plunger, and we have precise co-ordination of the intake of air and fuel.

This description of the intake control is based on the **Bosch K-Jetronic system**, which in its plain version relies simply on mechanical control and is capable of functioning very well as such. It can be refined, if desired, with the addition of some electronic equipment.

One such device consists of a solenoid valve and a hydraulic arrangement, and is attached to the fuel distributor. This equipment performs finer adjustments to the action of the fuel metering slits, and can be installed in combination with sensors of the type that send out an electronic signal, such as the Lambda sensor.

The L-Jetronic: this system has a greater degree of electronic control than the K system. It uses semi-conductor technology, combining its component parts into integrated circuits. Most of its active components are operated by the simple choice between 'on or off', which greatly simplifies the electronics of the control unit.

The L system advances a little further into the realm of high technology, measuring the impulses in the ignition system and instructing the injection valves to spray their fuel in exact time. As the engine turns faster, the ignition pulses grow shorter, and they switch the charging and discharging current of a capacitor alternately.

It follows that one of the chief distinctions between the K and L systems is that the K injects fuel continuously, while the L sprays intermittently as it follows ignition timing. The Motronic, too, sprays intermittently.

As well as being so eminently precise this equipment is today extremely reliable. It also gives great flexibility, and such are its electronic refinements that it can adjust the injection of fuel to the temperature of the engine, and of the intake air.

Bosch have developed their airflow sensors as a separate and interchangeable piece of equipment. For electronic control, a potentiometer is fitted which converts the flap angle into a DC voltage. Wear and noise have been reduced by the introduction of better materials: a relatively friction-free plastic, and silver-palladium alloy for the electric contacts.

Before the equipment leaves the factory, a computer is used to trim the final settings of the valves, which it does by means of a laser. The computer stores all the information about the settings as they vary from engine to engine, and any alterations desired by the manufac-turer of the vehicle or engine can be programmed in at the keyboard.

Bosch Motronic: the most advanced form of fuel injection to date is the Bosch Motronic. This is the system that has its own complete computer in the car and combines the functions of ignition and fuel injection into a single operation, resulting in the advertising claim that with the Motronic, a car's engine tunes itself – seventy times a second.

The heart of the Motronic is indeed a microcomputer, situated in the electronic control unit. It is small but it qualifies fully as a computer, with its microprocessor, programme and data memory, plus the input and output circuitry for incoming information and outgoing commands. Its memory can store spark advance curves, and the characteristic curves relating time and temperature.

Air intake quantity, engine speed, the position of the crankshafts and the temperatures of the engine and the intake air are all reported to the microcomputer. In a flash, it calculates the ignition point and the amount of fuel to be injected, and sends out the commands to the equipment.

The Motronic also has the remarkable facility of intervening in the performance of the engine, boosting torque at low and high engine speeds. During over-run the fuel supply is temporarily shut off and then finely cut in.

Injection versus the carburettor: there are some very interesting contrasts between injection and carbu-ration. In engine design the differences result from two different approaches to the introduction of fuel and air to the chamber.

(1) With a carburettor, fuel is drawn out of a jet by the vacuum in the intake manifold; in fuel injection it is fed either to the intake manifold or, as in large diesel engines, directly into the combustion chamber.

(2) The carburettor determines the quantity of fuel in a simple, mechanical fashion, either by means of the throttle plate, which changes the strength of the vacuum, or by varying the cross section of the flow, as in

the case of the constant vacuum carburettor. The fuel injection system takes more variables into account: besides measuring the airflow more precisely, it allows for engine and ambient temperatures and air pressure, in adjusting the flow of fuel.

(3) With a carburettor, air and fuel are mixed upstream of the throttle, while the fuel injection system conducts air and fuel separately all the way to the engine – either the manifold or the chamber itself.

(4) In the carburated system, different amounts of fuel find their way to each cylinder, while total similarity of combustion for all cylinders is obtained in fuel injection.

Three special inefficiencies are inherent in the carburettor, resulting from the fact that fuel is only partially vaporized on its way to the cylinders. First, it often happens that some of the fuel remains in the form of a film on the manifold walls. Then, as all the cylinders are inhaling at different times and different angles to the manifold, each tends to receive a different type of mix through the manifold. Experiment has shown that this variation increases as the intake pressure rises, in other words as the engine runs faster. This is bound to lead to waste: the overfed cylinders could in principle get insufficient air to burn all their fuel, while the underfed ones will not contribute the power they should with better fuel/air mixture.

The variation in mixture between cylinders can also make a nonsense of the process of tuning the engine. The smaller these differences are, the closer the engine can be tuned towards its misfire and knock limits, in order to obtain a lean mixture for fuel economy. Here fuel injection scores really high marks.

Injected engines start more quickly than carburettor engines, because among other things the injected engines have fuel pumps that operate under their own electric power, whereas it happens that the carburated ones usually have mechanical fuel pumps that are driven by the engine. An engine driven pump will not always provide the steady fuel pressure that is required for starting. The injected engine must have steady fuel pressure, its valves requiring a specific pressure or else they will not work, and this applies just as much during starting as at any other time.

The electric fuel pump usually comprises a permanent magnet electric motor with rotary pumps, combined in a very compact unit which lies immersed in the petrol tank. The armature of the motor even runs in fuel and is cooled by it.

To sum it all up, the advantages fuel injection can offer make truly compelling reading:

(1) lower fuel consumption,
(2) more torque,
(3) better cold and hot starting,
(4) smoother acceleration and deceleration,
(5) uniform distribution of fuel to the cylinders,
(6) spark control coupled to the injected fuel quantity and the engine speed, and
(7) no servicing required except changing fuel filters and spark plugs.

Class 7 Sports Cars

INTRODUCTION

The meteoric development of brake horse power, and its co-ordination with suitable suspension systems to produce vehicles which now progress down the Mulsanne straight at over 200 mph, has been due largely to sports car and endurance racing. Obsessional engineers, designers, drivers and manufacturers have worked in concert to achieve this. Levassor won the Paris–Bordeaux–Paris in 1895 with a 1.2 litre Panhard which developed 3.3 bhp/litre, while the cars which now win at Le Mans produce in excess of 260 bhp/litre.

Sports cars in the past have had a strong machismo image, but it is changing. Originally sports cars were for racing and/or leisure activities. They are now used for racing *and* as the executive's express. Using planes and hire cars or taxis does not solve all travel problems for executives, and many now prefer to use fast cars. Sports cars with high performance are now being equipped with interiors of great comfort for these purposeful directors. Research by Mercedes, Porsche and Ferrari shows that annual mileages that are double and treble previous figures, and at very much higher average speeds.

The development of more power in the engines has been the work of outstanding engineers like Marc Birkigt, Chief Engineer to Hispano Suiza, whose Alfonso of 1911, as well as being one of the most beautiful, was also the most efficient of the early sports cars. It had a 7.6 litre four-cylinder in line engine with twin overhead camshafts and four valves per cylinder. Ettore Bugatti, who produced the marque which stands for one of the highest expressions of sports car design; from the 16 valve 1.4 litre Brescia of 1919 to the type 35 which won the World Championship in 1926, the Type 51 which won it again in 1930, and the Type 55 (which had the same engine as the 51); W. O. Bentley whose cars achieved five victories at Le Mans. Ferdinand Porsche who was at Mercedes in the 1920s with the super-

charged six litre cars, and inspired the Porsche cars carried on by his son; Vittorio Jano, Chief Engineer to Alfa Romeo from 1924, whose straight eight engine of 2300 cc developed 142 bhp and won at Le Mans four years running (1931–34) followed by his six-cylinder engine also of 2300 cc which formed the basis of Alfa sports cars until 1938.

Jano also concerned himself with suspension systems; and Dr. Porsche again in the 1930s with the Auto-Unions made a radical step forward in design of engine chassis and bodyshell. Meanwhile Duesenberg and Miller were both very much concerned with the increase of bhp and speed, in the USA, at Indianapolis.

In the 1950s Eric Uhlenhaut designed the 300 SL gullwing sports car, with a 3 litre, 6-cylinder fuel injected engine of 215 bhp, followed by the eight-cylinder of 300 bhp 300 SLR. This car was involved in a disastrous crash at Le Mans in 1955, which caused Mercedes to abandon racing.

Jaguar cars won at Le Mans in 1951, 53, 55, 56 and 57 with the XK 6-cylinder engine of 325 bhp, the chief engineer being W. M. Heynes. Colombo and Alfieri have been the designers most concerned with the success of Maserati and Ferrari. Wally Hassan and H. Mundy designed the Coventry-Climax engine which was used by C. Chapman in F1 as well as sports cars. Dr. Porsche's son Ferdy masterminded the development of the Porsches.

The Italians pioneered the changes in the 1950s, from open to closed cars, and the practice of placing the engines behind the driver but ahead of the rear wheels. Enzo Ferrari, with his remarkable postwar record of Grand Prix wins, established a reputation as the supreme builder of sports cars. The double change of open to closed for aerodynamic reasons, and the central engine position give a better weight distribution. It is changes of this type which have created the real synthesis of engine, suspension and bodyshell.

AUDI QUATTRO

The Quattro is a high-powered passenger car with permanently engaged four wheel drive, which is powered by a 2.2 litre five-cylinder fuel injection engine developing 147 kW (200 bhp) with a turbocharger and air charge cooling, enabling speeds in excess of 220 km/h (137.5 mph).

The torque from the five speed gearbox is transmitted to all four wheels, to the front wheels, as with the Audi 200, and to the rear differential via an inter-axle differential. Instead of the normal output shaft, the gearbox employs a tubular shaft which enables an inter-axle differential to be integrated in the gearbox, which distributes the torque evenly to the front and rear drives, compensating for changes in weight distribution when the car is unevenly laden, or due to acceleration.

The propeller shaft connected to the inter-axle differential has constant velocity joints at each end and a cardan-type universal joint in the centre. There is of course a weight penalty for having drives to front and rear but it is small – 75 kg (165 lb) more than a front

wheel drive and 35 kg (70 lb) more than a rear wheel drive car.

The advantages in traction outweigh this penalty. For greater adhesion in extreme conditions, there is a locking mechanism on the inter-axle differential between front and rear drives, and a separate lock for the rear differential. Dashboard lights indicate when the differential locks are engaged.

The suspension system is simple and effective. The MacPherson strut front suspension of the Audi 200 is used, together with the same system at the rear, except that it is turned through 180°. A similar method was used for the two sub-frames. The suspension struts of the Audi 80 and 200 were used on the Quattro.

The brake system consists of ventilated floating caliper brakes with 280 mm diameter discs at the front, with unventilated 245 mm diameter discs at the rear.

The asymmetric power assisted rack and pinion steering, with its servo cylinder integrated in the cast aluminium steering box casing, was specially developed.

Opposite above: *Already achieving success in rallies, the Quattro has more power and more traction due to its turbo engine and four wheel drive*

Right: *The principles of the turbocharger are similar. The basic idea can be seen from the diagram of the Lotus. This diagram also shows the turbine itself, to the right of the picture*

Opposite below: *The simple suspension system, with MacPherson struts all round, supports a machine made up to a large extent from existing components*

Audi Quattro

Engine: Five cylinders in line, ohc, turbocharger giving max. boost (0.85 bar) at 3500 rpm. Intercooler allows high boost and increased bhp
Capacity: 2144 cc
Bore; stroke: 79.5 mm   89.4 mm
Compression ratio: 7.0 to 1
Injection: Injection via turbocharger
Max. power at 5500 rpm: 200 bhp   147 kW
Max. torque at 3500 rpm: 210 ft/lb   285 Nm

Transmission: 5 speed manual to four wheel drive with three differentials the centre and rear lockable

Suspension: All independent with MacPherson struts front and rear

Steering: Rack and pinion, power-assisted

Brakes: Power-assisted dual circuit. All disc brakes front ventilated. Split front/rear

Dimensions:
Kerb weight: 2840 lb   1290 kg

Performance:
Maximum speed: 137 + mph   220 + km/h
0–60 mph: 6.8 sec
Fuel consumption
   at 56 mph: 35.7 mpg   7.9 litres/100 km
   at 75 mph: 27.2 mpg   10.4 litres/100 km
   urban: 18 mpg   15.7 litres/100 km

Insurance Rating: 8 +

Derived Data:
bhp/litre (kW/litre): 93.3   68.6
bhp/ton (kW/tonne): 146.2   105.8
Speed × acceleration: 20.1
Performance Dimension: 13.8
Petrol consumption/ton at 56 mph (10/F): 5.77   (1.73)
Change in petrol consumption between 56 & 75 mph: 32%

High-powered cars of conventional type approach their limit when the driven wheels spin, which on front wheel drive cars causes loss of steering control, and with rear wheel drive, a loss of directional stability. Similarly, when the throttle is opened or closed in a corner, the change in the dynamic balance can cause under or oversteer with two wheel drives, whereas with four wheel drive, the torque being similar on all wheels produces a neutral response.

The five-cylinder engine is basically the same as that in the Audi 100, where it develops 100 kW (136 bhp) in standard form, the Audi 200 5T where it develops 125 kW (170 bhp) with an exhaust driven turbocharger, and in the Audi Quattro where it develops 147 kW (200 bhp) with no radical changes, but painstaking development, as follows: a cooler reduces the temperature of the intake charge by 50 to 60°C. This makes the air more dense than it otherwise would be, allowing a higher fuel intake of higher compression without pre-ignition. (See Heat and Work in the Engine, p. 68.)

The intake charge cooling is controlled by a sensor in the induction manifold to register temperature variations and relay them to an electronic processor which continuously calculates and adjusts the ignition timing. The stainless steel exhaust system (which has twin tail pipes) also contributes to the power increase through reduced back pressure. The 0.39 coefficient of drag, normally an important issue, seems almost irrelevant.

In 1977 Volkswagen had completed the development of the VW Ilitis 4 wheel drive vehicle for the German army. At the same time they were developing the turbocharged engine for the 200 5T, the basic layout of which, an in-line engine with its gearbox just behind the front axle, was eminently suitable for a four wheel drive.

So the Quattro is a new car produced from parts of existing VW products, engineered into a unity and developed on road and track into a car which is about to rewrite the motoring rule books – its traction, road holding, handling and performance showing the unique standard of engineering at VW/Audi.

BMW M535i

The 535i, a product of the Motorsport GmbH division of BMW, is recognizable from the front by its deep vented spoiler. It joins the M1 coupé in carrying a capital M as a prefix to the model code. Eighty-five per cent of it is built on the production lines and the final fifteen per cent by the Motorsport division. This is a logical development for the company, whose reputation in competition is extraordinarily high, to link the motorsport division to customer production. In the section on rally cars we have pointed out the disparity between production and rally vehicles but in this case they are one and the same.

The 3.5 litre engine is basically the same as that fitted to the 635 CSi and 735i models. This engine develops 218 bhp at 5200 revs, and 224 lb/ft of torque at 4000 rpm in the M 535i. With close ratio five-speed box, four ventilated disc brakes, uprated suspension, power assisted recirculating ball type steering, and a lighter bodyshell with spoilers front and rear, the M 535 has a claimed top speed of 136+ mph and 0–62 in 7.5 seconds. Handling and ride are unfaultable and

unforgettable at all speeds, with balance and stability in cornering and braking. The Recaro seats for pilot and passenger are the best available and give support of a superior kind. All instruments and controls are precise and impeccable.

While BMW have produced the M 535i by linking the production and Motorsport divisions so that customers are nearer to the heart of competition motoring, there is still one further stage towards the ultimate offered by Burkhard Bovensiepen and his Alpina factory in Buchloe, Bavaria.

The Alpina BMWs use the 635 CSi bodyshell and the B7/Turbo 3.0 litre power unit which achieves 250 km/h (156 mph), or with the B6/2.8 litre six-cylinder unit, a maximum speed of 220 km/h (137.5 mph). The Alpina factory produces about 300 of these highly desirable cars a year.

Of all the cars we tested over a period of two years, this one gave us the most pleasure. Impeccable. Power and sweetness of response beyond expectations.

Opposite: *The bodyshell is efficient and is the container of an engine and suspension system rather than being a flying work of art*

Above: *The engine is the six cylinder, 218 bhp unit as used in the M1, with fuel injection, naturally, and ease of access to all units*

BMW 535i

Engine: 3.5 litre, 6 cylinders in line, ohc
Capacity: 3453 cc
Bore; stroke: 93.4 mm   84 mm
Compression ratio: 9.3 to 1
Injection: Bosch L-Jetronic
Max. power at 5200 rpm: 218 bhp   160 kW
Max. torque at 4000 rpm: 228 ft/lb   310 Nm

Transmission: 5 speed manual gearbox

Suspension:
Front: independent on inclined spring struts, coil springs, stabilizer bar
Rear: independent on rubber-mounted semi-trailing arms, coil springs, stabilizer bar

Steering: Power assisted
Turning circle: 36 ft 7 in   11.2 m

Brakes: Dual twin circuit servo assisted. 11 in (27.9 cm) front discs vented, 10.7 in (27.2 cm) rear discs

Dimensions:
Length: 15 ft 2 in   4.62 m
Kerb weight: 3416 lb   1550 kg

Performance:
Maximum speed: 138 mph   222 km/h
0–60 mph: 7.8 sec
Fuel consumption
   at 56 mph: 27.7 mpg   8.53 litres/100 km

Insurance Rating: 8

Derived Data:
bhp/ton (kW/tonne): 142
Speed × acceleration: 17.9
Performance Dimension: 12.6
Petrol consumption/ton at 56 mph (10/F): 5.59   (1.79)

BMW 635 CSi

The 635 CSi can be bought only with a 5 speed Getrag manual gearbox, which gives an instant indication of its efficient and keen spirit. The engine is basically the same as that used for the M1 mid-engined coupé. The seven main bearing 6-cylinder in-line engine, with a compression ratio of 9.3:1, has electronic contact breakerless ignition and Bosch L-Jetronic injection; it produces 218 bhp at 5200 rpm, and 224 ft/lb of torque at 4000 rpm.

The driver has everything a driver could wish for in addition to this power unit. Visibility is excellent, the seat is completely adjustable for position, rake and tilt, pedals are large and well placed, the binnacle holds in clear view the speedometer, rev counter, tank and water indicators, with other controls such as heater/ventilation/fan on the angled facia. There is also the BMW check panel covering all systems.

The clutch needs some muscle, like all clutches concerned with engines of over 200 bhp, and the Getrag gearbox, like the ZF, has stronger springs than normal common or garden boxes, and requires fifteen minutes

of conscious practising, like a pianist with a Bechstein. The ratios are 1st 3.717:1, 2nd 2.403:1, 3rd 1.766:1, 4th 1.263:1 and 5th 1:1. The claimed 140 mph (225 km/h) maximum is reached at 5900 rpm in 5th.

One hundred and twenty is a relaxed cruising speed for the engine, and the acceleration of 0–60 in 7.5 seconds shows its mettle. Engines of this calibre invariably have flexibility, and it is always a pleasure to find out quite how much. The 635 will pull in 5th gear at tickover speed without stalling, which shows a level of engineering which both H. Royce and F. Porsche would have liked.

The car is a joy to drive at all speeds, helped by the limited slip differential when in the mountains and on rough roads, which was part of our long test drive. The ride is taut, but showed tendencies for the nose to dive and the rear to squat, unlike the 7 series, but this was terrain around Snowdon where a 7 would not have been taken. It is another of the 2 + 2s – large children for the back seats, or small, acquiescent adults.

152

Opposite: The fastest and most fabulous of the production models, excepting the M1, the 635 CSi is in the same category as the best of the Porsches

Right: A beautifully organised arrangement of engine with accessories: impeccable and at the same time with everything visible and available

BMW 635 Csi

Engine: 6 cylinders in line
Capacity: 3453 cc
Bore; stroke: 93.4 mm   84 mm
Compression ratio: 9.3 to 1
Injection: Bosch L-Jetronic
Max. power at 5200 rpm: 218 bhp   160 kW
Max. torque at 4000 rpm: 228.6 ft/lb   310 Nm

Transmission: 5 speed manual gearbox

Suspension:
Front: independent with sprung legs, torsion bar stabilizers and positive and negative stroke dampers.
Rear: independent axle carrier/gearbox unit 3 point suspended spring legs with angled trailing arms. Anti-roll bar

Steering: ZF recirculating ball powered

Brakes: Dual twin circuit servo assisted. 11 in (27.9 cm) front discs vented, 10.7 in (27.2 cm) rear discs vented

Dimensions:
Length: 15 ft 7 in   4.75 m
Weight unladen: 3308 lb   1500 kg
Performance:
Maximum speed: 138 mph   222 km/h
0–60 mph: 7.4 sec
Fuel consumption
    at 56 mph: 27.7 mpg   8.5 litres/100 km
    at 75 mph: 22.8 mpg   10.3 litres/100 km
    urban: 12.2 mpg   19.3 litres/100 km
Insurance Rating: 9
Derived Data:
bhp/litre (kW/litre): 63   46.3
bhp/ton (kW/tonne): 138.2   99.9
Speed × acceleration: 18.6
Performance Dimension: 13.5
Petrol consumption/ton at 56 mph (10/F): 5.39   (1.85)
Change in petrol consumption between 56 & 75 mph: 22%

The 635 CSi is equipped completely. There is no need to list the normal luxury car's inventory – it is all there. If the Grand Tour were still a part of European high life, it would be just the vehicle to use. Put in a museum beside one of the broughams they used for the tour, it would show similarities but mostly positive improvements in all directions.

A workmanlike set of controls which is so logical in every detail that it is never necessary to search for anything

153

FERRARI 308 GTB and S

One of the most beautiful of the Italian supercars, and a piece of running sculpture of the highest order, the Ferrari 308 GTB is one of the ultimate and all-time greatest of driving machines. Ferrari have been winning sports car races for thirty years, and pioneered the practice of putting the engine in the central position, that is behind the driver but ahead of the rear wheels. The power train, suspension and steering are very much a unity with the aerodynamic shell by Pininfarina and the pilot and his one passenger have the best of all facilities to negotiate the world's roads.

The engine is a 90° V8 of 2927 cc capacity, with 255 bhp at 7700 rpm and 210 ft/lb of torque at 5000 rpm. The maximum speed is 150 mph (241 km/h) and 0–60 in 6.7 seconds with an overall fuel consumption of 13.8 mpg. This is the speed which separates the cars of tomorrow from the cars of yesterday.

The ignition is transistorized Marelli, but as Ferrari and Weber are old friends and even went to school together, there are 4 twin choke Webers instead of the

fuel injection which would give slightly more power. The noise from the 4 OH camshafts with thimble tappets is splendid, as are all the various sounds emanating from this power unit. 'The real Gran Turismo Ferrari is an offshoot of my racing cars' says Enzo Ferrari, and there is certainly more than a hint of an orchestrated Formula 1 in the sound of the 308 GTB.

In 1969, Enzo Ferrari sold part of his holdings to Fiat because he needed the money and support, without interference on the technical or racing side; so Ferrari is a part of the Fiat/Lancia/Ferrari triumvirate. In 1969 he had 500 working for him at Maranello; now there are 1250. Enzo Ferrari is probably the last of the larger than life hero figures in the car world. It was his passion, pride, stature, and vision, which produced the whole Ferrari legend, which was always backed up by engines with more power to the litre than any others. To date Ferrari is the winner of 22 world championship awards, and his chief designer for most of the time, Giachino Colombo, is one of the greatest engine designers of this century.

Opposite: *Although this car was originally intended as Ferrari's answer to Porsche, it was never given sufficient factory development nor enough sponsorship for it to be a serious contender in sports car races. It is therefore more in the nature of a lovely might-have-been so far as real competition is concerned. This does not stop it from being one of the most beautiful of the Italian supercars. Designed by Pininfarina*

Right: *The Ferrari Dino 308 GT4, designed by Bertone*

Ferrari 308 GTB

Engine: 90° V8 twin dohc belt drive. Light alloy. Centrally mounted
Capacity: 2927 cc
Bore; stroke: 81 mm   71 mm
Compression ratio: 8.8 to 1
Carburation: 4 twin choke Weber 40 DCNF
Max. power at 6600 rpm: ~ 250 bhp (240 SAE)   186.5 kW

Transmission: 5 speed manual gearbox

Suspension: Independent front and rear

Steering: Rack and pinion
Turning circle: 39 ft 4 ½ in   12 m

Brakes: Dual circuit servo assisted. Ventilated discs front and rear

Dimensions:
Length: 13 ft 10 in   4.22 m
Kerb weight: 2403 lb   1090 kg

Performance:
Maximum speed: 153 mph   246 km/h
0–60 mph: 6.7 sec
Fuel consumption
   at 56 mph: 28.2 mpg   10 litres/100 km
   urban: 13.9 mpg   20.3 litres/100 km

Insurance Rating: 7

Derived Data:
bhp/litre (kW/litre): 85.4   63.7
bhp/ton (kW/tonne): 213.2   156.5
Speed × acceleration: 22.8
Performance Dimension: 10.7
Petrol consumption/ton at 56 mph (10/F): 8.54   (1.12)

There are few, if any, cars to match the 308 GTB in all round driving performance, and many say that it is Ferrari's answer to Porsche. Without full factory development and testing, however, little could be expected in the way of overall victories against a total commitment such as Porsche's and it has raced very seldom due to lack of sponsors.

There have been rumours of a 710 bhp twin-turbo 308 GTB which would run at Le Mans, but although it is known to exist it has not been raced as yet. It is interesting to speculate on the possible performance figures. Meanwhile, the chassis of the 308 has been the basis for several *carrozzeria* projects. One of these is the 'Rainbow' by Gandini, of Bertone, a Spyder version with a Targa roof which drops neatly into the space behind the seats in one motion when the catches are released. It is a pity that the 308 GTB, which has such good performance figures and looks so completely right, has not had the total Enzo Ferrari obsessional development treatment which produces total success in racing.

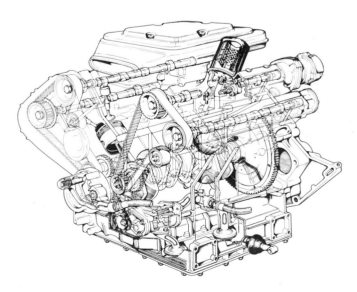

The 8 cylinder, 2927 cc engine of the 308 GTB with belt-driven overhead camshafts and harmonically balanced crankshaft developing 250 bhp

FIAT X1/9

A tour-de-force by Gandini, chief designer for Bertone, the Fiat X1/9 is a two-seater sports car equipped with a 1498 cc engine developing 85 bhp. Sixty per cent of the weight is borne by the back axle, giving improved traction to the drive wheels during acceleration. First produced in 1972, the design is similar to the Autobianchi runabout 'Barchetta' of 1969 also by Gandini. Variation models include the 1750 cc 200 ps 'Abarth', and the 'Dallara' with a rear wing. There is a targa top which can be stored in the boot.

The X1/9 is a miniature version of the exotic Maserati sports cars, using the same basic principles including the mid-engine layout but with smaller dimensions and reduced power.

The X1/9 (which is simply a code number applied by Fiat and has no significance regarding capacity or performance) has a top speed of 108 mph (174 kmh). With maximum bhp at 6000 rpm of 85, there is some noise from the engine at high speeds, but the handling and ride quality are such that this is acceptable,

more especially as this is an open sports car. The 5 speed gearbox is a pleasure to use, the ratios being well organized. The brakes are discs all round and give complete confidence. The car is essentially another well designed spartan with a weight of 920 kg (2028 lb) but with a strong body designed to comply with the exacting USA standards.

The driving position, facia and instruments are all very satisfactory, as are the seats with integral head restraints, designed to keep pilot and passenger secure. Luggage space is ample with two compartments, front and rear.

The 'new classical' sports car format is a very satisfying device to drive at all the speeds of which it is capable. It is exhilarating, completely dependable, and also economical. Naturally it does not have the power and high jinks of the incorrigible Maserati exotica which turn a blind eye to all financial considerations in reaching for the stars, but it is one of the better small sports cars of the eighties.

Opposite: *Fiat X1/9. Designed by Gandini at Bertone*

Right: *After several previous designs, the side elevation is now impeccable*

Below: *Fiat X1/9 with targa top removed (takes as little as five seconds)*

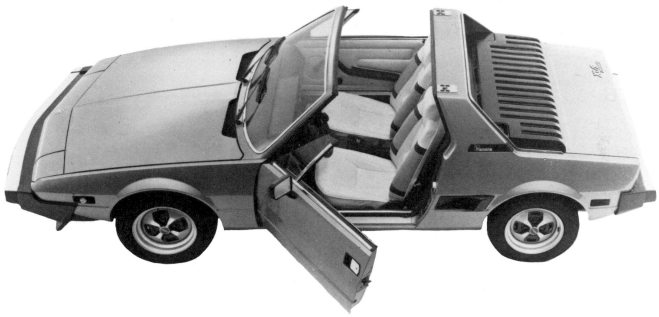

Fiat X1/9

Engine: 4 cylinders, belt driven sohc, alloy head, transverse mid mounted
Capacity: 1498 cc
Bore; stroke: 86.4 mm   63.9 mm
Compression ratio: 9.2 to 1
Carburation: twin choke Weber 34 DATR
Max. power at 6000 rpm: 85 bhp   63.4 kW
Max. torque at 3200 rpm: 86.8 ft/lb   117.8 Nm

Transmission: 5 speed manual

Suspension:
Front: independent, coil spring, MacPherson struts with tie rods.
Rear: independent, coil spring, MacPherson struts with lower wishbone and track control arm

Steering: Rack and pinion

Brakes: Dual circuit front/rear. 8.9 in (22.6 cm) front and rear discs

Dimensions:
Length: 13 ft   3.96 m
Kerb weight: 2027 lb   919 kg

Performance:
Maximum speed: 108 mph   174 km/h
0–60 mph: 9.9 sec
Fuel consumption
    at 56 mph: 47.2 mpg   6.0 litres/100 km
    at 75 mph: 36.8 mpg   7.7 litres/100 km
    urban: 26.6 mpg   10.6 litres/100 km

Insurance Rating: 6

Derived Data:
bhp/litre (kW/litre): 56.7   42.3
bhp/ton (kW/tonne): 84.6   62.1
Speed × acceleration: 10.7
Performance Dimension: 12.8
Petrol consumption/ton at 56 mph (10/F): 5.97   (1.67)
Change in petrol consumption between 56 & 75 mph: 28%

JAGUAR XJS

Jaguar cars won the Le Mans 24 hour race in 1951, 53, 55, 56 and 57. Jaguar also dominated British saloon car racing in the 1950s. There was a brief resurgence in 1977 with Leyland's Jaguar XJ12, in international saloon car racing, but the car was forced into retirement at the end of one unsuccessful season. The chief engineer of most of the successful Jaguars was William Heynes.

The Jaguar XJ5.3 and XJS have V12 engines. Twelve cylinders are justified by the need to keep each cylinder small, the rotating masses low and revving capabilities high. Engines with 12 cylinders are invariably smooth-running, powerful and extravagant with fuel.

There is near unanimity of opinion among British motoring journalists that Jaguar saloons have a quality of ride and handling which puts them in a very special category, beside the Mercedes S class and the Rolls Royce Silver Spirit.

The trouble with Jaguar has been lack of continuity. There have been superlative engines on numerous occasions, coupled with the right suspension systems,

but at no time except the 1950s, when Lofty England had control, has there been that indefatigable and ceaseless continuity of intent, backed by research and development, which produces the ultimate in automotive technology.

The 5.3 litre V12 engine is magnificent. It has that illustrious predecessor, the XK, 6-cylinder engine which won so many times at Le Mans. It was conceived as the cornerstone of Jaguars plan to re-enter motor racing, by W. M. Heynes and C. W. L. Bailey, vice chairman and chief designer respectively of Jaguar cars.

The first engine had a capacity of 5 litres, ohc, petrol injection and transistorized ignition, and was producing well over 500 bhp when the decision was taken to abandon the idea of racing. At this point, the two men who had designed the Coventry-Climax Formula one engine (which powered the cars which gave GB four World Driver and Manufacturers' Championships) joined the design team. These were Wally (WTF) Hassan and Harry Mundy. This new team were given the brief of

Opposite and right: *This bodyshell lacks the distinction of the power train and suspension system it conceals*

Jaguar XJS

Engine: 60° V12 aluminium alloy block and head 2 sohc
Capacity: 5343 cc
Bore; stroke: 90 mm   70 mm
Compression ratio: 9 to 1
Injection: Lucas electronic
Max. power at 5800 rpm: 285 bhp   212.6 kW
Max. torque at 3500 rpm: 294 ft/lb   399 Nm

Transmission: 4 speed manual gearbox (or automatic GM40 3 speed)

Suspension:
Front: independent semi trailing wishbones and coil springs. Anti-roll bar.
Rear: lower transverse wishbones with drive shafts as upper links. Twin coil springs and anti-roll bar

Steering: Adwest power-assisted. Rack and pinion. 3 turns lock to lock

Brakes: Dual circuit front/rear. Servo-assisted. 11.2 in (28.5 cm) ventilated front discs, 10.4 in (26.4 cm) solid rear discs

Dimensions:
Length: 16 ft   4.87 m
Kerb weight: 3710 lb   1687 kg

Performance:
Maximum speed: 155 mph   250 km/h
0–60 mph: 6.7 sec
Fuel consumption
   at 56 mph: 21.4 mpg   13.2 litres/100 km
   at 75 mph: 18.2 mpg   15.5 litres/100 km
   urban: 10.8 mpg   26.2 litres/100 km

Insurance Rating: 8

Derived Data:
bhp/litre (kW/litre): 53.3   39.8
bhp/ton (kW/tonne): 162.3   119.2
Speed × acceleration: 23.1
Performance Dimension: 14.2
Petrol consumption/ton at 56 mph (10/F): 7.52   (1.33)
Change in petrol consumption between 56 & 75 mph: 17%

designing a new engine capable of giving Jaguar Saloon and sports cars performance and reliability.

The brief for the new engine called for a design offering a greater degree of smoothness, silence and flexibility than the current engines and also to be able to produce higher bhp and torque figures than the 6-cylinder XK unit, hence the V12. The XK 6s, in competition form, at the time produced 325 bhp and the new V12 when first designed, developed something very near to it.

The V12 engine has an included angle of 60° and a single OHC to each bank. The face of each cylinder head is flat, and the shallow depression in the piston crown, together with the clearance between the head face and piston at TDC form the combustion chamber. It is consequently called a flat head.

Bore and stroke of 90 × 70 mm give a capacity of 5343 cc. With a compression ratio of 9:1 the gross power output is 314 bhp at 6200 rpm, with a torque of 349 ft/lb at 3600 rpm. The gross BMEP is 161 psi at 3800 rpm. The Lucas transistorized ignition, initially designed for the F1 racing engine, was retained.

The complete unit weighs 680 lb (308 kg), with all auxiliaries except the gearbox, due to the extensive use of light alloys in block and head and elsewhere. The block is ribbed for strength, with the lower face well below the crankshaft centre line to provide support and rigidity for the 7 main bearings. Wet type cylinder liners are used. The 3 plane crankshaft is statically and dynamically balanced and carried on 7 lead-indium bearings, steel backed.

In line valves are used, the inlet of 1.625" dia and the exhaust 1.375". Twin valve springs and bucket tappets are operated by the camshaft which is a chilled cast iron unit. The camshafts are operated by Duplex chains, which also drive the distributor by a jackshaft.

Lubrication is by a crescent type oil pump driven by the crankshaft. A by-pass valve diverts the oil through an oil-to-water type cooler located behind the filter. The long inlet manifolds, with originally four carburettors,

It is a pity this one has not been put to the test more consistently in competition

now have fuel injection.

The designers Hassan and Mundy admitted that they had carried out extensive research while designing the successful Coventry-Climax engine and used the experience with the Jaguar V12. They also stated that the engine was designed originally to produce substantially more power than its present rating, so it is unstressed even at maximum power.

So much for the engine. As we said at the beginning, it is magnificent, and the technology for improving the fuel consumption is at their disposal in the form of the May Fireball head. Jaguar already use a microprocessor to control the digital Lucas fuel injection system which not only provides better economy, but also reduces exhaust emissions. The compression ratio has been raised from 9.1 to 10.1 with the result of raising power and torque by 5.4 and 8.2 per cent respectively.

Unfortunately (see *Automatic v Manual Transmission*), a GM 400 3 speed automatic replaced the manual in 1979. That particular manual was rather botchy. It should have been replaced with a Getrag 5.

The current engine develops 300 bhp at 5400 rpm and 318 ft/lb of torque at 3900 rpm. *Motor* state that they were unable to record a true maximum speed at Mira, but they achieved 140 mph (225 km/h) and feel that Jaguar's claim of 150 mph (241 km/h) may be obtainable. The acceleration from 0–60, 0–100 and 0–120 is 7.6, 18 and 29.7 seconds. The Aston Martin V8 takes 7.5, 16.4 and 25.7 seconds. The 'old' manual XJS accelerated from 0–60 in 6.7 seconds, in 1976.

Everyone without exception speaks of the *quality* of the ride the XJS achieves; the quietest, the smoothest. There is also a total lack of bad habits or operatic temperament. 'Silky potency' is a phrase used constantly.

The overall consumption of 13.5 mpg is better than the Aston Martin's 10.7, but not so economical as the Porsche 928 at 18.5 mpg.

The Adwest power-assisted steering is often criticized as too light, but in general the car is well balanced,

The XJS looks rather anonymous beside one of its ancestors

showing only occasional signs of float because of the soft damping. The car is not a true four seater, but neither are its rivals. The driving position and arrangement of the controls is classical and completely satisfactory. The equipment is comprehensive, with air conditioning, electric window lifts, centre locking, adjustable steering, power steering, leather trim and a radio, all as standard fitments.

The unfortunate fact about the Jaguar XJS is that while the engine, suspension and running gear are nothing short of impeccable, because the team who designed them, especially Hassan and Mundy, rank among the world's best, whoever was responsible for the remainder was not in that category, and consequently this is a car which is perfect so far as the engineering goes, but rather a disaster with regard to everything else.

There is a chapter in this book about the Italian coachbuilders in which it is shown that car design is an art form. If you put the Jaguar bodyshell alongside a Gandini you will see what we mean. Similarly, the interior fittings are not the sort of thing to be seen in the same context as that magnificent engine, which deserved the best but got something very different.

The engineering is so outstandingly good that it should be given a new bodyshell, and now that the HE version with the May 'Fireball' head has been put into production with satisfactory results making the XJS HE one of the best power units in the world, the need for a totally new bodyshell is even greater. Why should such power hide itself under such a dull bushel?

A beautiful shape in silhouette. The welded steel backbone chassis is noticeable in addition to the potency of the engine

LOTUS ESPRIT SERIES 2.2

The pedigree of the series 2.2 cars reaches back through long experience with the steel backbone chassis, suspension systems borne out of success on the race track, well tried and yet interesting developments in glass fibre reinforced plastic body moulding and superb engine design.

Tony Rudd appears to have had a great deal to do with engine design development since he joined Lotus in 1969 but despite his undoubted enterprise it is experience gained on the race track which allowed the 907 engine, a road version of the LV 220 2 litre unit, to be announced only two years after he joined Lotus. Within a further three years this sixteen valve four-cylinder twin overhead camshaft engine was the heart and soul of the first of the new big Elites.

With quite incredible energy several other radically different engines have since been developed. We have seen not only the 911 used in the Chrysler Sunbeam, but now this larger 2174 cc unit still further developed as the 912 for the new 2.2 marque.

The Series 2.2 Esprit is remarkably flexible, given how oversquare the 912 engine is. Though its maximum torque, 160 ft/lb, arises some 2000 rpm below the peak revs, both power and torque are distinctly improved relative to the old 907 unit: peak power now being increased to 160 bhp at 6500 rpm.

Ignition is by an infra-red triggered contactless system and carburation by two Dellorto 45D HLA units more than capable of feeding the system efficiently, though we find it hard to believe that we will have long to wait before the cars in the series use fuel injection.

While the 912 remains moderately stressed at 73 bhp/litre, the 910 in turbo charged form flies more in the face of nature at very nearly 100 bhp/litre. While more could be got out of the 912 this would certainly be at the expense of reduced flexibility and long life.

Turning to the welded steel chassis, this has been improved for the Esprit Turbo, but has more than adequate torsional stiffness for the 2.2 litre, 912, power output. This backbone of a rustless plastic shell

162

There is a family relationship in all good engineering. Compare this with the BMW and Porsche engines, they are brothers – except that this one still uses carburettors

---

Lotus Esprit Series 2.2

Engine: '912': aluminium 4 in line dohc 4 valves/cylinder
Capacity: 2174 cc
Bore; stroke: 95.25 mm   76.2 mm
Compression ratio: 9.4 to 1
Carburation: 2 Dellorto 45 DHLA
Max. power at 6500 rpm: 160 bhp   119 kW
Max. torque at 5000 rpm: 160 ft/lb   217 Nm

Transmission: 5 speed all synchromesh Getrag type 265

Suspension: All independent. Coaxial coil springs.
Front: upper and lower wishbones and anti-roll bar.
Rear: trailing arm

Steering: Rack and pinion 3.5 turns lock to lock

Brakes: Servo assisted, split front/rear. 9.7 in (24.6 cm) discs front, 10.6 in (26.9 cm) discs rear

Dimensions:
Length: 13 ft 9 in   4.19 m
Kerb weight: 2249 lb   1020 kg

Performance:
Maximum speed: 138 mph   222 km/h
0–60 mph: 6.7 sec
Fuel consumption
    at 56 mph: 38.7 mpg   7.3 litres/100 km
    at 75 mph: 33.3 mpg   8.5 litres/100 km
    urban: 19.7 mpg   14.3 litres/100 km

Insurance Rating: 9

Derived Data:
bhp/litre (kW/litre): 73.6   54.7
bhp/ton (kW/tonne): 145   106
Speed × acceleration: 20.6
Performance Dimension: 14.2
Petrol consumption/ton at 56 mph: 6.6
Change in petrol consumption between 56 & 75 mph: 16%

---

necessarily provides its strength. As, however, in all the cars in the marque, great care has been taken to increase its lifetime. This is important in a vehicle in which there are distinct limits for the weight increases which can be allowed through using thicker steel tubes and box sections, because of the concomitant reduction in performance. The chassis is given the best conceivable protection by galvanised zinc coatings of thickness four or five times that generally used in other commercial applications of the material. The suspension system is superb and it is this, second only to the engine, which makes the Esprit such a pleasure to drive. A feature of Lotus design philosophy lies in the use of their glass reinforced plastic bodyshells.

Turning now to the performance of the Esprit series 2.2, it has a performance figure better than that of the 5.3 litre Daimler Jaguar, but not so good as that of the Jaguar XJS. All the Porsches except the 911 Turbo are surpassed by the Esprit Turbo.

It is in all the Lotuses' Performance Dimensions that they really score: they perform better (by nearly 20 per cent) than might be expected for their power to weight ratio. While the good absolute performance figures are determined by the low weight of the vehicles, this is not the explanation for the good Performance Dimension. It is here that we see the proof of Chapman's and Lotus design experience in the racing car business. The petrol consumption figures are by no means bad since the incorporation of the 912 engine. Amusingly, the very low 16 per cent increase in fuel consumption between 56 and 75 mph is consistent with the high top speed (see *Fuel Efficiency*, page 92).

It is difficult to find anything but the most trivial of faults with such a piece of machinery. In a mid-engined two seater car the only major problem is the lack of a view to the threequarter rear, but then who is going to be there apart from the odd flamboyant XJS driver?

Above: *This five-litre coupé has a V8 engine with 280 bhp, a five-speed gearbox and a maximum speed of 169 mph (272 km/h). Air conditioning is standard and Khamsin, incidentally, means a hot desert wind*

Right: *The V8 engine with chain-driven oh-camshafts and four twin-choke Webers. Note the shape of the piston crowns and enormous balance weights on the crankshaft*

Opposite: *Three litres and 208 bhp produce 153 mph (246 km/h)*

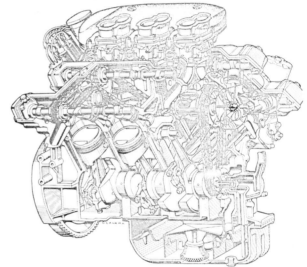

MASERATI KHAMSIN

The name Maserati means to most people the Grand Prix Maseratis which were winning between 1947 and 1957.

Or, to those interested in *Carozzeria Italiana* it means the extraordinarily beautiful cars with engines by Maserati and coachwork by Frua, Bertone, Vignale and Allemano of the 1960s. They were fast as well as visually fabulous. The Ghibli designed by Giugiaro in 1966 could produce 174 mph with real elegance.

A short history of Maserati, full of the slings and arrows of outrageous fortune, is as follows:

There were six Maserati brothers. Five of them were interested in metal and machinery. The eldest, Carlo, was a racing driver as early as 1900. Alfiari, Ettore, Ernesto and Bindo made a car which won its class in the 1926 Targa Florio, driven by Alfieri. They produced several outstanding GP cars between 1936–40, and won at Indianapolis in 1939 and 40. In 1947 the Maserati brothers sold the business to the Orsis, and returned to Bologna where they founded a new marque – the OSCA

(Officine Specializzate Construzioni Automobile).

Maserati GP cars won many races during 1947–57; in fact this is their high water mark when racing meant largely Ferrari versus Maserati.

In 1957 they almost gave up racing, after disastrous bad luck at Caracas, Venezuela, when three Maseratis crashed and the Ferraris finished 1-2-3 and won the Constructors' Championship. They then concentrated on the fast grand touring cars and it was during this period that the sports-racing car affectionately known as the 'bird-cage' was produced – so named because its frame was made up of tubes welded together like a cage. There were several versions – the type 60, 61 and 63 – and in 1960 and 1961, the Maserati Birdcage won the 1000 kilometre race at the Nurburgring.

Citroën took over Maserati from 1969–75, during which time the Citroën SM6 was produced with Citroën bodyshell and suspension, and a Maserati engine with an output of 188 bhp.

In 1975 Maserati was taken over by Alesandro de

Maserati Khamsin

Engine: V8, block and head of aluminium alloy with dohc per bank chain driven
Capacity: 4930 cc
Bore; stroke: 93.9 mm   89 mm
Compression ratio: 8.5 to 1
Carburation: Four twin choke Webers
Max. power at 5500 rpm: 280 bhp   209 kW
Max. torque at 3400 rpm: 330 ft/lb   448 Nm

Transmission: 5 speed manual gearbox

Suspension:
Front: independent by double wishbones with coil springs.
Rear: anti-roll bar

Steering: Power assisted rack and pinion

Brakes: Dual front/rear circuit, servo assisted. Ventilated discs all round, 11.5 in (29.2 cm) on front and 11.2 in (28.5 cm) on rear

Dimensions:
Length: 14 ft 4 in   4.37 m
Kerb weight: 3763 lb   1707 kg

Performance:
Maximum speed: ∼ 160 mph   257 km/h
0–60 mph: 6.6 sec
Touring fuel consumption: ∼ 17 mpg

Insurance Rating: 8

Derived Data:
bhp/litre (kW/litre): 56.7   42.4
bhp/ton (kW/tonne): 157.3   115
Speed × acceleration: 24.2
Performance Dimension: 15.4

Tomaso, with aid from Gepi and the Italian Government. They are marketed in the UK together with the de Tomaso range, by Subaru International Ltd.

The Merak is an example of Italian mobile sculpture based on its predecessor, a mid-engined coupé designed by Giugiaro, named the Bora. The Merak uses the SM6 V6 engine developed for the Bora by Alfieri, but increased to 2965 cc.

Maserati has maintained the Citroën connection, but the car is different from the SM6 in many ways. It actually follows the concept laid down by the Ghibli and the Indy, but uses Citroën hydraulics for the suspension, together with Citroën steering and brakes. The Khamsin is a conventional exotic, with a front mounted engine using a five speed box to drive the rear wheels.

Although this Maserati has rivals with a higher top speed, it performs in such a way, with roadholding, acceleration and a generally idiosyncratic style which only the Modenese cars can produce, that it is unique.

The Khamsin's acceleration and performance over 120 mph puts it into the highest category, and of course the 0–60 of 6.6 seconds, 0–100 in 15.9 and 0–120 in 24.7 seconds are very good indeed, although again the Aston Martin can achieve 0–60 in 5.8, 0–100 in 13.6 and 0–120 in 20.7. The Jaguar XJS cannot achieve comparability, nor can the Bristol 412, nor the Mercedes 500 SL, because of their automatic transmissions, which have no place in sports cars at all (see *Automatic v Manual* page 126).

Motor road tested the Khamsin in September 1980 and we are indebted to them for all the performance figures.

While we think that Porsche achieve a perfection with their sports cars which has no faults whatsoever, due to everything being right from concept to detail control, Maserati cars always possess grandeur. A concept of visual aesthetic appeal, mated to heroic engine power which really is glorious. The fact that the minor switch gear is a little confusing can be excused – rather like Tito Gobbi having one shoe missing.

MAZDA RX7

The Mazda RX7, designed and built by Toyo Kogyo of Hiroshima, Japan, has a Wankel twin-rotor engine with a power output of 105 bhp at 6000 rpm and maximum torque of 106 ft/lb at 4000 rpm. Top speed is a claimed 120 mph (193 km/h) and acceleration 0–60 mph is 9.6 seconds. The bodyshell of this beautiful 2 + 2 sports car has a drag coefficient of 0.36. Splendid results in competition emanate from a 200 bhp track version against the standard 105 bhp road car. Ear plugs are *de rigueur* with the competition model.

The Wankel engine has a normal four-stroke cycle, but instead of pistons it has a rotor, which in plan is a convex-sided triangle. This rotor moves within a chamber and each corner of the rotor maintains contact with the chamber wall throughout each re-volution. The fuel is ignited by spark plugs.

The rotor is directly connected to the transmission. There are fewer moving parts than in a conventional engine. There have been several technical difficulties to overcome, a) the seals must be durable and gas tight, b) there are severe temperature gradients in the chamber casing and c) there is a higher petrol consumption than piston engines of similar power. The Mazda RX7 has successfully solved a) and b).

The Mazda RX7 is well designed in all respects. The handling and performance are excellent, the clutch is light and positive and the gearchange is smooth. The controls are well laid out and easy to use, and the car is a continual delight with one enormous failing, a fuel consumption of 18.2 mpg which relates unfavourably to the Porsche 924 of 27.8 mpg – the Porsche also having a top speed of 126 mph (203 km/h).

Opposite and below: *A beautifully conceived sports car, not designed by the Italians, and successful in competition*

Right: *The Wankel engine. Rotary power, with a triangular rotor on a crankpin. In each of three spaces between rotor and casting, fuel/air mixture follows the stages of the Otto cycle. In place of poppet valves there are ports and the rotor uncovers them at appropriate stages in the working cycle*

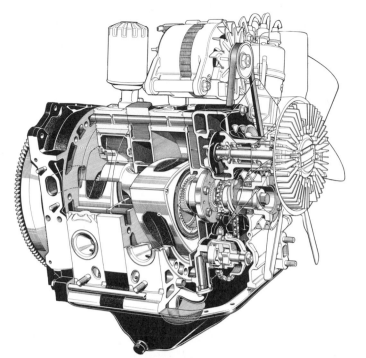

Intake

Compression

Expansion

Exhaust

Mazda RX7

Engine: Twin rotor Wankel
Capacity: 2292 cc
Compression ratio: 9.4 to 1
Carburation: 2 stage 4 barrel downdraught
Max. power at 6000 rpm: 105 bhp   78.3 kW
Max. torque at 4000 rpm: 106 ft/lb   143.8 Nm

Transmission: 5 speed manual gearbox

Suspension:
Front: independent by MacPherson struts, coil springs and anti-roll bar
Rear: live axle located by upper and lower trailing arms and Watts linkage. Anti-roll bar

Steering: Recirculating ball 3.7 turns lock to lock
Turning circle (kerb): 31 ft 6 in   9.6 m

Brakes: Dual circuit servo assisted. 9 in (22.9 cm) front ventilated discs, 8.9 in (22.6 cm) rear drums

Dimensions:
Length: 14 ft 1 in   4.28 m
Kerb weight: 2206 lb   1001 kg

Performance:
Maximum speed: 117 mph   188 km/h
0–60 mph: 9.6 sec
Fuel consumption
   at 56 mph: 33.2 mpg   8.5 litres/100 km
   urban: 18.1 mpg

Insurance Rating: 7

Derived Data:
bhp/litre (kW/litre): 45.8   34.2
bhp/ton (kW/tonne): 96.8   71
Speed × acceleration: 12.2
Performance Dimension: 12.6
Petrol consumption/ton at 56 mph (10/F): 7.84   1.27

MERCEDES-BENZ 500 SL

Mercedes-Benz designers headed by Werner Breit-schwerdt have spent seven years on the development of the new 3.8 and 5.0 litre engines for the new S class. These engines produce more power and torque for less weight and fuel consumption. The 380 develops 160 kW (218 bhp) and the 5.0 litre 177 kW (240 bhp) at a modest 4750 rpm and torque of 404 Nm at 3200 rpm.

At the same time a new four speed automatic box was developed with an improved torque converter of smaller diameter which reduces mechanical losses in the transmission and consequently works more quickly and more efficiently, and over a wider range.

The new 5 litre engine together with the four speed automatic gearbox has been placed in the chassis of the 2.8 litre SL two seater. The 5 litre eight-cylinder weighs no more than the 2.8 litre six-cylinder, but develops 55 more brake horsepower. There is also more torque, 164 Nm of it, and this makes a vivid impression on driving the 500 SL.

The eight foot wheelbase and length of 14 ft (4.3 m)

seem very small for such an almighty engine, but the luxurious appointments bring up the weight to 3395 lb – 1½ tons/30.3 cwt. Luxury is a heavy commodity apparently, and this is a luxurious vehicle. With technology of Mercedes order, it could go a lot faster than 145 mph with very little alteration; the potential is there, but there has been an obvious decision to make this car highly civilized, which it is.

This power unit together with a five speed gearbox and a bodyshell based on any one of the Mercedes CIII cars, so aerodynamically sound and already proven in world record runs, would produce a sports car in the same category as the BMW M1 but probably better. No doubt the Mercedes directors have thought of this already and rejected it. As it stands, the Mercedes 500 SL is a superb sports car – neither of us knows many people who could drive it to its full potential in any case. Understressed as it is, it will last for ever.

Opposite: *Three impeccable Mercedes roadsters. Hard top, soft top, and the top model, the 500 SL in the foreground, recognizable by its back spoiler*

Right: *The hard top 500 SL has an enormous five litre V8 engine*

Below: *Cross-section and end elevation of the engine. If you use a magnifying glass you can see all the details of the engine and fuel injection system*

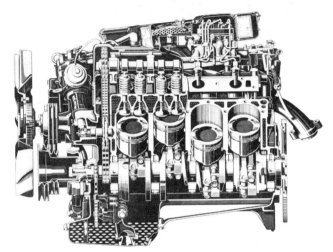

Mercedes-Benz 500 SL

Engine: V8 all light alloy, cylinders protected by silicon, sohc/bank
Capacity: 4973 cc
Bore; stroke: 96.5 mm   85 mm
Compression ratio: 8.8 to 1
Injection: Mechanical fuel injection
Max. power at 4750 rpm: 240 bhp   177 kW
Max. torque at 3200 rpm: 297.7 ft/lb   404 Nm

Transmission: MB automatic 4 speed to rear wheels

Suspension:
Front: axle with double wishbones, coil springs and anti-roll bar
Rear: diagonal swing axle, coil springs, and anti-roll bar

Steering: MB power assisted 2.75 turns lock to lock
Turning circle: 40 ft 3 in   12.16 m

Brakes: Dual circuit, discs front and rear

Dimensions:
Length: 14 ft 5 in   4.39 m
Kerb weight: 3395 lb   1540 kg

Performance:
Maximum speed: 140 mph   225 km/h
0–60 mph: 7.6 sec
Fuel consumption
    at 56 mph: 25.4 mpg   11.1 litres/100 km
    at 75 mph: 21.2 mpg   13.3 litres/100 km
    urban: 13.7 mpg   20.6 litres/100 km

Insurance Rating: 9

Derived Data:
bhp/litre (kW/litre): 48.2   35.6
bhp/ton (kW/tonne): 148.5   107.8
Speed × acceleration: 18.4
Performance Dimension: 12.4
Petrol consumption/ton at 56 mph (10/F): 6.87   (1.45)
Change in petrol consumption between 56 & 75 mph: 20%

Above: *A beautiful British sports car, like a Lotus-Jaguar, but it must prove itself*

Opposite: *The convertible looks good with the hood up or down*

TVR TASMIN

For those who want a hand-built, low-volume sports car with all the refinement of a grand tourer, and yet with service facilities everywhere, a fuel consumption of 24–30 mpg and a cruising speed in excess of 120 mph (193 km/h), the Tasmin is that car.

The Tasmin's designers were ex Lotus and Jaguar, Oliver Winterbottom and Stewart Halstead, so it is no surprise to find that it handles like a Lotus–Jaguar, and that the cockpit is bisected by a handsome high backbone chassis. The interior is marked by a high standard of trim with burr walnut *à l'anglais*, but this is no cocktail cabinet, it is an extremely well designed car in every detail which handles like a pure bred sports car.

In particular, there is a tailgate like the Lamborghini Espada, with self-supports, which is functional beyond its capacity as a hatchback—the all round vision is improved by it. There are excellent 7 inch (18 cm) alloy wheels, halogen headlamps which are retractable, and twin fuel tanks with individual fillers on each side of the car with a total of 14 gallons (64 litres).

With a car of this nature, the designer has an opportunity to choose the best components from different manufacturers in order to create a car which will have a unique quality although built up from known components.

Although they did not manage to get a Weissach axle, the collection of sensible pieces of engineering is splendid. First, the cradle mounted 3.07:1 Salisbury axle, as used on the Jaguar XJS, which has inboard rear disc brakes. The clutch is hydraulically operated by the Broadspeed system of co-axial slave cylinder acting on the clutch thrust bearing as used on the XJ5.3C type.

The instruments are American, Stewart Warner, which are also used on the legendary Countach. The front uprights of the suspension, hubs and brake drums are from the Ford Granada, and the upper wishbones are lower links from the Cortina. The steering is Cortina rack and pinion. The rear end is a co-ordination of Jaguar and Lotus, with Jaguar differential and Lotus radius arms, the hub carriers being cast in alloy specially

TVR Tasmin +2 Convertible Manual

Engine: V6 cylinder
Capacity: 2792 cc
Bore; stroke: 93 mm   68.5 mm
Compression ratio: 9.2 to 1
Injection: Bosch K-Jetronic
Max. power at 5700 rpm: 160 bhp   117.8 kW
Max. torque at 4300 rpm: 162 ft/lb   219.7 Nm

Transmission: 4 speed manual (3 speed automatic optional)

Suspension:
Front: independent by upper wishbone, stabilized lower level coil springs and anti-roll bar.
Rear: lateral links, trailing arms and fixed length drive shafts, coil springs

Steering: Rack and pinion 3.7 turns lock to lock
Turning circle (kerb): 31 ft 6 in   9.5 m

Brakes: Dual front/rear, servo assisted. 10.6 in (26.9 cm) discs on front, inboard 10.9 in (27.7 cm) discs on rear

Dimensions:
Length: 13 ft 5 in (13 ft 2 in)   4.08 (4.01) m
Kerb weight: 2340 lb   1062 kg

Performance:
Maximum speed: 133 mph   214 km/h
0–60 mph: 7.7 sec

Insurance Rating: 7

Derived Data:
bhp/litre (kW/litre): 57.3   42.7
bhp/ton (kW/tonne): 139.8   101.3
Speed × acceleration: 17.3
Performance Dimension: 12.3

for TVR. The top of the differential is bolted to a cast-alloy cross member, which is bolted to the chassis. The bottom of the differential is attached to two brackets providing the mounting points for the transverse links.

It is a well designed and convincing chassis design with total integrity and it had to be, because the 3.07 to one Salisbury differential achieves 22.18 mph/1000 rpm which in turn allows cruising of 127 mph (204 km/h) at 5700 rpm.

The engine is the Ford 2.8 litre with 160 bhp and 162 ft/lb of torque. At present with a 4 speed box. It needs 5 gears. Bosch K-Jetronic fuel injection system is used, together with a Bosch fuel pump, fuel filter and accumulator. There is also electronic ignition. The GRP (glass reinforced plastic) body is moulded in two halves and bonded along the waistline, and combined with the multi-tubular steel backbone chassis with outriggers complete with fuel and passengers, the weight distribution is 50/50.

The instruments include speedometer, tachometer, oil pressure gauge, water temperature gauge, fuel gauge and voltmeter, with warning lights for hand brake, ignition and low fluid level.

The use of the Ford 2.8 litre engine is astute. It is a splendid engine, fuel injected, and comes with an enormous service network which covers so many parts of the suspension. The work carried out at TVR itself does not look as though it would need further attention – it is solid, positive and long lasting.

So the Tasmin is a very good sports car, but to stick to our principles, we must repeat that simple phrase which we have been grinding out like a Greek Chorus throughout the book 'only the white heat of competition motoring can produce a sports car'. TVRs have already proved themselves in the past in production sports car racing, but to keep it all together, they must continue. The Tasmin is fine as it is, but given the Hart Formula 2 engine and a Getrag 5 speed gearbox, it might well prove itself in the white heat.

SPORTS CARS: SUMMARY

Here we have perhaps the most disparate group in the book, in terms of pure performance. The point is perhaps that enjoyment in driving can come as much with the smooth and yet shattering capabilities of a BMW 528i or Daimler Double Six, neither of which could be remotely described as sports cars, as with the 20 mph Go-cart. Perfectly sensibly, there can thus be cars here which, though outperformed by conventional saloons, are still desirable as mouthwatering adrenalin raisers.

The concept can perhaps be taken too far however. Some of the smaller two seaters can be just a bit too slow, while some of the hyped up tiny saloons just a bit too frightening. At the upper end of the former market we would put the X1/9 because it *is* fun and one could almost imagine that the engine beside one's ear was bigger than in fact it is.

We do hope that the XR3 turns out to be as good as is hoped, since it could almost be the genuine escape from the sporty saloons, but we fear that it isn't.

The old Datsun 280 ZX in the mid size range does, we feel, have a genuine point or two in its favour in the group, but it is still outrun by several members of class 5 – as would be the RX7, included mainly as an epitaph for the rotary engine. How sad that this masterpiece of engineering appeared just at the time when we all were forced to start thinking seriously about fuel consumption. In fact, for its performance and power to weight ratio, its fuel efficiency is not terribly bad.

Putting the Audi Quattro in this class is arguably as confusing as putting it beside the Range Rover. It really should be in with the other turbocharged petrol driven cars, like its stable mate the 200T. We have, however, included it here for two reasons. Firstly, it really could be the way sports cars of the future will go, and, secondly, it is rather nice to have a direct comparison with the super BMWs, which it outranks with relative ease. We don't think BMW will take such treatment lying down!

Turning to more conventional sports cars for a moment, it is a pleasure to see the TVR with quite respectable performance, its PD being of the same order as that of the Mercedes 500 SL.

For sheer style, coupled with performance, the Ferrari must remain the horse to make the nostrils flare, but it is a little sad to see that for its power it should go a little faster. Perhaps it does, and no one's managed to find out! For the really brave, and those who eschew town driving, the Khamsin can only be beaten by the Porsche 911 Turbo and the Lotus Essex Esprit turbo. From what we gather the main aspect of the bravery involves red lining the rpm; behaviour surely only for the very rich or sadistic!

Meanwhile Porsche will keep trying to escape the 911. They just about manage it with the 924, which nearly matches its forebear for handling, but not of course for performance. The 911 remains superb, and much as we admire the Esprit 2.2 which betters its performance and fuel efficiency it would, we think, take more finish than the Esprit can muster to convert the 911 fanatic.

Having been passed, and at a fair howl, while having the great pleasure of driving an Esprit 2.2, by a three year old XJS (admittedly only in the upper speed range) we have to take serious cognisance of that V12 engine. It really is quite remarkable. Personally we don't exactly admire the XJS to look at, but for sheer performance a glance at the data should be sufficient. This car has breeding as good as any in the list; can we hope for more style as well?

Class 7	**Data Summary**				
Datum Point		*Perform-ance*	*Power Weight*	*PD*	*FE*
A	Audi Quattro	20.1	146	13.8	1.73
B	BMW 535i	17.9	142	12.6	1.79
C	BMW 635 Csi	18.6	138	13.5	1.85
D	BMW 732i	14.9	123	12.2	1.80
E	Ferrari 308 GTB	22.8	213	10.7	1.12
F	Fiat X1/9	10.9	85	12.8	1.67
G	Jaguar XJS	23.1	162	14.2	1.33
H	Lotus Esprit 2.2	20.6	145	14.2	1.51
I	Maserati Khamsin	24.2	157	15.4	*na*
J	Mazda RX7	12.2	97	12.6	1.27
K	Mercedes-Benz 500 SL	18.4	149	12.4	1.45
L	TVR Tasmin	17.3	140	12.3	*na*

na = not available

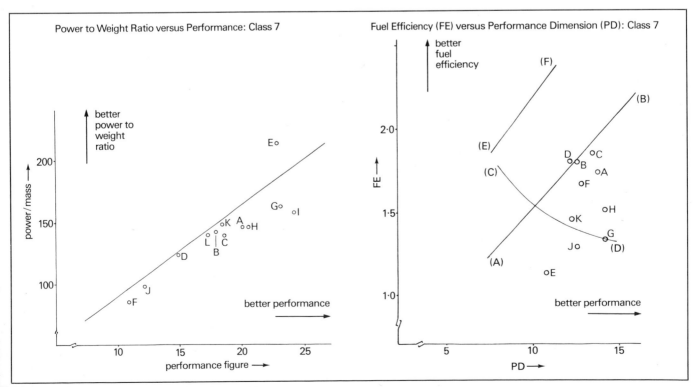

Above: *TVR Tasmin –
beginning to show its quality
in competition*

Right: *Audi Quattro*

Power to Weight Ratio versus Performance: Class 7

better
power to
weight
ratio

power/mass →

better performance

performance figure →

Fuel Efficiency (FE) versus Performance Dimension (PD): Class 7

better
fuel
efficiency

FE →

better performance

PD →

7 Motor Sport for Better Motoring

HOW MOTOR SPORT HAS HELPED DESIGN TODAY'S PRODUCTION CAR

Motor sport has been one of the prime movers in the development of the motor car. If the research and development to produce four wheeled vehicles with the speed, traction and manoeuvrability which they now possess had been carried out at a normal rate, as in other fields, without the impetus of winning races, it would have taken a thousand years.

The sums of money invested by manufacturers is incalculable. Ford invested five hundred million pounds in the research, design and development of the front wheel drive Escort. Imagine how much it has cost to develop Mercedes cars from the 1885 Benz to the S class, or Rolls-Royce from the first two-cylinder to the Silver Spirit. Add to that all the Bugattis, Ferraris, Cadillacs, Duesenbergs, and all General Motors products, plus landspeed record cars, and we reach a galactic total which makes the cost of development of today's jalopy add up to more than a fleet of space ships.

Whatever the cost, it has been in a good cause. The mobility of the individual, which has made the last half century different from any previous period of civilization, has been provided by the motor car. The world has become smaller because of it.

It did not take long after the invention of the horseless carriage in 1885 for the idea of racing them to arise. It started with the huge 1895 monsters, driven often by their creators, like Emile Levassor, driving 732 miles single handed at an average speed of 15 mph, from Paris to Bordeaux and back, in the first road race. The Renault brothers carried out similar feats. So did Henry Ford, driving his '99' 'Special' himself, across a frozen lake where he had congregated his financial backers.

The reason why the early racing cars were so monumental was because the volumetric efficiency was so low. Today's everyday cars produce a minimum of 40 bhp/litre, but the 1896 Benz only developed 2 bhp/litre, Panhard-Levassor 4 bhp, and the de Dion Bouton of about 1906, 7 bhp/litre; so in order to develop

sufficient power, the engines had to be 14 or 20 litres in capacity. One of the largest was probably the 1906 Metallurgique which was equipped with a 21 litre Maybach engine in 1910, capable of 73 mph at only 1000 rpm.

The first events were mainly road races between cities. This was followed by the 'heroic' races like the Peking to Paris won by Prince Scipione Borghese in an Itala 1907, and the St Petersburg–Moscow and New York–Paris, before it all became more organized, by the French. Grand Prix racing was organized by the *Automobile Club de France* and the first Grand Prix, at Le Mans, was won by Szisz in a Renault at 62.88 mph.

Prior to this, James Gordon Bennett, the proprietor of the New York Herald, had started the idea of international motor racing with his trophy races, but the *Automobile Club de France* put a stop to these, clearly anxious that France, as the premier car manufacturing country, should organize international motor racing, rather than an American newspaper proprietor.

So the ACF – *Automobile Club de France* – set up the AIACR, *Association Internationale des Automobile Clubs Reconnus*, in 1906, as an international body of motoring sport. This became CSI, *Commission Sportive Internationale*, in 1922, and FIA, *Fédération Internationale de L'Automobile*, in 1946, which, with FOCA, organizes all the world championships today.

Since its inception in 1906 until today this French institution has helped to direct the development of racing cars over the years by laying down laws, restrictions and limitations, which ultimately have affected everyman's car. The first law they laid down concerned weight. In order to change the monsters into light, easy to handle racing cars, they limited their weight to 1000 kg. This immediately produced unbalanced cars with light chassis inadequate for their enormous engines, so in 1908 they restricted cylinder bores to 155 mm and the total capacity to 4½ litres. This was a master stroke and produced years of constructive development and national rivalry.

Kaiser Wilhelm (as had Prince Heinrich of Prussia) took an intelligent interest in motor cars, and owned

1950 Ferrari Mondial

several Benz. One of them was powered by a Maybach racing engine, and he decided to award a Kaiserpreis to the winner of a race over the Taunus mountains. This was a moment when Maybach was probably working on the Zeppelin engines however, and the race was won by Felice Nazzaro in a Fiat at 52.5 mph.

In 1912 and 1913 Georges Boillot won the French Grand Prix in a 150 bhp Peugeot, and in 1913 Rolls-Royce won the Spanish Grand Prix in the Guadarrama mountains, with the Rolls-Royce which was a Silver Ghost engine fitted with a light and beautiful open tourer body. In 1914 Daimler-Benz had completed their research and development, and Mercedes were first, second and third in the French Grand Prix, the winner Lautenschlager at a speed of 65.66 mph.

The 1914–18 war put an end to Grand Prix and competition motoring for four years or more, but the Rolls-Royce Silver Ghost proved its qualities by providing engine and chassis for staff cars, armoured cars and ambulances. T. E. Lawrence (of Arabia) had some particularly good things to say about the Rolls-Royce Silver Ghost as a machine gun carrier.

Germany found Mercedes to be equally serviceable, as did France with Renaults and Peugeots. The First World War also redirected many of the engine designers to aircraft engines – Henry Royce designed his Eagle aero-engine for example, and W. O. Bentley, Henry Birkigt and Wilhelm Maybach were all achieving more bhp per litre and dependability from their designs for aero-engines. The urgency of designing engines for fighter aircraft was greater than winning Grand Prix races, and the rate of development increased, afterwards benefiting car engines.

Meanwhile the development of small cars was helped, not so much by the ACF, but by the French motoring journal *L'Auto*, which sponsored a *Coupe des Voiturettes* for small and lightweight cars. Hispano-Suiza, Peugeot, Salmson and Amilcar all developed in this direction, improving the design of the small production cars which have been an important part of life in Europe since the thirties, and in the USA since 1973.

Endurance racing began in 1923 with the Le Mans Grand Prix d'Endurance, which is still an annual event, in June. Porsches now progress down the Mulsanne Straight, in the Vingt-quatre heures du Mans, at 230 mph, which was the world land speed record in 1930. In 1980, this race was won by a Rondeau which was powered by a Cosworth engine identical to those used in F1 races.

Rallies are another way in which cars are constantly being forced to develop or disintegrate, causing the development of suspensions for wildly uneven surfaces as well as tarmac, and in general concerning the driver and designer in much wider parameters than the grand prix race track. There are now international rallies, like the Safari, the One Thousand Lakes and the Monte Carlo, which test cars and drivers in snow, ice, tropical heat and conditions in regions which are suitably hostile and awkward, like the Sahara, the Alps in winter, Finland, Patagonia and East Africa.

Today's car then has been developed by benefits derived from Grand Prix racing, which has improved the aerodynamic structure and the brake horsepower of the engine as well as the transmission and suspension systems. Rallies have also helped to make cars better in every way, but especially in developing steering and suspension systems, and improving the structure and the power/weight ratio. In both Grand Prix and Rallies there has been an emphasis on the necessity for integrity of design and workmanship based on the right concepts. It is this which has ultimately benefited the everyday car, making it now a remarkably successful and efficient machine.

This is not intended to be anything more than a very brief introduction to the history of Grand Prix racing and autosport in general as there are plenty of books available for those who wish to read about it in detail. However, as Formula One racing is something of a crystal ball, it would be useful to look at it more closely, to see how it may affect the future.

In 1965, it was announced that the 1½ litre formula would be changed to 3 litres in 1966. Coventry-Climax, who had been making the most successful engines for British machines for several years, decided at this point

The Cosworth DFV engine – the most consistently successful Formula One engine

to withdraw. This left the British teams in a dreadful situation, for none of them was capable at that time of either designing or building their own engines. BRM, HWM, Connaught and Vanwall were all gloomy reminders.

Walter Hayes of British Ford at this point persuaded Ford to invest £100,000 in a project with Cosworth Engineering to design a 3 litre engine for F1 racing. The trade name Cosworth is made up of the linked names of the production engineer, Mike Costin, and the designer, Keith Duckworth. Unquestionably one of the best 3 litre engines of the period 1967–81, this successful DFV (double-four-valve) V8 engine was produced with Ford money, Duckworth design and Cosworth engineering in Northampton. Many people imagine that it was made at Dagenham, but this is not so as Denis Jenkinson has pointed out in *Motorsport*. Ford, having paid for design and development, have had thirteen years of publicity for sponsoring, but not manufacturing, the engine.

British Leyland then immediately confused the issue

again by sponsoring the successful Williams team, which now have the name Leyland in large black letters on the sides of their cars. The lay public must be certain that the cars are using some sort of British Leyland engine. Simultaneously, the Ensign team are receiving sponsorship from Unipart, a subsidiary of BL, so the red, white and blue Unipart logo helps to confuse the spectators still further, thinking that BL have two engines competing with one another in Grand Prix racing.

Years ago, in 1903, when Jenatzy was photographed winning the Gordon Trophy race at Ballyshannon, there was a cotton banner hanging between two trees in the distance with the words Dunlop Motor Tyres. Advertising had begun. It has grown, however, and in a weird, wonderful and totally unethical way. While the financial help to autosport by advertising sponsorship is vital, it is time the FIA laid down a simple rule about it, if only to stop confusion and misunderstanding among the spectators and retain some ethical standards.

The history of forced induction in Grand Prix racing –

176

Cutaway of Cosworth DFV engine

that is, supercharging or turbocharging – has been interesting but spasmodic. In 1966, when the new Formula was introduced, supercharged 1 ½ litre engines were considered to be equivalent to 3 litre normally aspirated engines, but as the latter could now develop 400 bhp, there was not too much interest in forced induction.

For once, F1 and GP were behind instead of ahead of the times. Research in turbo and supercharging had been going on for years in other areas. Everyone can remember about the screaming compressors of Manfred von Brauchitsch and Rudi Caracciola in their Mercedes-Benz in the thirties of course, but exhaust driven turbochargers were used in several German aircraft during the Second World War and also in the American Air Force's Flying Fortresses. For years, turbocharging had been used in all drag racing, at Indianapolis, in endurance races and in most Can-Am events. Porsche, Renault, Lancia and BMW have all been developing it in events other than F1.

Also, in the industrial world, turbochargers have been developed in particular for diesel engines which need them. In America, there is the Garrett AiResearch Corporation, with branches in many countries, which specializes in turbocharging to such an extent as to make it almost a monopoly, but there are two other firms – KKK (Kuhnle, Kopp and Kausch) in Germany, and in Switzerland Brown Boveri who manufacture a pressure-wave supercharger named Comprex.

It would appear that the next few years of Formula One racing may become centred around turbo and supercharging. Renault have already developed their own V6 turbocharged engine, Alfa Romeo their V8, Brabham the 4-cylinder BRM, Toleman the 4-cylinder Hart engine, and Ferrari's V6 now has the Brown Boveri pressure wave supercharger. The FIA have ordained that the period of aerodynamic research and concern with 'ground effects' has gone on long enough, the designers will most probably concentrate on increasing brake horsepower again, and this time via forced induction.

Class 8   Turbo-driven Cars

INTRODUCTION

There are purists about who seem to consider that turbos do not constitute an acceptable means of increasing brake horsepower and torque; an anti-turbo lobby in fact. Among these, strangely, is L. J. K. Setright who is one of the best living authorities on the internal combustion engine. He states (*Car*/August 1980/ Trouble-charging) about turbochargers 'I dislike each and every one that I have encountered'.

He is concerned with the spasmodic and variable response from the throttle, but so are we all. He would prefer a Roots or Lysholm supercharger, or that which Lampredi is working on at Fiat, and so would we all. But, turbochargers have a long way to go, and surely it would be better to carry out the developments they so obviously need than to abandon them, like the Gobron-Brillié. Keep at it, like those who are still working with the Stirling engine.

Turbines are one of the facts of life and have been for some time. They have made life easier by increasing kinetic energy derived from other sources, for hundreds of years. The exhaust turbo has obvious limitations at present, but they can all be cured. Meanwhile, if we start more or less at the beginning, we will see that other turbines have had their problems.

Hero of Alexandria made a kind of turbine 2000 years ago, with a steam ejection which rotated a ball. No one has recorded why such a useful device was abandoned, without Scopas becoming interested, at least. Then, throughout the Middle Ages and Renaissance, water wheels were used which were a form of turbine, the water transferring to the wheel a part of the energy dependent on its speed – the kinetic energy – Concelet curved the blades so that they were tangential to the velocity of the water, energy loss caused by the frontal impact against the blades being reduced. Naturally, Leonardo da Vinci had something to say about it in his *Codice Atlantico* in which he drew a hydraulic wheel like a turbine.

There were a number of improvements to water wheels throughout the 16th century, but the first example of a true reaction turbine occurred with the Segner wheel in 1750. This was improved by Fourneyron

with a radial reaction type, and by Jonval in 1843 with his axial reaction turbine.

One branch of the research and development of turbines was used to obtain power from water. Fourneyron made use of mathematical calculations made by Euler and Manoury, and applied them to his turbine of 1813. James Francis designed the first radial reaction turbine (1840) with external distributor and internal runner, the prototype of the Thomson turbine of 1852. This in turn was developed by Callon & Girard into the Pelton turbine which came into general use all over Europe in the latter half of the nineteenth century, providing power for industry and generating electricity.

The other branch of turbine development took place with the steam turbine. Charles Parsons produced the first efficient steam turbine in 1884. Unlike the hydraulic turbine, which in the 19th century was utilizing the waters of mountain torrents to power paper factories (the thought of producing electricity coming much later), Parsons designed the steam turbine expressly for the production of electric power but got side-tracked into using it for marine propulsion. It is a beautiful story, told to us by an ancestor who worked with Parsons as a draughtsman.

The Parsons turbine had been perfected in the same way that all inventions are developed, by models, which got larger as the designers felt more convinced that they were finally getting it all together. It was suggested that the largest model to date should be installed in a pinnace called *Turbinia*, to see what would happen. The results were incredible and the trial runs down the Tyne and out to sea were apparently breathtaking.

Charles Parsons, not yet knighted, wrote to the Admiralty saying that he had discovered a new source of marine power and an Admiral came to see him in a steam driven battleship. The *Turbinia* was watched doing her fantastic speeds, but the Admiral felt certain that it was more of a gimmick than a phenomenon, and set off down the North Sea to the Admiralty. Parsons and his draughtsmen – they were not yet called designers – sat about discouraged until one of them suggested overtaking and accompanying the battleship.

Instantly the *Turbinia* was fuelled up and set off. For mile after sea mile when they had caught her up, they circled the battleship making different geometric shapes and patterns around her, Parsons himself at the wheel. The Parsons turbine was installed in the ships of the Navy, the *Mauretania*, and by the introduction of reduction gears, into many merchant ships, and subsequently for the purpose it was originally intended – generating electricity. Then there are gas turbines of course, but let us return to that exhaust turbine.

The turbocharger extracts more power from the engine without the penalty of increasing the capacity and the fuel consumption. An important characteristic of a turbine is its ability to extract energy from even low-pressure gas. In the 1940s and 1950s turbochargers were developed for large constant speed diesels (stationary) then for diesel trucks. In the 1960s General Motors produced turbocharged engines for the Chevrolet Corvair and the Oldsmobile, but did not continue, as fuel was not in short supply then.

The difference between turbos and superchargers is that turbos are driven by the exhaust gas, and superchargers are mechanically driven by the engine and consequently have the penalty of absorbing power, but the advantage of being always positively engaged and ready to produce instant power. In the case of the turbocharger, the exhaust gases are providing the power, *free*, as the water in the mountain streams was free, to power turbines which create electricity.

There are several diagrams in this section which show graphically how the turbocharger works. The components are a turbine wheel mounted on a short shaft and a compressor with its impeller mounted on the other end of the shaft. The compressor increases density in the air-fuel charge entering the engine, exhaust gases being used as the power to rotate the turbine wheel. Inconsistent quality of the fuel, which could lead to detonation, is controlled by knock sensors of various kinds. As with any supercharging system,

manifold pressure must be controlled, and this is done by the wastegate. This is a safety valve. At a specific pressure it opens and allows some of the exhaust gases to bypass the turbine, to retain intake manifold pressure at a preset figure.

The major manufacturer of turbochargers is the AiResearch Division of the Garrett Corporation, which produces most of those employed by manufacturers. The KKK turbocharger is made in Germany. In the same way that Robert Bosch does the research, develops and makes fuel injection systems as a specialist activity, Garrett and KKK develop and make turbochargers, working with the engine designers of each firm to produce the most appropriate design.

This sounds acceptable, but it is not really good enough. No major manufacturer except Lotus has, as yet, designed an engine specifically as a turbocharged engine. The turbocharger is still a bolt-on item. Admittedly, the Mercedes 300 D was modified in various ways, to accept the turbocharger, but not as an integral part of the original concept.

Imagine how much better it will be when the manifolding, engine castings, and turbo components are all integrated with a turbocharged engine. Then there will be the use of ceramics. With the turbine revolving at 120,000 rpm, the housing has to be strong enough to stop it causing a disaster in the event of failure. A ceramic wheel could do the work and be light enough to be contained by a much lighter housing, such as another ceramic. Air bearings might be used eventually.

The whole thing has just started. Think of that waterwheel, turning in the medieval streams and eventually becoming a Pelton turbine. And, as we have pointed out elsewhere, research and development work is carried out much faster with the internal combustion engine than in any other field. By 1990 everyone will have exhaust turbos and not even be aware of it.

This saloon is in the same category as the large Mercedes and the 7 series BMWs, but it is turbopowered and front wheel drive

AUDI 200 S TURBO

Motor states that they lapped Mira's circuit with this car at 119.7 mph (193 km/h) and there is a claimed top speed of 121 (195). The fuel consumption is the one area where there have been no miracles with the 200 T. Our overall was 18 mpg which compares with the Opel Senator, also 18, and the BMW 528i with 18.5 mpg. A five speed gearbox together with a higher final drive would help to improve this.

The Audi 200 Turbo has the almost universal MacPherson struts with coil springs and anti-roll bar at the front, with a dead axle, coils and trailing arms at the rear, together with a Panhard rod. The rear coil springs are wider at both ends and thinner in the centre (GM's are wider at one end). The ride is exceptionally satisfactory and so is the neutral handling.

The engine, a 2144 cc five-cylinder in-line, is a development of the 80 engine with a longer stroke. The fuel injection system is Bosch K-Jetronic, and the turbocharger is a KKK. The engine, due to the turbocharging has thicker gudgeon pins, sodium cooled

exhaust valves and a nickel/iron alloy exhaust manifold.

The braking system is similar to the Quattro's in that there is a pump in tandem with the steering and the amount of power supplied to the brakes is naturally controlled by the brake pedal. Citroën employ a similar tandem between power brakes and steering which is more positive at all times. Audi's braking is good when everything is going and they are warm, but poor in the early morning when they are cold.

This is a beautiful, safe, comfortable motor car, well equipped and uncriticizable. Professional drivers whom we very much respect, rave about it even. Something, however, is missing. Something which appears when you are sitting in a Mercedes or a BMW. A tangible feeling of security due to a bit more weight perhaps, or a slight disquiet at not being used to so much power driving the front wheels.

Above: *This cutaway engine shows the belt drive to the camshaft, fuel injection system and a view of the impeller and turbine*

Right: *An unconventional car, its high technology encapsulated by a quite conservative body design*

Audi 200 S Turbo

Engine: 5 cylinders in line, sohc
Capacity: 2144 cc
Bore; stroke: 79.5 mm 86.4 mm
Compression ratio: 7 to 1
Injection: with exhaust driven turbocharger
Max. power at 5300 rpm: 170 bhp 125 kW
Max. torque at 3300 rpm: 186 ft/lb 265 Nm

Transmission: 3 speed automatic transmission to front wheels via double joint semi axles

Suspension: Coil springs
Front: independent MacPherson struts and lower wishbones and anti-roll bar.
Rear: torsion beam axle located by Panhard rod

Steering: Power assisted rack and pinion
Turning circle: 37 ft 1 in 11.3 m

Brakes: Dual diagonal servo assisted. Front ventilated discs, rear solid discs

Dimensions:
Length: 15 ft 6 in 4.69 m
Weight unladen: 2772 lb 1260 kg

Performance:
Maximum speed: 121 mph 195 km/h
0–60 mph: 9.4 sec
Fuel consumption
  at 56 mph: 28.2 mpg 10 litres/100 km
  at 75 mph: 21.9 mpg 12.9 litres/100 km
  urban: 18.3 mpg 15.4 litres/100 km

Insurance Rating: 8

Derived Data:
bhp/litre (kW/litre): 79.3 58.3
bhp/ton (kW/tonne): 127 92
Speed × acceleration: 12.9
Performance Dimension: 10.1
Petrol consumption/ton at 56 mph (10/F): 7.48 (1.33)
Change in petrol consumption between 56 & 75 mph: 29%

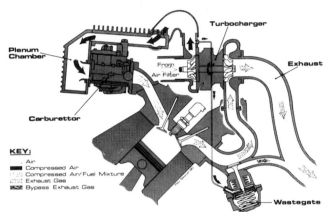

LOTUS ESPRIT TURBO

This is a car of superlatives and its heart is, of course, the 910 engine. The main problem with turbocharged engines more simple in concept is that at low engine rpm the power can be mundane. The compression ratio has to be reduced to prevent preignition when the turbocharger is at full power. Lotus have kept to conventional aspiration, two twin choke Dellorto carburettors are used, and argue that with the Garrett turbocharger blowing *into* them they get improved air/ fuel distribution and good throttle response.

The engine as a whole is very different from the 912. The larger piston bowl volumes provide the necessary lower compression ratio but it is in the shaping of this region that the engine designer has to show his mastery of the fuel air mixture when turbocharged.

While higher lift camshafts have helped the unboosted performances as radical changes on the old 907 2 litre unit include a new coolant circuit in the head and sodium filled exhaust valves which can cut their head temperatures by nearly 100°C. The Turbo Esprit engine

is as unconventional in the way it deals with the blow-off gases from the wastegate which are fed back into the silencer rather than to any earlier point. This improves high rpm power by reducing exhaust back pressure.

The design solutions that have gone into the 910 make it a unit which will be admired for many years. The position of the car on our graph of speed × acceleration against power to weight ratio is with a performance dimension of 15.6, quite exceptional. The car is, in this sense, better than the 3.3 litre turbocharged Porsche 911 which although marginally faster only manages this with a power to weight ratio of some 30 per cent better.

Only brief familiarity with the further changes between the Esprit 2.2 and the Essex Turbo demonstrate the way in which the new car is a complete design concept.

To start with the chassis and suspension: the well tried Esprit steel chassis has been extensively modified, with a new space frame engine and transmission cradle

Opposite above: *Giugiaro designed the Lotus Esprit Turbo and many consider it to be one of his best designs*

Opposite below: *This diagram shows the basic principles of the turbo engine*

Right: *The massive 210 bhp Lotus Esprit Turbo engine*

Lotus Esprit Turbo

Engine: '910' aluminium 4 in line, 4 valves/cylinder (exhaust sodium cooled)
Garrett AiResearch T3 turbocharger pressurizes air to carburettors at boost pressure of 8 lb/in²
Capacity: 2174 cc
Bore; stroke: 95.29 mm   76.2 mm
Compression ratio: 7.5 to 1
Carburation: 2 Dellorto 40 DHLA H
Max. power at 6500 rpm: 210 bhp   156 kW
Max. torque at 4500 rpm: 200 ft/lb   271 Nm

Transmission: 5 speed manual

Suspension:
Front: all independent, coil springs, upper wishbone lower transverse link with anti-roll bar.
Rear: double unequal non-parallel transverse links, with radius arm

Steering: Rack and pinion (not power assisted)

Brakes: Split front/rear system. All disc
Dimensions:
Length: 13 ft 9 in   4.19 m
Weight (midladen): 2690 lb   1220 kg
Performance:
Maximum speed: 152 mph   245 km/h
0–60 mph: 5.55 sec
Fuel consumption
    at 56 mph: 28.4 mpg   9.9 litres/100 km
    urban: 15.7 mpg   18 litres/100 km
Insurance Rating: 9
Derived Data:
bhp/litre (kW/litre): 96.6   71.7
bhp/ton (kW/tonne): 175   128
Speed × acceleration: 27.4
Performance Dimension: 15.6
Petrol consumption/ton at 56 mph: 8.2

giving a wide four point mounting system, while the torsional stiffness has been improved by widening the front box section. The front suspension is of course independent with upper wishbones, single lower links, anti-roll bar, coil springs and telescopic dampers. Both the front and rear track have been increased, but the rear suspension has seen the more extensive changes. Here new forged aluminium hub carriers lie between non-parallel transverse links of unequal length, the coil springs picking up ahead of the hub carriers and tilting inwards at the top.

The car now has wrap around front and rear bumpers with a new front and rear spoiler as well as deeper sills. The low weight of the Lotus bodies is a key point in their outstanding performance. The most important changes that have been made to the Turbo's body are in its aerodynamic form.

While the drag coefficient at 0.35 is fine, the designers have paid extremely careful attention to front and rear lift effects at speed. These are now exactly balanced and limited to only 50 lb at 100 mph. This necessitated reducing the effect of the rear spoiler in Giugiaro's prototype, partially by adding a smaller one at the rear of the roof and front of the engine cover. The chin spoiler also had to be reduced in depth and we see the compromises so essential in the design process in that it also had to be made more effective as an air feed for the massive radiator, oil cooler and front disc brakes. The underneath of the car is as clean and free from turbulence as one might expect and we see the purpose of the sills in that NACA ducts are moulded into them to provide cooling air for the engine.

The technical refinement of this car is extensive: the gear shift is delightfully to hand and the seats supportive. From here, however, the space age takes over; not only is the rich and deep Connolly leather of the seats surrounded by carpeting nearly as deep, but features such as air conditioning as standard affirm the car's position in the price hierarchy.

This Porsche looks familiar because it is their fifteenth year without a significant body change

PORSCHE 911 TURBO

In the end, the ultimate in performance cannot be obtained without a heavy fuel input; this is a natural consequence of the first law of thermodynamics. So the 911 turbo has a useful maximum speed of 162 mph (260 km/h), but it drinks fuel like the best of them. Weissach *can* produce cars which are not so dreadfully thirsty, e.g. 924 Turbo, 160 mph and 21 mpg.

The 911 is in its fifteenth year of development without having a major body change. Might as well try to change the shape of Brancusi's famous fish; the 911 is almost in the same work of art category. The overall concept is also unchanged with the flat six air cooled engine overslung, driving the rear wheels through a 5 speed gearbox transaxle, with MacPherson struts and torsion bars at the front and semi-trailing arms/torsion bar rear suspension, plus anti-roll bars at both ends.

The difference is the turbo, which has increased the bhp to 300 from the 204 of the 911 SC, and the maximum speed from 148 to 162 mph (238–260 km/h). Now, in 1981, engineers are pointing out that 150 mph

(241 km/h) is the speed which separates these from those. For example, the Ferrari 308 GTB and Maserati Merak have maximum speeds of 150 but they do it with normal aspiration, putting them in a class apart.

The driving position in the 911 is ideal, but with the pedals offset to the left. The dials are circular and clearly marked. There is no wind noise, but the engine and wheel roar are there as you might expect. This car has superb handling and traction. The wheel communicates everything about the road and the tyres and how they are getting along together, and all the time there is a perfect neutral situation. In the wet more care needs to be taken.

Braking is impeccable, without drama, and providing a reassurance which uplifts the spirit. The clutch, like all Porsche clutches, requires strength. In all, this really is a supercar. Many are given this name because of their exotic appearance or their purchase price, but the 911 achieves it by power, speed and efficiency.

Complicated in the extreme but with no loose ends, the turbo produces 300 bhp and a maximum speed of 162 mph (260 km/h)

Porsche 911 Turbo

Engine: 6 cylinders horizontally opposed, sohc/bank chain drive. Turbocharged with induction. All light alloy. Rear mounted. Air cooled
Capacity: 3299 cc
Bore; stroke: 97 mm   74.4 mm
Compression ratio: 7 to 1
Injection: Bosch K-Jetronic
Max. power at 5500 rpm: 300 bhp   221 kW
Max. torque at 4000 rpm: 303.6 ft/lb   412 Nm

Transmission: 5 speed manual gearbox to rear ½ axles with double universals

Suspension: Anti-roll bars front and rear.
Front: torsion bar.
Rear: one torsion bar per wheel

Steering: Rack and pinion
Turning circle: 36 ft   10.9 m

Brakes: hydraulic dual circuit with vented discs on all 4 wheels. Servo assisted

Dimensions:
Length: 14 ft 1 in   4.29 m
Kerb weight: 2866 lb   1300 kg

Performance:
Maximum speed: 162 mph   260 km/h
0–60 mph: 5.3 sec
Fuel consumption
    at 56 mph: 23.9 mpg   11.8 litres/100 km
    at 75 mph: 19.9 mpg   14.2 litres/100 km
    urban: 14.4 mpg   19.6 litres/100 km

Insurance Rating: 8

Derived Data:
(for weight ½ laden (3285 lb))
bhp/litre (kW/litre): 90.9   67
bhp/ton (kW/tonne): 204.5   148.3
Speed × acceleration: 30.6
Performance Dimension: 14.9
Petrol consumption/ton at 56 mph (10/F): 8.05   (1.24)
Change in petrol consumption between 56 & 75 mph: 20%

PORSCHE 924 TURBO

The 924 Turbo has a rear spoiler of polyurethane which lowers the drag coefficient from 0.36 to 0.35, and a Naca duct in the bonnet directing air to the turbocharger. These two external features identify it as the turbo. The engine is tilted to the right, and the turbocharger, which is a KKK, is mounted on the underside, beside the exhaust manifold. While the cylinder block, crankshaft and connecting rods are 924 units, there is a new cylinder head, combustion chamber conformation and pistons. The spark plugs are platinum tipped and the ignition is transistorized, and there is Bosch K-Jetronic fuel injection.

The turbo develops 170 bhp and 181 ft/lb of torque compared with the normal 924's 125 and 122. To cope with the increased horsepower, a larger clutch (the same as the 911 SC) is fitted, and the propshaft has been increased in diameter from 0.78 inches to 1.0 inches, running in three bearings within a torque tube. The gearbox has been adapted from the 911 unit, whereas the 924 gearbox is based on the Audi box. The brakes

from the 911 are used at the front, and from the 928 at the rear, all ventilated. Equipment within the car is luxurious and complete.

Performance is naturally impressive: 140 mph (225 km/h) top speed, 0–60 in 7 seconds, 120 mph in 29.1 seconds. The power produces 24.4 mph/1000 rpm at full song, but unfortunately the power dwindles at low engine speeds, because there just isn't enough bang in the exhaust gases to produce turboboost.

We have mentioned, in the section on diesel engines, the necessity of learning how to get the best out of diesels, and it is the same with turbochargers. The real power comes in at 3000 rpm, and above this, everything happens as and when you want it to happen, with no time lag. In order to get the best out of its biased performance, you must stay in the lower gears and keep the revs up. Maximum power is at 5500 rpm so it is pointless to push the needle above that towards the red 6500 rpm (there is in any case a rev-limiter at just over 6000).

Opposite: *One of the best cars in the world*

Right: *Still very much under development, modifications to this engine will steadily produce more power, torque and flexibility*

Porsche 924 Turbo

Engine: 4 cylinders in line. Aluminium alloy head, belt drive sohc. Exhaust driven turbo charging. Front mounted
Capacity: 1984 cc
Bore; stroke: 86.5 mm 84.4 mm
Compression ratio: 7.5 to 1
Injection: Bosch K-Jetronic
Max. power at 5500 rpm: 170 bhp 125 kW
Max. torque at 3500 rpm: 180.5 ft/lb 245 Nm

Transmission: Rear mounted 5 speed manual gearbox

Suspension: Anti-roll bar front and rear.
Front: independent, coil springs, MacPherson struts and wishbones.
Rear: independent, semi trailing arms with torsion bar power wheel

Steering: Rack and pinion
Turning circle: 32 ft 9.5 in 10 m

Brakes: Dual servo assisted. Ventilated discs front and rear

Dimensions:
Length: 13 ft 8 in 4.21 m
Kerb weight: 2601 lb 1180 kg
Performance:
Maximum speed: 140 mph 225 km/h
0–60 mph: 7.6 sec
Fuel consumption
    at 56 mph: 36.2 mpg 7.8 litres/100 km
    at 75 mph: 26.9 mpg 10.5 litres/100 km
    urban: 23.0 mpg 12.3 litres/100 km
Insurance Rating: 7
Derived Data:
(as for ½ laden 2954 lb)
bhp/litre (kW/litre): 85.7 63
bhp/ton (kW/tonne): 128.9 93.3
Speed × acceleration: 18.4
Performance Dimension: 14.3
Petrol consumption/ton at 56 mph (10/F): 5.91 1.69
Change in petrol consumption between 56 & 75 mph: 35%

The 924 T has a wider rear track than the 924, and a thicker anti-roll bar, together with reinforced semi-trailing arms. The steering has lower gearing by the use of longer steering arms, and is very precise indeed. The suspension and steering provide neutral handling, with mild understeer in the wet. The instruments are perfect – simple and circular – as on all the best cars. There are one or two reasonably good cars with over stylized instruments, but very few.

The 924 T is capable of 140 mph yet has a fuel consumption of 21 mpg. This is unprecedented, except for the Lotus Esprit. One of the first production line 924 turbos was driven by Lins and Plattner in one of the cruellest tests for any car. In one of the longest and hardest winter drives recorded, they covered 37,000 km (23,125 miles) in America, Africa and Europe. En route to Fairbanks, Alaska, they drove through one of the worst snow-storms recorded in recent years, at a temperature of minus 51°C. This was followed by the constant darkness of the Polar Circle, and the rain, mud and dust

of Africa. With an average fuel consumption of 22.78 mpg the 924 Turbo returned without a fault.

This is typical of the whole Porsche ethic – through trials of all kinds towards perfection. The way in which Porsche cars have at various times dominated endurance racing has made it appear that they were designed primarily for racing, but this is not the case. They have made use of the facts discovered on the track to produce cars which are safer, faster and more fuel efficient than most. When visiting various firms one notices different attitudes – some are concerned with shifts in design and others in market changes, but Porsche are always thinking about the next developments which will make their cars more invincible than ever at Le Mans, and then how to use those facts in their current production cars.

Opposite and above: *Another conventional bodyshell covering a powerful new turbocharger*

RENAULT 18 TURBO

The Renault 18 Turbo is a production car which makes use of the research from turbocharged competition cars, the Renault 5 Turbo – the splendid muscle-bound dwarf – and the more or less successful Formula one racing cars. By choosing the 1600 cc 18 model, which is a straightforward three-box family saloon, Renault are bringing their turbo experience to everyman and his family. It is the cheapest turbocharged car on the market, but the normal 1600s cost at least a thousand pounds less. It is an economical car for its size and performance.

This 18 turbo does not use the same engine as the Renault 18 TS, which is 1647 cc, but a 1565 cc unit from the R12 Gordini, which already possessed the necessary pistons and connecting rods for a turbo engine, a cross flow head and hemispherical combustion chambers. The Garrett turbocharger blows into the single choke Solex through a necessary intercooler, otherwise, with the high compression ratio, the charge would detonate. The 18 turbo produces 110 bhp and 134 ft/lb torque compared with the standard 18's 79 bhp/86 ft/lb – an outstanding improvement, but surprisingly, the identical bhp and less torque than the fuel injected VW Scirocco.

The maximum speed of the Renault 18 T is 115 mph (185 km/h) and 0–60 mph time is 9.7 sec, but more important than this is its flexibility at lower speeds. Peak power is at 5000 revs and anything above this produces nothing but noise and fury. Driven as a sports turbo, the 18 T returns 24 mpg, but with more calm, 30–35 mpg. The overdrive fifth gear gives 20.9 mph (33.6 km/h) per 1000 revs. There is a low level of engine and wind noise at the cruising speed of 90–100 mph (145–160 km/h).

This car is satisfactory in all respects with the exception of the gearchange. Perhaps it will soon have an improved gearbox – the power deserves something better.

Right: The engine
1 *air filter*
2 *turbine compressing air to intake*
3 *air cooler*
4 *carburettor with air blowing into it*
5 *inlet valve*
6 *exhaust valve*
7 *exhaust manifold*
8 *turbine powered by exhaust gas*
9 *regulator for exhaust gas*
10 *pressure capsule for regulation*

▷ *air at atmospheric pressure*

▧ *compressed air*

◼▶ *compressed air (cooled)*

◼▶ *exhaust gas*

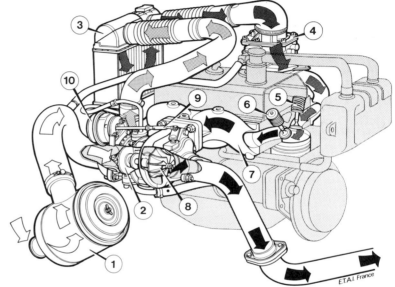

Renault 18 Turbo

Engine: 4 cylinders in line, longitudinally mounted; chain driven camshaft in block. Block and head alloy. Garrett blows into carburettor at up to 0.6 bar
Capacity: 1565 cc
Bore; stroke: 77 mm   84 mm
Compression ratio: 8.6 to 1
Carburation: Single barrel Solex 32DIS
Max. power at 5000 rpm: 110 bhp   82 kW
Max. torque at 2250 rpm: 133.8 ft/lb   181.6 Nm

Transmission: 5 speed manual gearbox

Suspension:
Front: independent, coil springs, four bar linkages by double unequal wishbones. Anti-roll bar.
Rear: rigid beam axle with 2 trailing radius arms and one triangulated arm. Coil springs. Anti-roll bar.

Steering: Rack and pinion power assisted
Turning circle: 36 ft 9 in   11.2 m

Brakes: Dual diagonal power assisted. 9.4 in (23.9 cm) ventilated front discs, 9 in (22.9 cm) rear drums

Dimensions:
Length: 14 ft 4 in   4.4 m
Weight unladen: 2293 lb   1040 kg

Performance:
Maximum speed: 115 mph   185 km/h
0–60 mph: 9.7 sec
Fuel consumption
   at 56 mph: 42.2 mpg   6.4 litres/100 km
   at 75 mph: 31.4 mpg   8.5 litres/100 km
   urban: 28.8 mpg   9.8 litres/100 km

Insurance Rating: 6

Derived Data:
bhp/litre (kW/litre): 70.3   52.4
bhp/ton (kW/tonne): 97.9   71.8
Speed × acceleration: 11.8
Performance Dimension: 12.1
Petrol consumption/ton at 56 mph (10/F): 5.7   (1.76)
Change in petrol consumption between 56 & 75 mph: 30%

SAAB 900 TURBO

There have been several improvements made to the Saab 900 Turbo since it was first introduced. The H type engine no longer uses an idler shaft for ancillary drives, these being driven by crank or camshaft. This has resulted in a lighter block. The turbocharger has a smaller turbine which improves power at low speed, and the wastegate is controlled by intake manifold pressure instead of exhaust. The five speed manual box has a better range of gear ratios, and this together with the fact that the turbocharger delivers boost from below 2000 rpm and reaches peak at 2500 rpm has improved acceleration vividly.

Naturally, with K-Jetronic injection, it starts immediately, and cruises at any speed up to its maximum of 119 mph (192 km/h) without noise, vibration or boom periods.

The steering is responsive and with total stability from the suspension, none of the road imperfections affect either controls or passengers, even on country roads of poor quality at speed. Motorway cruising is faultless.

The seats are well designed and comfortable, and the control layout noticeably good. The heating and ventilation has seven positions to select various combinations of fresh or heated air. The four-cylinder engine shows refinement at all times.

The new 4-door coachwork with a boot, together with the option of automatic transmission, moves Saab nearer to the mainstream of consumer demand. The automatic transmission does not provide the same exhilarating acceleration as the five speed manual which we found had a 0.6 second advantage to 60 mph. The interior of the new body has an extraordinarily comfortable rear seat, designed by Dux, a Swedish furniture manufacturer, and the front seats have been good from the beginning.

The Saab 900 Turbo is a well designed car in every way. It is also positively different in every way. There is something reminiscent about small aircraft in the shapes and curves and the instrument binnacle, which is echoed in the quality of the ride.

Above and left: *Saab have achieved an original design, both with the large hatchback and the four-door saloon*

Right: *The Saab turbo engine has succeeded in producing a wider range of power with fewer problems than other turbos*

Saab 900 Turbo (5 door)

Engine: 4 cylinders in line inclined 45°. Light alloy cylinder head, sohc
Capacity: 1985 cc
Bore; stroke: 90 mm   78 mm
Compression ratio: 7.2 to 1
Injection: Bosch K system
Max. power at 5000 rpm: 145 bhp   108.2 kW
Max. torque at 3000 rpm: 174 ft/lb   236.1 Nm

Transmission: Five speed manual gearbox, front wheel drive

Suspension:
Front: coil springs with transverse wishbones.
Rear: dead axle with four links and a Panhard rod, coil sprung

Steering: Power assisted rack and pinion, 3.6 turns lock to lock

Brakes: Dual diagonal servo assisted. 11 in (27.9 cm) front discs, 10.6 in (26.9 cm) rear discs

Dimensions:
Length: 15 ft 6 in   4.74 m
Kerb weight: 2820 lb   1279 kg

Performance:
Maximum speed: 120 mph   193 km/h
0–60 mph: 9.3 sec
Fuel consumption
    at 56 mph: 41.3 mpg   6.8 litres/100 km
    at 75 mph: 32.5 mpg   8.7 litres/100 km
    urban: 20.3 mpg   13.9 litres/100 km

Insurance Rating: 8

Derived Data:
bhp/litre (kW/litre): 73   54.5
bhp/ton (kW/tonne): 106.7   78.4
Speed × acceleration: 12.9
Performance Dimension: 12.1
Petrol consumption/ton at 56 mph (10/F): 5.03   (1.98)
Change in petrol consumption between 56 & 75 mph: 28%

TURBOS: SUMMARY

The turbocharger, so natural on a diesel, requires engineering of 'state of the art' levels to work successfully on a petrol engine. The point of course is that it is no good just ramming the mixture into the cylinder, because it will simply preignite when the pressure is increased about tenfold. We want as high a compression ratio as possible, but we have the general difficulty that if work is done on a gas to compress it, it warms up, thus exacerbating the problem.

How then does a turbocharger do any better than a simple increase of compression ratio? The principles are very straightforward. If the fuel and air mixture can be at least part compressed out of the cylinder, using the waste energy from the hot exhaust gases, then the reciprocating motion of the piston has to do less work. Furthermore, the more the gas is compressed away from the engine, the more the opportunity to cool it before allowing it into the combustion chamber already part compressed. This, then, allows more fuel and air to be put into the cylinder for a given critical compression for preignition. Of course in the diesel preignition is not the problem! In the early petrol engine turbochargers, little was done to cool the compressed gas, and in consequence the gains were not substantial.

Not surprisingly, since turbocharging is essentially about increasing the efficiency of an engine, we find the principle applied to both standard saloons and the ultimate performance cars. Efficiency does neither any harm! The current image of turbocharging as solely for the hot shots will undoubtedly change over the next year or two, though there are problems about making the system work well over a wide engine rpm range.

The cars we have described fall into three groups. There are the saloons for which the system has had fairly minimal effect, and those for which fairly dramatic improvements have proved possible in both performance and fuel efficiency. There are also the sports cars for which what had previously been considered to be the ultimate has become fairly mundane.

Firstly then, comparing the Audi 200 ST with its unturbocharged brother the Audi 100 GL5E, it is clear that though the performance has been improved, this has required a substantial increase in the power to weight ratio, with a lowering of the performance dimension. The same could be said for the Broadspeed Granada. The decrease in the fuel efficiency (at 56 mph) for the former car is the natural result of a lowering of the compression ratio to cope with the turbine input pressure at higher rpm. In fact the cars which manage increased low speed fuel efficiency have thus had very clever engineers indeed!

This has been done on the new Renault 18 Turbo, though without a spectacular performance improvement, and even more astonishingly on the Saab 900 Turbo, though in this case with more substantial performance improvements relative to the unturbocharged engines. In a sense Saab had to do it with their old engine, and progressively over the last few years they have gained the necessary experience to market a system which is now both smooth and efficient. It is a pleasure to drive, not as a sports car, but as a performance saloon.

Not a lot need be said about the Lotus Essex Esprit and the turbocharged Porsche 911, both are clearly fantastic cars, though in turbocharged form the 911 has the clear mastery of its much smaller engined competitor. Just who could claim to drive well enough to scratch the surface of the potential of such machinery? At a rather lower, but still not that low, level of performance, the Porsche 924 in turbocharged form is a significant improvement on the 924, but still no match for the Audi Quattro.

Class 8	Data Summary				
Datum Point		Perform-ance	Power Weight	PD	FE
A	Audi 200S Turbo	12.9	127	10.1	1.33
B	Lotus Esprit Turbo	27.4	175	15.6	1.22
C	Porsche 911 Turbo	30.6	205	14.9	1.24
D	Porsche 924 Turbo	18.4	129	14.3	1.69
E	Renault 18 Turbo	11.8	98	12.1	1.76
F	Saab 900 Turbo	12.9	107	12.1	1.98

Audi 200 Turbo

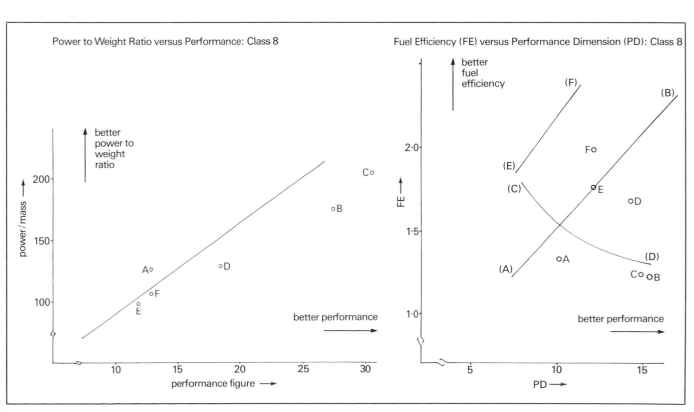

Power to Weight Ratio versus Performance: Class 8

Fuel Efficiency (FE) versus Performance Dimension (PD): Class 8

8 Diesels-The World's Workhorse

Rudolf Diesel (1858–1913) who invented the diesel, said 'Inventing is the process of sorting one good idea out of a multitude of mistakes, and pursuing it through a series of failures and compromises to practical success'. He published his first paper *Theory and construction of an efficient heat engine* in 1893. After countless experiments, which all took place in the Maschinenfabrik Augsburg, most of them unintentionally explosive, Diesel began to collaborate with Robert Bosch, who at that time was designing magnetos, but had already been experimenting with injection pumps. Between 1923 and 1927 Bosch designed a successful fuel injection system. Soon, the diesel engine became the workhorse of the world. It is the driving force in ships, submarines, trains, buses, cement mixers, tractors, trucks, taxis, and now private cars with increasing numbers annually. There are diesels from 60,000 bhp to 1 bhp (42,000 kW to 0.7 kW).

The 'one good idea' which Rudolf Diesel was talking about was the high compression engine and the thermal efficiency that went with it. It was getting the fuel into the high compression area – an extremely dangerous and hostile environment – which caused the problems and the explosions. Having solved diesel injection, Bosch moved to petrol injection and electronic ignition, which are described elsewhere in this book.

There is engineering finesse of a high order in the latest passenger car diesel engines. Injection must be accurate to within 0.1 milliseconds (0.0001 sec). The fuel spray from the injection must have a very exactly defined shape, direction, penetration energy and atomization. Gas temperatures reach peak values of 2000°C and pressures up to 90 bar. It is not surprising that injection pumps which encapsulate this order of sophistication are normally sealed.

Since diesel engines have been used for passenger cars, research has been carried out in an effort to make them run quietly. There is also interest in fuel economy and the suppression of exhaust pollutants. Further research with the fuel injection nozzles may solve these problems.

Before considering the operation of a diesel injection nozzle, one must be clear about the atomization and combustion processes in the turbulence chamber, or prechamber. We cannot crawl into the combustion chamber to see what is going on. Bosch have therefore made oversize models – a 25 × magnified model of the injection nozzle. This model, which looks like a space rocket, is fitted with sensors and gauges. With a model of these dimensions it is possible to use about 100 measuring points – an achievement that would be quite impossible with the actual size nozzle. With the large model, engineers can measure flow quantities, velocities and pressure distributions at all points for any conceivable number of shapes of nozzle body and valve.

Another method of research is to use stroboscopic photography, by which means it has been possible to get an idea of the contours of the fuel jet and its dispersion patterns. Exact synchronization of the photographic exposure with the pulse of the injection nozzle makes it possible to photograph the fuel stream inside the chamber. But this kind of photography, ingenious though it is, is still not sensitive enough to enable the engineers to follow the precise movements of the particles inside the fuel spray itself; they wish to know about – and to rectify – any variations in fineness and distribution within the tiny cloud of spray.

Recently astronomers have started to make use of photographic techniques using the negative to establish light intensity in bodies in space, for instance in a comet, and learn about the material composition of these bodies. This is called equidensitometry. Chemists have helped in this issue and a special emulsion has now been made for film used in this research. In diesel engineering, it was found possible to apply equidensitometry to analyze the fuel spray's structure, using precisely timed stroboscopic lamps. The black and white pictures are then printed on to the special film with various exposure times, and from this it is indeed possible to see the individual equidensities – that is, areas of the same grey shade.

The new process also enables the engineer to distinguish a conical segment of finely atomized fuel

194

that surrounds the more compact stream and is not visible in normal photographs. This segment helps to determine the 'ignition delay' – the time between the injection of fuel and the start of combustion. The task is to control ignition delay precisely to at least one thousandth but not more than two thousandths of a second; if it is too long or short, the engine will run rough and knock.

So much for the fuel injection nozzles. At the same time, the pump components themselves – the precisely drilled, machined and honed steel cylinders, in which the cross-sections and control edges govern fuel flow so that the engine gets the right amount of fuel at the right time – are also subject to more research.

The facts as they are made known are fed into a computer which helps to design improved systems; it can compare new designs with 2000 others, whose characteristics are stored in its memory bank, and if it cannot select a suitable design already available, it even produces a sketch diagram itself.

The latest computers simplify this dialogue: when an engineer puts forward a new design, this appears on the display and the computer adds its knowledge immediately. Computers are also used in the final assembly of injection pumps, controlling manufacture with the accuracy already mentioned, to milliseconds.

The 'idle knock' of the diesel engine results from the combustion process. Between the start of fuel injection and effective ignition, as we know, there is the ignition delay. This pause is at its greatest with a cold engine or under low load. The longer the delay, the more fuel enters the combustion chamber, and so it ignites violently, instead of smoothly – hence the diesel clatter. Do not think Mercedes are not aware of this ghastly noise. They have been working at it for many years, together with Bosch. Research continues in the development of the glow plugs, which heat the combustion chamber before starting. The new pencil-type glow plug, which uses a glow tube of heat resistant steel, bedded and electrically insulated in magnesium oxide powder, has dramatically reduced the waiting time before the engine fires.

Will the results from all this research – the oversize model of the nozzle, stroboscope photography, the use of equidensometric methods and film, and computerized redesign of pump components – will these things turn the cheerfully clattering diesel work-horse into the silent wonderhorse? The gusto with which Mercedes and VW are attacking world records for diesels has led to startling improvements in their engines, and there is a dramatic increase in diesel sales in the USA, but the incentive is not entirely profit. There is also pride in engineering and innovation, which are not quite the same. The use of turbos has raised the maximum speeds, but turbocharging is a boost which automatically produces better results, whatever the basic system to which it is added. It is the diesel engine itself and its injection system which must be improved before everyman and his wife will accept it more readily. The noise is decreasing and will shortly be a mere whisper. Would you believe that research could remove the smell and the smoke? It has already, we are told, but the price is prohibitive.

Diesel engines are becoming more compact and have longer service intervals. Next step: more turbo-diesels

TURBO DIESELS

THE MERCEDES-BENZ 300 TD TURBO DIESEL AND THE
PEUGEOT 604 SLD TURBO

Turbocharging has a long way to go. No manufacturer has yet designed a production engine specifically as a turbocharged engine. When they do, the turbo will be integrated with the manifolding and engine castings, making a unity of the engine with the turbocharging components. One of the difficulties of achieving this ideal is the fact that the Garrett AiResearch Corporation, the world manufacturer of turbochargers, provides the research, designs and often manufactures the parts for most of the turbos made. Garrett have manufacturing facilities in the USA, in Britain, France, Brazil and Japan. It is not surprising to find that Garrett provided the turbochargers for both of the engines under review.

Turbo diesels incorporate a synthesis of two features very appropriate for the eighties, fuel economy with performance. The impressive torque potential, fully on tap even in the lower engine speed range, with both models, removes the truck and taxi stigma always associated with diesels. Sadly, it does not remove the smell.

In both cases, the turbos were added to existing engines. In the case of M-B it was the 300 D and for Peugeot the XD2, which powered the 504 diesel. The addition of the turbo made massive improvements in all areas, and also necessitated almost identical changes to the components to cope with the increased output: both engines had to be given oil-cooled pistons with jets in the crown, larger gudgeon pins, reinforced inlet and exhaust valves and strengthened crankshafts. In the case of the Mercedes the crankshaft is also nitrided which doubles the fatigue strength and the exhaust valves are sodium-filled. This extra care can be seen with every detail of M-B engineering practice.

Bosch provided the injection equipment for both engines, as Garrett designed the turbos. The comparison therefore relates to the respective engines, Peugeot and Mercedes, the gear train in each case, and the suspension.

In the case of the Peugeot, there is a choice of the BA10/4, BA10/5, of four or five gears respectively, and the ZF3HP22 automatic which has three gears. The M-B uses a new four-speed automatic transmission of their own design, modified to suit the power and characteristics of the turbo-diesel engine. It is impeccable and there is no other option, understandably.

The transmission of the Peugeot includes a torque tube with constant velocity sliding joints. The suspension consists of MacPherson struts and an anti-roll bar front and trailing arms at the rear, with a second anti-roll bar. The front and rear shock absorbers are Peugeot double-acting telescopic hydraulics. The ride and handling of the Peugeot is in a very high category; few cars with a comparable power/weight ratio of 54.8 bhp/ton achieve this degree of comfort, stability and smooth effortless handling.

If it were being compared with any other car of comparable size and power, the Peugeot might well have been considered outstanding, but it is being compared with a car in which the engine holds some of the relevant world records, and a suspension which includes a self-levelling back axle which Mercedes have been quietly improving for several years. It is being compared with the car which has achieved the unimaginable, of providing large weight volume and carrying high cruising speed, precise handling and limousine charisma with, of all things, economy.

No crystal ball is needed to forsee a prolification of turbo-diesels, but it is unlikely that they will be in the same category as the Mercedes, which achieved its elite position by unremitting perfectionism, from the original concept down to every detail of its composition. At present, this car is only available in the USA.

When the crystal ball *is* used, it shows turbines more closely co-ordinated with the engine, ceramics being used for both turbines and their housings, and an improved power-weight ratio, bringing more performance plus economy. It also shows aerodynamic shapes, closely resembling the M-B CIII which has been used by Mercedes as a mobile test-bed for years, being adapted for passenger cars.

The single seater ARVW has an impressively low Cd × F of 0.11 m². The six-cylinder turbocharged diesel engine is behind the cockpit and has its charge air cooled by a water spray. The low profile tyres, size 195/50 VR 15, are completely covered by wing flaps

DIESEL RECORDS

Doktor Klaus of Volkswagen was asked why VW have become involved in world records for diesels. 'Because we want to find what speeds can be achieved with a minimum of fuel consumption. Whatever course the fuel crisis takes, there will always be a demand for fast cars, but in the future they must be economical.' The project was therefore concerned not with speed alone, but speed in relation to fuel consumption. Goldie Sardener achieved 206 mph (331 km/h) with an 1100 cc MG, boosted to 200 bhp, but his fuel consumption was 5 mpg on methanol, whereas the VW turbo-diesel was returning 50 mpg at 150 mph (241 km/h).

The purposeful single seater body of the Aerodynamic Research Volkswagen (ARVW) is in carbon fibre reinforced plastic (CFRP). It has a 6-cylinder 2.4 litre turbo-diesel engine, taken from the VW LT Commercial, and the standard gearbox from the Audi 100. The output of the engine is 129 kW (175 bhp), and the weight 1040 kg. The car thus has a power/weight ratio of 0.125 kW/kg and a brake horse power per litre 72.9. The bodyshell of the ARVW is aerodynamically reminiscent of Fritz von Opel's rocket car with its short anti-lift front wings, and the vertical tail fins are like Malcolm Campbell's Bluebird, but the whole device is small – length 5000 mm, width 1132 mm, height 837 mm.

The most impressive fact is that the basic power train is in existence already, in a VW Commercial and the Audi 100. When VW's ancestor Auto Union achieved 265 mph in 1938, it was with a very sophisticated petrol engine developing 600 bhp together with a special aerodynamic body.

The records were broken at the Fiat Nardo track near Brindisi in Southern Italy, where Mercedes had recently broken them with the five-cylinder 300 D turbo-diesel, using the CIII bodyshell. Mercedes continued to hold world records in the longer distances:

Mercedes records

	mph
5000 miles	157.800
10,000 km	157.730
10,000 miles	157.370

The records held by the VW diesel are as follows, also given in mph:

Volkswagen records

Flying start:	mph	Previous record (mph)	
1 km	214.405	190.300	
1 mile	215.405	190.043	
Standing start:			Class records
10 km	152.750	139.820	
10 miles	162.930	143.640	
100 km	210.570	197.930	
100 miles	215.780	198.790	
500 km	214.530	199.875	World records
One hour	219.890	200.020	

Class 9 Diesel Cars

INTRODUCTION

For ten years, from 1949 to 1959, Mercedes had something near to a monopoly of diesel engined passenger cars in Europe. At the end of 1959, Peugeot produced a diesel, and for eleven years Mercedes and Peugeot produced sufficient for the demand. In 1972, Opel launched their Rekord Diesel, and then there were three. By 1980, however, almost all manufacturers had produced diesel passenger cars.

Before the fuel crisis in 1973, the proportion of diesel cars was constant, at around two per cent of the total. It took some time for the diesel development to get started, naturally, but it soon grew to seven per cent in 1977, and the figure is now much higher than that.

There are many issues in the diesel situation which are difficult to comprehend. First, the differentiation in cost of fuel. At present, this can be represented as follows:

		West				
GB	France	Germany	Italy	Belgium	Sweden	Holland
+5%	−27%	0%	−54%	−32%	−49%	−31%
more	less	the same	less	less	less	less

A common policy for the Common Market should have included transport, surely, so that driving a diesel across Europe should not bring out such pointless divergences of fuel costs. It must be more irritating still for the manufacturers, and shows that they must have little impact in the corridors of power, or this hotch-potch would have been cleared up.

Secondly, the use of diesel vehicles shows a wide divergence. This table shows the numbers of thousands for 1979 for the countries in Europe:

GB	Holland	Belgium	Italy	France	Germany
4.7	35	45	87	144	184.8

Diesel engines are described fully in *Diesels – The World's Workhorse* (page 194), but we will remind you that a diesel engine has no carburettor, no spark plugs, no coil, no distributor, no condenser, and is therefore less likely to go wrong. The real advantages of a diesel engine are its longevity, reliability, lower maintenance costs, and clean exhaust emissions medically (actually they do look blacker). It is possible, by choosing a good one, to drive through Switzerland without being caught for infringing their stringent stationary noise levels, but the diesels mentioned here meet all exhaust emission laws throughout the world.

Diesel engines cost more to produce because of their robust construction, sophisticated fuel injection system, heavy duty battery and starter, but the service life is at least double that of a conventional petrol engine.

Furthermore the diesel owner starts with a healthy advantage in terms of efficiency. It will be remembered (*Heat and Work in the Engine*, page 68) that very roughly the thermodynamic efficiency E of an engine is related to the compression ratio R by the expression:

$$E = 1 - \frac{1}{\sqrt{R}}$$

Consequently since compression ratios are limited to values around 10 in petrol engines, because of preignition, but can commonly be 20–25 in a diesel, the diesel engine can naturally be as much as 10 per cent more efficient absolutely, or relatively about 15 per cent less voracious in terms of fuel usage than the petrol engine.

Mercedes-Benz 300 Turbo-diesel

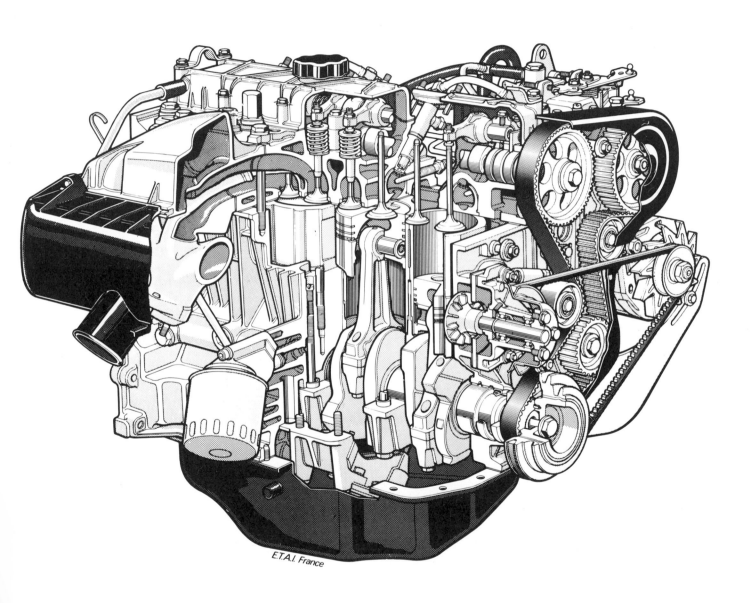

Renault 2 litre diesel engine. Note the robust connecting rods and the ingenious coordination of auxiliaries

AUDI AVANT L-5D

The VW Golf D came as a surprise and a pleasure in that it combined diesel economy with comfort, small dimensions and a degree of performance. It was therefore very successful. VW consequently introduced the Passat LD, using the same 1470 cc engine with 50 bhp as the Golf D.

The Audi Avant L-5D is larger and more luxurious than the Golf and the Passat diesels. The 1986 cc engine is a five-cylinder version of the Golf. Longitudinally mounted, this engine drives the front wheels through a four speed gearbox. The suspension is MacPherson struts at the front and dead axle at the rear, with power assisted rack and pinion steering. The brakes are disc front and drums rear. The Audi 100 series are all remarkably well designed, made and equipped, and priced accordingly.

The engine develops 70 bhp at 4800 rpm and 91 ft/lb of torque at 3000 rpm, which produces a performance better than one would expect, but not so good as the Citroën Diesel. Top speed is 93 mph (150 km/h), and

acceleration 0–60 mph of 17.5 seconds is certainly adequate for a diesel. Like all diesels it improves in every way if the engine is kept at it as hard as it will go, and will cruise at 80 (129) plus for as long as you wish, and still give over 38 mpg.

Handling is completely satisfactory, due to the well designed suspension and the power steering, together with progressive, positive braking. The whole car has been thoughtfully put together, with spaciousness, comfort and functional organization everywhere. The low centre of gravity gives it a feeling of stability at all times.

The driver is well equipped. Instruments are clear, pedals at the right positions and the four stalks and switches are all to hand. Heating and ventilation are adequate. Arranged with the rear seats folded, as a form of estate car, the space is long, flat, but rather narrow.

In all, there is nothing phenomenal about this car, but it is more of a pleasure to drive and to live with than many cars we can think of, in that it has no bad habits or

Right: *This 2 litre, five-cylinder engine develops 70 bhp and is a much cleaner unit than the diesels of the past*

Audi Avant L5D

Engine: 5 cylinders in line, ohc belt driven
Capacity: 1986 cc
Bore; stroke: 76.5 mm 86.4 mm
Compression ratio: 23 to 1
Injection: Bosch indirect diesel
Max. power at 4800 rpm: 70 bhp 51 kW
Max. torque at 3000 rpm: 90.4 ft/lb 123 Nm

Transmission: Front wheel drive, 4 or 5 speed manual gearbox via differential and double joint semi axles

Suspension: Coil springs.
Front: independent MacPherson struts, lower wishbones and anti-roll bar.
Rear: torsion crank axle with Panhard rod

Steering: Rack and pinion
Turning circle: 37 ft 8.5 in 11.3 m

Brakes: Dual diagonal servo assisted. Front discs and rear drums

Dimensions:
Length: 15 ft 0.5 in 4.59 m
Weight unladen: 2668 lb 1210 kg
Performance:
Maximum speed: 93 mph 150 km/h
0–60 mph: 17.5 sec
Fuel consumption
   at 56 mph: 45.5 mpg 6.2 litres/100 km
   at 75 mph: 33.2 mpg 8.5 litres/100 km
   urban: 31.4 mpg 9.0 litres/100 km
Insurance Rating: 6
Derived Data:
bhp/litre (kW/litre): 32.2 25.6
bhp/ton (kW/tonne): 54.2 38.9
Speed × acceleration: 5.3
Performance Dimension: 9.8
Fuel consumption/ton at 56 mph (10/F): 4.8 (2.08)
Change in fuel consumption between 56 & 75 mph: 37%

obnoxious elements of bad design anywhere. The fact that it is a diesel does not obtrude either, which shows that the Bosch researchers are moving slowly but steadily to that diesel nirvana they are promising (see *Diesels – The World's Workhorse*), when the radio can be playing Satie or Chopin without a Wagnerian anvil chorus accompaniment from the combustion chambers and the connecting rods.

Right: *The five-cylinder diesel engine. The cutaway section shows one piston with its strengthened connecting rod, the massive balance weights of the crankshaft, the heater plug and injector valve*

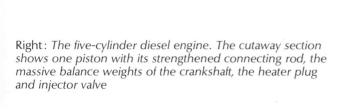

CITROËN CX 2500D PALLAS

The Citroën Pallas Diesel has exceptional qualities. It starts quickly, with a warm up by the glow plugs of thirty seconds, there is little audible evidence of the high compression engine, and knocking can be eliminated by driving within the limits of the governor, which cuts in at 4900 rpm, giving maximum speeds of 25, 43, 63 and 84 mph (40, 69, 101 and 135 km/h) through the gears.

Its top speed of 92 mph (148 km/h) compared with the 94.9 mph (152.7 km/h) of the turbocharged Peugeot, and acceleration from 0 to 70 mph taking 14 seconds or three seconds faster than the Peugeot, makes one interested in how it is achieving this. Normally aspirated engines should not be capable of outaccelerating turbos.

The Citroën engine first appeared eight years ago in the C35 light utility vehicle and has been developed from that. It uses a CAV Roto-diesel injection system. The overhead valves are operated by pushrods. The camshaft is driven by an intermediate gear, not chains. It develops 75 bhp at 4250 rpm, and 111 ft/lb of torque at 2000 rpm, whereas the Peugeot develops more bhp *and* torque – 80 bhp output at 4150 rpm and torque of 136 ft/lb at 2000 rpm.

The high performance (by diesel standards) is not at the expense of high fuel consumption. During seven days of very diverse driving it recorded 34.5 mpg and this could have been improved to around 40 by omitting the peak revs for an exuberance of driving not usually possible with diesel power. That is economical motoring and in style.

The design of the interior is ergonomically and aesthetically on the highest level. The ride, with Citroën's hydropneumatic suspension is superb. The brakes are incredibly efficient. In every way it shows design and engineering refinement of a high order. This Citroën is so lively that few passengers realize that it is a diesel; the driver forgets it as well most of the time.

Opposite: *Other manufacturers are now catching up with Citroën's aerodynamic bodyshells. The hydropneumatic suspension system is still avant garde, however, and in this case so is the diesel engine*

Right: *The concave window has not been copied yet*

Below: *The estate version is, in our opinion, an exceptionally well designed and desirable vehicle*

Citroën CX 2500D Pallas

Engine: 4 cylinders in line, transverse mounted, ohv
Capacity: 2500 cc
Bore; stroke: 93 mm 92 mm
Compression ratio: 22.25 to 1
Injection: Roto-Diesel
Max. power at 4250 rpm: 75 bhp 55.9 kW
Max. torque at 2000 rpm: 111 ft/lb 150.6 Nm

Transmission: Five speed gearbox to front wheels (C-Matic 3 speed torque converter optional)

Suspension: Independent self-levelling hydropneumatic. Front: equal length double wishbones. Rear: trailing arms and anti-roll bars

Steering: Fully power Varipower. 2–5 turns lock to lock
Turning circle: 35 ft 9 in 10.9 m

Brakes: Powered dual circuit. 10.2 in (25.9 cm) front ventilated discs, 8.8 in (22.4 cm) rear discs

Dimensions:
Length: 15 ft 2.5 in 4.63 m
Weight unladen: 2866 lb 1300 kg

Performance:
Maximum speed: 92 mph 148 km/h
0–60 mph: 17.5 sec
Fuel consumption
  at 56 mph: 46.3 mpg 6.1 litres/100 km
  at 75 mph: 34.9 mpg 8.1 litres/100 km
  urban: 31.8 mpg 8.9 litres/100 km

Insurance Rating: 5

Derived Data:
bhp/litre (kW/litre): 30 22.4
bhp/ton (kW/tonne): 54.3 39.9
Speed × acceleration: 5.26
Performance Dimension: 9.7
Petrol consumption/ton at 56 mph (10/F): 4.42 (2.26)
Change in petrol consumption between 56 & 75 mph: 33%

MERCEDES-BENZ 300 D

Mercedes-Benz have immense experience in the design and manufacture of diesel engines. They also hold several long distance diesel records, and forty-five per cent of their total production is diesels.

The 300 D has five cylinders, but the design is actually the same as the 240 D with an extra cylinder. The performance is considerably better than the 200 D. This we can state with some authority, as we actually bought and used a Mercedes 200 D a few years ago as a second car, partly because we are interested in cars and had never owned a diesel, partly because we thought it might prove to be economical, and finally because we thought it would be a new experience in motoring. It was not economical because of the curious fuel tax structure of the UK, and you could say it was more in the nature of a continuously sad experience.

The performance of the 300 D, however, is much better than the 200 D, and consists of a maximum speed of 96 mph (155 km/h), 0–30 mph of 4.9 plus 0–60 of 17.5 seconds. The real performance actually appears on motorways, where it will cruise for nights and days on end at 85 mph (137 km/h), getting steadily sweeter and more acceptable every hundred miles and with no wind noise at all.

While doing so, there is time to enjoy the car, apart from its engine. The power-steering is accurate and pleasant to use, the suspension, by double wishbones and semi-trailing arms, provides a neutral ride, and the brakes are superb, being discs all round. There is space everywhere and to spare. Passengers are all comfortable and the enormous boot will carry everything they may need. The controls and instruments are well placed and uncriticizable. Heating and ventilation are in the perfect category and even the automatic transmission seems to work remarkably well with the diesel engine.

Mercedes have also designed a turbocharged diesel which has been available in the USA for some time, after the development of the engine and world record runs in the CIII with an output of 170 kW (230 bhp).

The turbocharged 300 D has bath-nitrided crankshaft

Opposite: *A diesel-powered saloon visually similar to the S-class*

Right: *Rear view of the saloon with voluminous boot*

Mercedes-Benz 300 D Manual (Automatic)

Engine: 5 cylinders in line
Capacity: 2998 cc
Bore; stroke: 90.9 mm   92.4 mm
Compression ratio: 21 to 1
Injection: diesel injection mechanical
Max. power at 4400 rpm: 88 bhp   65 kW
Max. torque at 2400 rpm: 126.7 ft/lb   172 Nm

Transmission: Rear drive via 4 speed manual gear box or 4 speed automatic with torque converter

Suspension:
Front: coil springs, stabilizer and double control arms.
Rear: MB diagonal swing with brake torque compensation coil springs, stabilizer

Steering: MB power steering, 4.3 turns lock to lock

Brakes: Dual circuit servo assisted. Discs on all wheels

Dimensions:
Length: 15 ft 6 in   4.72 m
Kerb weight: 3560 lb   1615 kg

Performance:
Maximum speed: 96 (93) mph   155 (150) km/h
0–60 mph: 17.5 (18.6) sec
Fuel consumption
    at 56 mph: 32.5 (31.4) mpg   8.7 (9.0) litres/100 km
    at 75 mph: 22.8 (22.4) mpg   12.4 (12.6) litres/100 km
    urban: 24.6 (24.6) mpg   11.5 (11.5) litres/100 km

Insurance Rating: 7

Derived Data:
bhp/litre (kW/litre): 29.3   21.7
bhp/ton (kW/tonne): 52.1   37.9
Speed × acceleration: 5.48 (5)
Performance Dimension: 10.5 (9.6)
Fuel consumption/ton at 56 mph (10/F): 5.15 (5.33) (1.94 (1.88))
Change in fuel consumption between 56 & 75 mph: 42% (40%)

---

which doubles the fatigue strength, the pistons are cooled with an internal oil spray and the exhaust valves given additional sodium for cooling.

One remarkable fact about the turbo diesel is that the fuel consumption is below that of the 300 D, and even more so at higher speeds.

The 300 D which we subjected to a long drawn out test drive, was very much better than the 200 D which I found to be such a millstone to carry about, but the turbo 300 D sounds like the definitive answer to diesel motoring. If you refer to the table of comparative diesel fuel costs in the introduction to this section, you will realize why Mercedes have not considered the UK to be a suitable place to export their turbo-diesel.

This is the turbo-diesel. The 300 D has the same engine and gearbox. The turbocharger can be seen in the centre of the engine block, together with the regulating valve and wastegate

PEUGEOT 604 D

The Spartans had nothing to do with the 604 Peugeot series; it was the Epicureans. Rarely have such comfortable seats been seen in any limousine. This total extravagance can be coped with in normal countries where diesel fuel costs less than petrol because a massive turbo-diesel like the 604 D is not thirsty, and so powerful that the weight and wind resistance of this palace of luxury on wheels, is nothing. It can propel it all at 95 mph (153 km/h) and cruise quietly and contentedly at 80 mph (129 km/h), and all within 30–35 mpg.

The comfort does not stop with the seats, which are extraordinarily restful and quite enormous, but goes on to include every limousine necessity, together with the space usually found in the long wheelbase variety, or so it seems.

Diesel engines are different from spark ignition petrol engines. If you read the article on diesels, page 194, you will discover the technical reasons for their slightly odd behaviour. There is nothing you can do about it except

to learn a new technique. At first it seems like driving a shire horse; powerful, positive and self-willed. The engine revs are governed and one has to anticipate the rev limit on all five gears and change up just before it. Momentum must be conserved whenever possible, and overtaking planned ahead.

Although diesels have been improved to a remarkable extent within the last five years, this Peugeot diesel turbo especially, they can never be driven with the gusto of a petrol car. They *can* be driven hard and for long distances however, and the faster and harder they are driven the more smoothly and effortlessly they go. This Peugeot reduces the gap between petrol and diesel engines considerably for two reasons. The turbo improves the engine performance, and the car itself, that is the interior, the suspension, the ride and handling all show such a degree of refinement that the minor disadvantages seem negligible.

The turbo is of Garrett AiResearch design and manufacture, giving torque of 136 ft/lb at 2000 rpm and

Opposite: *Massive boot*

Right: *An orderly, organized engine bay despite the enormous size of the turbo-diesel*

Peugeot 604 Diesel Turbo

Engine: Garrett AiResearch T03 turbocharger, 4 cylinders in line, pushrod ohv
Capacity: 2304 cc
Bore; stroke: 94 mm   83 mm
Compression ratio: 21 to 1
Injection: Bosch
Max. power at 4150 rpm: 80 bhp   59.7 kW
Max. torque at 2000 rpm: 136 ft/lb   184.5 Nm

Transmission: 5 speed manual gearbox

Suspension:
Front: independent by MacPherson struts, coil springs and anti-roll bar.
Rear: independent by semi-trailing arms, coil springs and anti-roll bar

Steering: Rack and pinion
Turning circle: 37 ft 9 in   11.5 m

Brakes: Dual split front/rear servo assisted. 10.7 in (27.2 cm) front and rear discs

Dimensions:
Length: 15 ft 6 in   4.72 m
Weight unladen: 3229 lb   1465 kg

Performance:
Maximum speed: 95 mph (153 km/h)
0–60 mph: 16.6 sec
Fuel consumption
   at 56 mph: 46.3 mpg   6.1 litres/100 km
   at 75 mph: 32.8 mpg   8.6 litres/100 km
   urban: 29.4 mpg   9.6 litres/100 km
(French Government test)

Insurance Rating: 7

Derived Data:
bhp/litre (kW/litre): 34.7   25.9
bhp/ton (kW/tonne): 51.9   38.1
Speed × acceleration: 5.72
Performance Dimension: 11
Fuel consumption/ton at 56 mph (10/F): 3.96   (2.52)
Change in fuel consumption between 56 & 75 mph: 41%

---

maximum output at 4150 rpm of 80 bhp. Fuel injection is by Bosch. The fuel consumption can be 30 mpg, but driven as we have advised, it gave 28 mpg in a week of varied driving including London, motorways and country roads.

The power assisted rack and pinion steering is effective, and directional stability is excellent. The fact that the engine is by no means light makes the car noseheavy, and although the large disc brakes front and rear are effective, these two factors can present minor equilibrium problems.

Ventilation and heating are good, and the night driving with the reassuringly adjustable (by a wheel below the column) headlights, is without problems. In fact the Peugeot 604 D has all the refinements; electric window lifts, centrelocking, quartz clock, well designed warning lights and a pleasant, well designed interior with comfortable seats.

In order to drive this excellent engine efficiently, it needs a tachometer. There is no ignition system to make this an easy problem to solve, but it could be run from the signals controlling the fuel injection system. The instrument panel, already good, would then be excellent and the main differences in adjusting one's driving habits to the diesel would disappear.

RENAULT 18 D

The Renault diesel can be obtained as a saloon and an estate, and with a four or five speed gearbox, or automatic. The engine is arranged longitudinally and drives the front wheels. In the same way that the Golf diesel was designed to fit into the normal petrol version, the Renault 18 D appears to have almost identical features to the rest of the 18 series. The maximum speed is surprisingly near to that of most of the series, being 97 mph (156 km/h). Fuel consumption is naturally very much better than the petrol versions.

At the launch in April 1978, the Press Release gave comparative figures with the Opel Rekord, the VW Passat and Peugeot diesels, but omitted the vivacious Citroën CX 2500. The Renault goes faster than all of those mentioned and uses less fuel, except in comparison with the VW.

The engine has a capacity of 2068 cc, the same as the Renault 20, and is made at 'Française de Mécanique' Douvrin. Power is 50 kW (66.5 bhp) at 4500 rpm. At the launch its two principal virtues were pointed out as

'vivacité et économie' and both of these are due mainly to the design and production of the Douvrin power unit.

The remainder of the vehicle is well designed due to the remarkably competent team at Renault. The staff of the design department consists of 19 bodywork and interior stylists, 11 volume research men, 4 colour stylists and 43 model makers. Normally, the design team of 100 produces 20 full scale projects a year.

Today's car has two skins – an outer and an inner, and the link between them is technics. The design and styling department are very competent and produce work of a high standard – look for example at the Renault Fuego – and they are of course noticeably French, with a flair for colour, form, texture and the general habitability of the vehicles which have a positively feminine atmosphere without in any way producing boudoirs – and one of the stylists is Mlle I. Glovinski.

There is also a department concerned with design and safety which has produced new and extremely

E.T.A.I. France

Above: _This drawing shows the extra thickness and strength to crankshaft and connecting rods and the ingenius way in which camshafts and auxiliaries are driven by a belt_

Opposite: _The well designed 18 series has only the smallest sign to show that this one is a diesel_

useful findings in this area. One of the most startling of these was the fact that the plastic and stuffed dummies representing human bodies used by many manufacturers in their crash tests, all had necks which were very much stronger than our rather fragile human ones, so putting very much at nought years of crash test results.

Renaults are noted for their ride, due to a well organized suspension system and dampers which are right. Softly sprung, pitch and bounce are still well controlled. The 18 D is well packaged, offering interior space for 5 people and an adequate boot.

So far as the driver is concerned, the relationship between seat, pedals, major and minor controls is very good. The instruments are well laid out and easily seen. Heating and ventilation were very much praised by our passengers who normally consider this to be their domain. They found them easy to adjust, responsive and efficient. Of the two models available we found the estate to be the most satisfactory.

Renault 18 TD and GTD (Renault 18 Diesel)

Engine: '852' 4 stroke diesel in line, longitudinal
Capacity: 2068 cc
Bore; stroke: 86 mm   89 mm
Compression ratio: 21 to 1
Max. power at 4500 rpm: 66.5 bhp   49.6 kW
Max. torque at 2250 rpm: 93.3 ft/lb   127 Nm

Transmission: Five speed manual

Suspension: Anti-roll bars front and rear.
Front: independent with coil springs acting on double wishbones.
Rear: coil springs. Rigid axle on longitudinal radius arms

Steering: Rack and pinion (negative offset geometry)

Brakes: Diagonally split circuit servo assisted. Front discs and rear drums

Dimensions:
Length: 14 ft 4 in   4.37 m
Kerb weight: 2315 lb   1050 kg

Performance:
Maximum speed: 97 mph   156 km/h
0–60 mph (estimated): 14 sec
Fuel consumption
    at 56 mph: 54.3 mpg   5.2 litres/100 km
    at 75 mph: 39.2 mpg   7.2 litres/100 km
    urban: 32.5 mpg   8.7 litres/100 km

Insurance Rating: 5

Derived Data:
bhp/litre (kW/litre): 32.1   24
bhp/ton (kW/tonne): 6.31   43
Speed × acceleration: 6.9
Performance Dimension: 10.9
Fuel consumption/ton at 56 mph (10/F): 4.6   (2.18)
Change in fuel consumption between 56 & 75 mph: 38%

VOLKSWAGEN GOLF DIESEL

There is more shoulder room in the Golf Diesel than in the Daimler Sovereign (*Autocar*) and as with all the Golf range, five full size passengers can ride in comfort. The fuel efficiency is a remarkable 43.5 mpg and the top speed of 88 mph (142 km/h), like all diesel top speeds, can become a smooth cruising speed in those countries which permit such a thing. Although the Golf looks short, there is an area of 12.4 cu ft at the tailgate, which can be extended to 38.9 cu ft by removing three of the full size passengers. Since their inception a few years ago, we have considered that rear-window wash wipes should be compulsory as standard equipment and it is good to see that all Golfs have this.

The driver's position is workmanlike and pleasant, except for that dreadful little stylized animal in the centre of the wheel. Is it a wolf examining its tail? Dr Ferdinand Porsche would have some meaningful and unprintable German words to banish it to hell. The facia, instruments and controls are all first rate, and so are the heating and ventilation arrangements. The suspension with MacPherson struts and coil springs at the front, trailing arms linked by a torsional crossbeam with coil springs at the rear, with rack and pinion steering and disc front/drum rear brakes, provides a balanced ride and good all-round driveability.

The Golf's suspension has obviously been a subject of steady development since its inception, because we can remember a combination of float and jitter in the early models which has gone, leaving a very satisfactory ride for this size and cost of car. The subject of noise is very straightforward. Wind noise is non-existent due partly to Giugiaro's aerodynamic design of the bodyshell, and also to sound manufacturing. Suppression of tyre roar is better than it was with the early models, but the engine can be heard in no uncertain way.

The torque has been increased from 82 to 100 Nm at 3000 rpm, since the engine's capacity was raised to 1600 cc. There are also four more horses with the bhp, and the difference is a noticeable improvement on the first model.

Opposite: *Diesel 'World Car'?*

Right: *The product of a team of designers with several world diesel records for both speed and amazingly economical fuel consumption figures.*

Below: *A Giugiaro bodyshell which shows no signs of dating.*

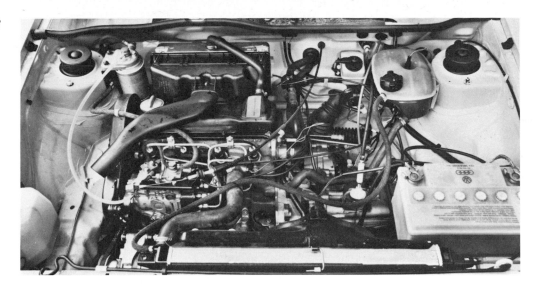

Volkswagen Golf Diesel (and E) 5 door

Engine: Four cylinders in line, transverse, front mounted
Capacity: 1588 cc
Bore; stroke: 76.5 mm   86.4 mm
Compression ratio: 23.5 to 1
Max. power at 4800 rpm: 54 bhp   40 kW
Max. torque at 3000 rpm: 73.4 ft/lb   100 Nm

Transmission: Four speed manual gearbox (4th overdrive on E) front wheel drive

Suspension:
Front: MacPherson struts and lower wishbones.
Rear: combined trailing arm torsion axle

Steering: Rack and pinion
Turning circle: 33 ft 9½ in   10.3 m

Brakes: Dual, diagonally divided and servo assisted. Front discs, rear drums

Dimensions:
Length: 12 ft 6 in   3.81 m
Kerb weight: 1863 lb   845 kg

Performance:
Maximum speed: 89 (86) mph   143 (138) km/h
0–60 mph: 16.8 (17.5) sec
Fuel consumption
   at 56 mph: 52.3 (61.4) mpg   5.4 (4.6) litres/100 km
   at 75 mph: 34.4 (41.5) mpg   8.2 (6.8) litres/100 km
   urban: 41.5 (47.1) mpg   6.8 (6.0) litres/100 km

Insurance Rating: 3

Derived Data: (using ½ laden weight)
bhp/litre (kW/litre): 34   25.2
bhp/ton (kW/tonne): 51.6   37.7
Speed × acceleration: 5.3 (5.0)
Performance Dimension: 10.3 (9.7)
Fuel consumption/ton at 56 mph (10/F): 5.16 (4.4)   (1.94 (2.27))
Change in fuel consumption between 56 & 75 mph: 52% (48%)

Whereas some diesels are gloomy, heavy handling and sluggish, the Golf diesel is positively merry. The gearchange being VW, is among the best of any car, front wheel drive or rear drive. The Beetle had an impeccable gearbox also.

Finally, there is a pleasant impression of space, solidity and quality, which is ultimately a better asset than digital clocks and electric window lifts.

DIESELS: SUMMARY

We have seen a little of the history of diesel development both in the introduction to this class and in chapter 8. While diesel fuel was so much cheaper, for political reasons, than high octane petrol, the diesel engine had its natural place as the powerful but somewhat sluggardly high mileage work-horse of the town taxis. Now that diesel fuel is more correctly priced in terms of its energy value, the diesel engine designers have had to think more carefully about how to take the natural advantage which should accrue from the greatly increased compression ratios which can be applied in such engines.

In terms of economy the advantage is obvious, given that the efficiency of an engine is very roughly $1 - 1/\sqrt{R}$, where R is the compression ratio. Typical values for R in a diesel are between 20 and 25, whereas a figure of 10 for a petrol engine is difficult to attain without considerable skill and lead additives in the fuel to inhibit preignition. It remains, however, appallingly difficult to get much power out of a diesel, mainly because of the engineering and materials problems associated with running them at high rpm. In the past they just haven't naturally competed on the performance front with petrol engines for the saloon car market.

It has taken the staggering, but, in terms of energy costs, realistic price increases of fuel generally over the last few years to force the manufacturers to think seriously about improving smaller diesel engines. Fortunately much larger, and hugely powerful turbocharged diesel engines have been marketed for some years for lorries, so at least some of the transition problems have been tackled relatively quickly and with more ease than with petrol engines.

This being, however, an essentially transitional period we see described in this class several of the older brethren, and only a few of the new generation.

Generally adequately pleasing cars to drive include, as always the Citroën CX 2500 D, and the Audi 100 LD, and both have the extremely high fuel efficiency figures to be expected for diesel powered vehicles. Mercedes have had it their own way for perhaps rather too long in this market, but the 300 D and the 300 TD estate (surely the right place for a diesel) certainly have comparatively speaking good PDs and reasonable fuel efficiency, provided that is we steer clear of the automatics. But this is of course true whether the car is petrol or diesel powered.

The more exciting developments in the field are of course the turbocharged diesels and we have described three, the Renault 18 TD, the Peugeot 604 TD and the Mercedes 300 TD turbo. As a group they make a particularly interesting comparison, in that they demonstrate that at least reasonable performances can be attained even with relatively small engines. The Mercedes figure of 7.1 with, admittedly, a large engine by comparison with that of the Renault, with comparable performance, is clearly by current standards admirable. With their big 604, Peugeot tend to the other extreme of improving still further the fuel efficiency with bearable performance.

Perhaps the most remarkable development has been the VW Golf diesel demonstrating that reasonable power can be delivered by even small engines of the unturbocharged type. The cars in E form further show that as more diesel cars are developed we will soon see the CD trend (*Fuel Efficiency*, page 92) for the diesels that has already been noted for petrol driven cars.

Class 9	Data Summary				
Datum Point		Perform-ance	Power Weight	PD	FE
A	Audi Avant L5D	5.3	54	9.8	2.08
B	Citroën CX 2500D	5.3	54	9.7	2.26
C	Mercedes-Benz 300 D	5.5	52	10.5	1.94
Ca	Mercedes-Benz 300 DA	5	52	9.6	1.88
D	Mercedes-Benz 300 TD	5.2	54	9.8	2.05
Da	Mercedes-Benz 300 TDA	4.7	54	8.8	1.74
E	Mercedes-Benz 300 TD	7.1	74	9.6	2.11
F	Peugeot 604 D Turbo	5.7	52	11	2.52
G	Renault 18D Turbo	6.9	63	10.9	2.18
H	VW Golf D	5.3	52	10.3	1.94
I	VW Golf D (E)	5.0	52	9.7	2.27

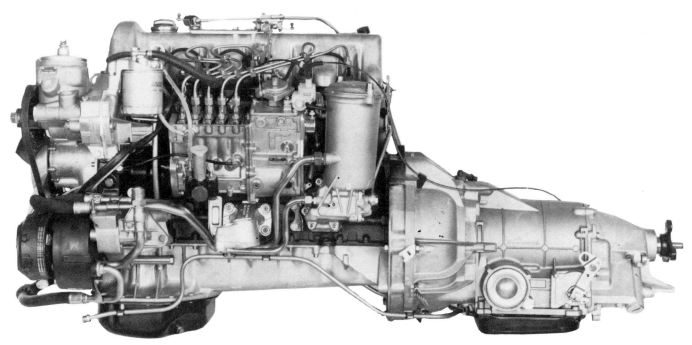

Mercedes 300 D turbo engine, with new four speed automatic gearbox

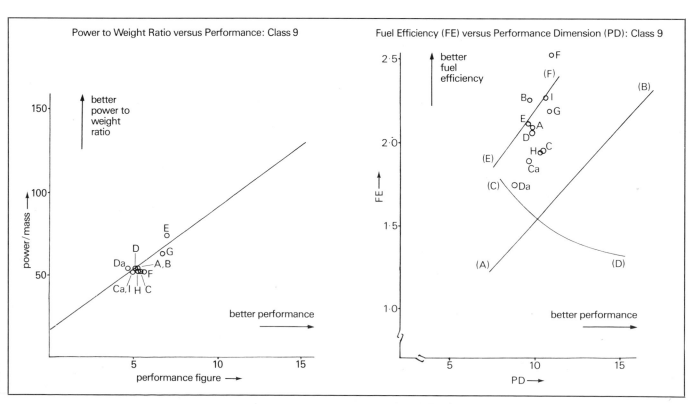

Power to Weight Ratio versus Performance: Class 9

Fuel Efficiency (FE) versus Performance Dimension (PD): Class 9

9 Carozzeria Italiana

Chariot racing and design reached its peak in Roman times when there were race tracks in all the large towns in Italy. They consisted of two long straights with semicircular ends; basic, like Indianapolis. Horses were bred for speed and power, light chariots designed for manoeuvrability, but with enough strength to take buffetting and shunting, and professional drivers went from track to track, like F1 drivers. Sociologists say that this was all organized by the ruling classes to keep the people happy – bread and circuses. If the Caesars had not built the tracks, the charioteers would have raced round the houses.

Racing is a perennial and inextinguishable passion, but the Romans gave it something extra with the splendour of their chariots and horse harness, and the bravura of the event. It was not just racing, it was charioteering with style and magnificence. The Italians have never let this exultation die. Drive any Ferrari, Alfa Romeo, Lamborghini, or a Fiat-Abarth and Ben Hur sits beside you.

Perhaps it is not surprising that in our century, year in year out, at the motor shows at Turin, Paris, Geneva, Frankfurt and Birmingham, it is the Italian coachbuilders who produce cars which are works of art. Pininfarina has celebrated his 50th anniversary of designing bodies for Ferrari, Peugeot and Austin-Morris, which are remembered with respect for their balanced moderation.

Bertone is the oldest of the existing Carrozzerias, with a history of 65 years in which they have not only designed, annually, the outstandingly best cars, but shown repeatedly a psychic instinct about the future forms of cars. Bertone prototypes at the shows always appear *too* avant garde. No manufacturer in his right mind would put them into production. Yet, two years later, they appear quite normally acceptable, with admittedly modified versions being driven everywhere.

The products of the Carrozzeria Bertone can be divided into four groups: 1, those designed by the founder, Giovanni Bertone until the Second World War; 2, the period when Scaglione was chief designer; 3, those produced with Giugiaro as the chief stylist; and 4, the current period with Gandini at the head. The

designers themselves at the Bertone carrozzeria always call their work running sculpture: and so, of course, does Henry Moore.

Of all the postwar stylists, it is Giugiaro who has had the most amazingly widespread effect. It is as though his work has hypnotized all Europe. A résumé of his life should be an inspiration to young artists and designers. Giorgetto Giugiaro was born in Piedmont, 7th August 1938. His father and grandfather worked at decorating churches and palaces. But further back, in Roman times, they were surely designing the best chariots. At age 12 Giugiaro went to Turin to study painting at the Accademia di Belle Arti, followed by a three year course in technical design. When 17, at the diploma show at the end of his training, Giugiaro met Dante Giacosa, head of Fiat *Centro Stile*, who offered him a job at Mirafiori. Giugiaro stayed at Fiat four years, when he moved to Carrozzeria Bertone's *Centro Stile*.

Working at Fiat had given him a basic training and he now began to work more freely without the restraint and conditioning of the large company. He produced several designs for Alfa Romeo – the 2000 Sprint, and the Giulia GT. Then the Aston Martin DB4, BM4 3200, Maserati 5000, Ferrari Asa 1000, Iso Rivolta, Ferrari 250 GT, and the Iso Grifo Coupe. In 1963 he designed the classic 'Testudo' for GM Chevrolet, shown at the 1964 Geneva show. This was followed by the Alfa Romeo Canguro, the Ford Mustang AQ, Fiat 850 Spyder, all in 1965, as well as the Fiat Dino Coupe.

Then Giugiaro moved to Ghia. The manager of the company was at that time Giacomo Gaspardo Moro, who appointed Giugiaro head of the *Centro Progetti e Stile*, at the age of 27. In 1966, he designed the de Tomaso 2000 and the Isuzu 117 Coupe, and for the Turin show the Maserati Ghibli, de Tomaso Mangusta, Pampero, and Fiat 850 Vanessa. In 1967 Giugiaro started his own studio, continuing with Ghia as a consultant.

In 1968 Giugiaro established Italdesign, with Aldo Mantovani in charge of car engineering and Luciano Bosio dealing with manufacturing processes and automation methods for mass production. Italdesign is a new kind of motor car company: it offers a complete

Alfa Romeo Caimano (prototype 1971) designed by Giugiaro.

Alfa Romeo Iguana (prototype), presented by Giugiaro at the Turin Show.

all-round service: not only styling and design, but the development of production equipment, the building of prototypes and the analysis of methods and costs for mass production processes. The first full-scale project of Italdesign was the entire pre-production phase of the Alfa Romeo Sud, including styling, designing, methods, equipment, time and motion study and costing. The Alfasud was presented for the 1971 Turin show, while for the same occasion Giugiaro had designed (together with the Alfasud Caimano) the Abarth 1600, the Alfa Romeo Iguana (prototype), the VW Porsche Tapiro and the VW Karman Cheetah.

In 1972 Giugaro brought out the Maserati Boomerang at Geneva, the Maserati Merak in Paris and the Lotus Esprit in Turin. In 1973 the designs for VW Passat, and in 1974 the Golf and Scirocco, were by Giugiaro. In 1976, at the invitation of the New York Museum of Modern Art, he built a taxi prototype for the eighties. At the 1979 Geneva show Giugiaro presented the Ace of Clubs, a four seater coupé designed with aerodynamic qualities and comfort combined.

Whereas Dr F. Porsche was probably the greatest engineer of the internal combustion engine and car designer of the early twentieth century, Giugiaro, commencing from the outside of the car as a stylist and moving inwards to power train and suspension geometry, has become the person with the widest visual influence over the car in the second half of the century.

Horseless chariots have seen many changes in the last 99 years. The fuel crisis has whittled away much of the ostentation and fantasy; and the stringent need to comply with acceptable power/weight ratios, together with the dictates of wind tunnel tests, have produced new, basic automobiles. Unfortunately, they are beginning to look, some of them, like the same basic automobile. If designers must use identical parameters, and they must, then the end products will have more than a few points of similarity.

The interior is determined by anthropometrics. An average sized seated figure is surrounded by the straitjacket of dimensions from head to roof line, knee to facia, shoulders to tumblehome, hands to wheel, and feet to pedals. This can be seen in all brochures from all manufacturers. The exterior in turn is determined very much by the coefficient of drag.

It would take a genius to comply with all these unavoidable points of reference, both inside and outside the bodyshell, and produce a work of art in fluid dynamics. This Giugiaro has done repeatedly and so has Gandini, chief designer for the Carrozzeria Bertone, whose works include the Lamborghini Countach, the Lancia Stratos and the Fiat X1/9. Giugiaro and Gandini have done more than design some of the best bodyshells. They have produced a style which in turn has influenced other designers in firms all over the world.

Class 10 Grand Cars

INTRODUCTION

Grand in conception and fabulous in the quality of design, engineering and craftsmanship, as beautiful to contemplate as to drive, and with no concern whatsoever with cost, is what we are dealing with in this class. We wrote to Ferrari, mentioning this, and they sent photographs and specifications of the Mondial 8. The Rolls-Royce Silver Spirit has recently been announced, and the new Mercedes S class, Porsche have produced the 928 S, and there are the 7 series BMWs.

They are all good, but there is the shadow of a depression about, and it was *the* Depression which made most of the grand cars disappear with a puff of smoke in the early thirties. There is also an irresistible social consciousness which is, with a force greater than the impending depression, undermining the exalted spirits of the designers and the potential buyers. Why are we not designing cars and agricultural machinery for the Third World?

There always has been a lot of exchange of ideas in the car design business. One of the ways in which cars have developed has been by copying new technology from the best ones whenever possible and it is still going on – car heating, synchromesh, better suspension systems, all started with the grand cars, as did tinted glass, electric window lifts and centre locking, and already they have reached across the market place.

The really early cars were all capable of the grand conception; Panhards, Renaults, Daimler-Benz, Rolls-Royce Silver Ghosts, looked and *were* grand without really trying – it was their métier to be bigger than life size. Pride in craftsmanship was an everyday practice.

The histories of architecture, furniture and jewellery give some indication of the life, ideas and spirit of people at various periods in time, but the history of the motor car gets nearer to the vitals and spirit.

This section is concerned with vehicles of the highest standards. We have dealt with cars for ordinary mortals elsewhere, in the categories 500–1200 cc, 1200–1400 cc, 1400–1700 cc, 1700–2200 cc, 2200–3 litres.

The builders of the beautiful early horseless carriages found Royal patronage came quite readily. Kaiser Wilhelm encouraged Wilhelm Maybach to put one of his racing engines into the royal landaulette. King George V always went to Ascot in his Daimler (still using the 1907 to the 1913 races we see, a careful monarch). King Alfonso XIII of Spain encouraged Marc Birkigt with his aero-engines and Hispano-Suiza limousines, so that Birkigt named his type T15 the Alfonso XIII in his honour. He then produced the type 68, a V12 of 9427 cc with a 100 × 100 mm bore and stroke, initially for Alfonso, but eventually for those commoners who could see a sensible way of life in a car weighing three tons with a top speed of 110 mph, 0–60 in 12 seconds and all with silence and less than 3000 rpm.

At the same time, Isotta-Fraschini were producing similar enormous masterpieces, like the 1925 Tipo 8 two seater convertible with a wheelbase of 145 inches, a seven litre, one hundred and fifty brake horsepower engine with the same simple beauty as a Bugatti, and a body by Castagna. While the type 41 Bugatti Royale, the ultimate car of this period, with an engine of 12,763 cc, did not meet with real demand, one of the engines showed its quality by pulling a train in the 1940s.

It is the vision, engineering efficiency, design and craftsmanship of the Bugatti's set standards, like those of Henry Royce and Marc Birkigt, which this section is about. There are many examples, but we think of Bugatti's 5 litre type 50, with Carrosserie by Profilée for example, and the 57c with coachwork by Gangloff.

Louis Delage also produced grand cars, with bodies by Letournier et Marchand and others. So did the Packard brothers, their quality receiving an accolade in the fact that Ettore Bugatti owned one and often used it for long journeys in preference to one of his own – Packards are very much in line with this small role of honour, the 1934 V12 sports sedan for example with coachwork by Dietrich. Many of these firms have died of course, or have been merged, or their names are used like flags, to suggest the old mystique by manufacturers.

We are now living, however, in the age of NACA, the shuttle, Concorde and enormous progress in electronics, together with the beginnings of a global social consciousness which will soon have more influence on the shape and design of the motor car than the

Aston Martin Volante

razzmatazz of the glorious but unthinking Edwardians had on the early engineers, or the millionaires of the thirties. Legend tells us that the wheel was invented by a Chinese philosopher who was watching the course taken by the corolla of a flower moved by the wind through the grass. Centuries later a wheel *was* made at Ur in 4000 BC (but as an ornament), and in 3500 BC it was used solid for heaving carts. It has gone a long way, that wheel, and might well concern itself back in China soon, where there are millions of people and enormous distances.

Meanwhile, there are the grand cars shown here,

which, like those which have been described for other periods in time, represent the standards of engineering, body design and manufacturing of the eighties. Museums of motor cars are appearing in most countries and it is interesting to see how the earliest models have a purity of form, and simplicity of design which shows their earnest and unswerveable intent; cars of the Edwardian period, reflecting the healthy flamboyance of their owners, the Duesenbergs reminiscent of the hoods of the Prohibition period because of their speed and efficiency, and through it all a few world marques retaining a consistency of thought and design.

ASTON MARTIN LAGONDA

The Lagonda has a potent thoroughbred engine in a chassis which provides it with the suspension it deserves, producing a ride and handling balance as good as that of any car currently available. The aesthetically commanding bodyshell by William Towns gives an immediate indication of its character. The Lagonda is a unique motorcar. The quality control in its construction is reassuringly continuous, for it is simply part and parcel of the integrity of the craftsmen who make the car. Each engine is made by, and is the responsibility of, one engineer, whose name appears on a small brass plate on each engine. The practice is reminiscent of Rolls-Royce while Henry was alive, as is the small factory in which the Aston Martins are made.

The Lagonda is a car as satisfying to drive as it is in which to be driven. It is satisfying to the driver because of its remarkable performance, fine steering and handling, due partly to the 50/50 weight distribution. It is satisfying for the passengers because of its stability, refinement and comfort. The car is taut, crisp and very much faster than luxury saloons are expected to be, and the passengers are not thrown about, however hard it is driven.

In the Lagonda one has a feeling of a new dimension in driving and being driven, a feeling of controlled other worldliness, of the achievement of near perfection in the car's most essential features – and these are surely the impeccable balance between power train, suspension and steering geometry, and the superbly co-ordinated aerodynamics of the bodyshell.

The Lagonda needs Bosch Motronic. It simply cannot afford to be without the best fuel injection system that is known, so near as it is to a rare kind of perfection.

Opposite and above: *An impeccable front end by William Towns*
Below: *The engineer will personally sign his engine with a brass plate*

Aston Martin Lagonda

Engine: V8 with dohc per bank. Alloy block and head, front mounted driving rear wheels
Capacity: 5340 cc
Bore; stroke: 100 mm 85 mm
Compression ratio: 9.3 to 1
Carburation: 4 Weber 42 DNCF/twin choke downdraught
No brake horsepower or torque figures are available

Transmission: 3 speed automatic/Chrysler Torqueflite

Suspension:
Front: independent by double wishbones, co-axial coil springs and dampers, anti-roll bar.
Rear: De Dion rear axle located by parallel trailing links and Watts linkage, co-axial coil springs and self-levelling dampers

Steering: Burman power rack and pinion

Brakes: Ventilated discs front and rear. Rear inboard

Dimensions:
Kerb weight: 4551 lb 2064 kg
Weight distribution: front and back 50/50

Performance:
Maximum speed: 145 mph 233 km/h
0–60 mph: 7.9 sec
Speed × acceleration: 18.3

ASTON MARTIN VANTAGE

The Aston Martin's 90 degree V8 engine of 5340 cc capacity is basically the same as that used in the Lagonda. Its output figures are undisclosed, but its acceleration and general performance are such that the brake horsepower must be in the region of 450. In fifth gear the engine pulls at 26.25 mph per 1000 rpm, and the car weighs two tons. The power/weight ratio is probably in the region of 225 bhp/ton, delivered through a five speed ZF box.

Whereas the Lagonda has a quality which is almost other worldly, the Vantage is all muscle and reality. The engine revs to more than 6000 rpm but only the best drivers will see 6000 in any gear, particularly fourth. 100 mph is less than third gear's maximum and less than its comfortable cruising speed. 5000 rpm in fifth gives 130 mph plus and a comfortable unstressed rate of progress. Another 1000 rpm (to the 6000 we were talking about) and it is 160 mph. From rest to 100 mph takes 13 seconds.

Whereas the Lagonda tends to isolate the driver from

the machinery, the Vantage communicates it in a very dynamic way and at all times. It is not through the medium of loud noise, for the car is fairly quiet at 100 mph; but one has an awareness of the power and glory of that estimated 450 brake horsepower which it produces without harshness or vibration.

The Vantage is devoid of vices and gives warning when it feels that it is being mishandled. Possessing one of the most powerful engines ever to be put into a road car, there is something heroic about it. In some ways it is a reincarnation of the Bentleys, brought up to date with more recent technology, but with the same virility and massive grandeur.

The Aston Martin V8 and the Volante also have the 5340 cc V8 engine, but in a less celestial state of tune. The following figures give the facts:

	Maximum speed	0–60/seconds
V8	145 mph (233 km/h)	6.6
Volante	130 mph (209 km/h)	7.0

Above: *The same fabulous engine, with various modifications, is used in all the Aston Martin/Lagonda cars, all with Webers and torque flite automatic gearboxes*

Right: *Aston Martin convertible*

Opposite: *Aston Martin Vantage saloon*

| Vantage | 160 mph (258 km/h) | 5.4 |
| Lagonda | 130 mph (209 km/h) | 7.9 |

These four cars all show integrity in design, engineering and craftsmanship, and the level of that achievement is shown in the above table of speed and acceleration times. Compare them with the statistics of all other cars and you will find that only the Porsche Turbo 3.3 can better the acceleration time of the Vantage, and the top speed is the same.

Right: *A facia similar to that of a Ferrari*

BMW 735i

BMW have adopted the advanced Bosch Motronic fuel injection together with transistorized ignition and the latest electronic engine management systems, which gives them performance together with good fuel economy. Their continual and successful involvement in motor sports means, of necessity, continual engine development and the connection between this and the 735i is positive and very real.

The 3.5 litre engine first appeared in the 635 CSi, then in the fabulous M1 mid engined coupé with the addition of a 24 valve head and dry sump which gave it 277 bhp as a road car and 400 bhp in Group 5 tune. The engine as used with the 735i has a single overhead camshaft and produces 218 bhp at 5200 and 228 ft/lb torque at 4000 rpm. The bodyshell could be improved aerodynamically by simply changing the nose, but the kerb weight is very good at 31.0 cwt. (Mercedes 500 SE 31.9 cwt.)

The performance is vivid and most impressive. Only 4400 rpm are needed for a constant 120 mph (193 km/h),

which it achieves effortlessly, but speeds beyond this are impeded by wind resistance which that improved nose would help to solve. The indirect fifth gear is excellent. Strong clutches are to be expected in engines of this calibre. While the overall mpg is officially stated to be 17.3, we achieved over 20 in three days of very mixed conditions – London, motorways and mountain roads in Scotland.

The BMW accepts the entire set of Bosch patents by also using the ABS anti-lock braking system which in the best of all possible worlds should be made compulsory, being not merely good but fabulous, achieving better than 1.0 g on retardation.

The car is well designed and completely equipped in every way. The electrically adjusted door mirrors, electric window lifts, centre locking doors, headlamp level adjustment, digital clock and 10 second interior light delay to give you time to insert the ignition key, together with a superb heating/ventilating system and ergonomically designed seats, are comprehensive aids

Opposite: *Just as they say, this saloon in many ways really* is *the ultimate*

Right: *The six-cylinder engine in 218 bhp form is masterly and uncriticizable*

BMW 735i

Engine: 6 cylinders in line
Capacity: 3453 cc
Bore; stroke: 93.4 mm   84 mm
Compression ratio: 9.3 to 1
Injection: Bosch L-Jetronic
Max. power at 5200 rpm: 218 bhp   160 kW
Max. torque at 4000 rpm: 228.6 ft/lb   310 Nm

Transmission: 5 speed gearbox (3 speed automatic with torque converter optional)

Suspension:
Front: independent sprung legs, torsion bar stabilizer. Positive and negative stroke dampers.
Rear: independent 3 point suspension of axle/gearbox carrier, sprung legs with trailing arms, swing brackets on differential

Steering: Powered ZF recirculating ball
Turning circle: 38 ft   11.6 m

Brakes: Dual diagonally split servo assisted. 11 in (27.9 cm) front ventilated discs, 11 in (27.9 cm) rear solid discs

Dimensions:
Length: 15 ft 11 in   4.86 m
Kerb weight: 3374 lb   1530 kg

Performance:
Maximum speed: 132 mph   212 km/h
0–60 mph: 7.3 sec
Fuel consumption
　at 56 mph: 27.3 mpg   8.6 litres/100 km
　at 75 mph: 21.8 mpg   10.8 litres/100 km
　urban: 20 mpg   11.8 litres/100 km

Insurance Rating: 9

Derived Data:
bhp/litre (kW/litre): 63.1   46.3
bhp/ton (kW/tonne): 135.7   98.1
Speed × acceleration: 18.1
Performance Dimension: 13.3
Petrol consumption/ton at 56 mph (10/F): 5.35   (1.87)
Change in petrol consumption between 56 & 75 mph: 25%

---

to total comfort and therefore efficient driving and/or being driven.

The pilot could well be a chauffeur, in this large BMW, designed for taking passengers to the theatre, or long distances up the motorways in a short time, like London to Aberdeen in 7 hours, including long stops for meals of course. And the chauffeur has a proper facia, tilted towards him and away from the front seat passenger. Pedals of the right size, feel and position, a wheel with the right lock, and two stalk primary switches. The whole is complemented by a facia with dash-mounted controls together with the visual check control of fluid levels and electric functions.

Enough, together with one of the best 6-cylinder engines in the world, to show the passengers how near to ultimate perfection this comfortable, safe, luxurious, high-speed saloon can achieve.

The computer will display the following information on the facia:

Outside temperature (with an audible warning when the temperature drops to near freezing and there is a risk of ice on the road).

Pre-set speed limit – with audible warning if speed is exceeded.

Fuel consumption; first, actual consumption at the instant of checking, and then average consumption over current journey. For economy driving, set yourself a specific mpg. A warning sounds when this figure is exceeded.

Estimated remaining mileage before refuelling needed.

Distance to the required motorway exit – with an audible warning prior to turn off.

Alarm clock. Audible warning when required time is reached.

Remaining distance to journey's end, plus estimated time of arrival.

DAIMLER 5.3 SERIES III DOUBLE SIX

The twelve cylinder engined series III Daimler Double Six with a Performance Dimension of 13.5 is better even than the 12.8 for the Mercedes 500 SEL. This is not to say that the S series, or any other Mercedes, is bad, nor for that matter is the BMW 735i with a PD of 12.5; it is simply that the series III 5.3 litre Daimler is a better car in this respect. Also the essentials of the car have been around for a long time. Once one has come to this conclusion on the basis of the car's stark performance data, one starts looking harder at this bit of English history.

At this point we should admit that we have not driven a 5.3 series III spruced up by BL. In fact the firm was nearly the only manufacturer which was not re-markably co-operative in letting us drive its cars. It should thus be clear that in no way are we exactly biased in favour of BL products. Fortunately, however, either by finding understanding salesmen or by badgering despairing friends with the right car we managed to try out all the firm's cars which could conceivably have

been interesting enough to discuss.

The discreet, smooth and yet firmly stated power of the Daimler makes us think seriously of finding some way of reaching the appropriate boardroom status to be given one. Reading other tests of both the 5.3 and the 4.2 straight XJ6 engined Jaguars and Daimlers, we detect the same feeling.

Nearly all writers end up by commenting on these cars' quietness and breeding, usually by using that word 'refinement'. For once we think that at least the 5.3 Daimler deserves it. More to the point, it accurately describes the process of development which the Daimlers have undergone over the last ten years. We can only hope that the evolution will continue in such a way that the Double Six remains better than anything that could be classed as a rival.

The process will not, however, continue unless British Leyland get back into racing their cars. It is on the race track that all the developments of Jaguar cars were made in the past and, as tax payers, we would welcome

Opposite: The Daimler Double Six has the advantage of an engine originally designed for Formula One

Right: As impeccable a piece of engineering as you are likely to see, before 1990. The V12, now with Lucas electronic injection at the heart of it

Daimler 5.3 Series III Double Six Vanden Plas

Engine: 60° V12 aluminium alloy block and head 2 sohc
Capacity: 5343 cc
Bore; stroke: 90 mm   70 mm
Compression ratio: 9 to 1
Injection: Lucas electronic
Max. power at 5800 rpm: 285 bhp   212.6 kW
Max. torque at 3500 rpm: 294 ft/lb   399 Nm

Transmission: Automatic GM40 3 speed is standard. A 5 speed manual box is optional for the 4.2 6-cylinders

Suspension:
Front: independent semi trailing wishbones and coil springs. Anti-roll bar.
Rear: lower transverse wishbones with drive shafts as upper links. Twin coil springs and anti-roll bar

Steering: Adwest power assisted rack and pinion. 3 turns lock to lock

Brakes: Dual circuit front/rear. Servo assisted. 11.2 in (28.5 cm) ventilated front discs, 10.4 in (26.4 cm) solid rear discs

Dimensions:
Length: 16 ft 3 in   4.96 m
Kerb weight: 4300 lb   1950 kg

Performance:
Maximum speed: 145 mph   233 km/h
0–60 mph: 7.6 sec
Fuel consumption
   at 56 mph: 19.3 mpg   14.6 litres/100 km
   at 75 mph: 16.7 mpg   16.9 litres/100 km
   urban: 10.9 mpg   25.9 litres/100 km

Insurance Rating: 8

Derived Data:
bhp/litre (kW/litre): 53.3   39.8
bhp/ton (kW/tonne): 141   103.6
Speed × acceleration: 19.1
Performance Dimension: 13.5
Petrol consumption/ton at 56 mph (10/F): 7.23   (1.38)
Change in petrol consumption between 56 & 75 mph: 16%

---

more investment of our money by BL on new projects of this type. Without this approach history demonstrates that the new product on the road is an untried and uncried over milksop to be buried in the commercial competition, or hard sold to the extent that the multitude of purchasers does the car testing!

We have said undeservedly little about the Double Six. Our apologies, but then the data and the pictures speak for themselves, and the magazines have done a fine job of picking out the car's few past faults, most of which seem now to be buried. Unlike most writers, and despite being all out for development in the appropriate place, we actually rather like not only the good hide upholstery, but also the slightly dated though very clearly equipped facia, reflections or not. In many ways one hears too much about such things – anyway, when it is sunny, what owner driver needs to keep his eyes glued to the instruments like a pilot on his first solo?

The engine has been described in the article on the XJS, and the ride and handling of the car are about as

good as one could imagine for a car of this size. We have only one suggestion to offer, and that is to make the 5 speed manual gearbox, optional on the XJ6, not just an option on the Double Six but standard. Until automatic gearboxes have undergone far more radical design changes than seem to be likely for some time, the best will only be got out of this, or any car, efficiently in an energy conscious world by giving up the children of the fluid flywheel, even if this too is a memory in Daimler's history.

Luxury and speed in equal proportions. Body by Pininfarina and power by Ferrari

FERRARI MONDIAL 8

A true thoroughbred in terms of power output, performance and roadholding, this new Ferrari is designed as a high speed GT with four seats, a large luggage compartment, a flexible and thoroughly soundproofed engine, and comprehensive equipment. Today, the market for high-class sports cars amounts to 0.7 per thousand in Italy, 0.9 per cent in France, 3.4 per cent in the UK and 8.8 per cent in West Germany. America of course is the largest and most important market. There has been an increasing tendency for motorists to expect a sports car to encompass the comfort and appointments of a luxury saloon. This car is therefore a combination of the performance of a sports car with the comfort of a saloon – a genuine grand tourer, and has succeeded in no uncertain way.

The Mondial has a tubular chassis frame, V engine with dual overhead camshaft on each bank, cylinder block and head in light alloy, five speed gearbox and limited slip differential. The engine is derived from that of the 308 (described under sports cars) but it has

benefited by several improvements.

The first development is the use of Marelli electronic ignition. Instead of a single spark advance curve found with conventional systems, this supplies 8 curves, each of them adequate for a predetermined level of vacuum in the induction manifold. The spark advance angle no longer depends on the number of revs alone, but on the vacuum also, i.e. on engine load. This provides improved performance together with reduced fuel consumption. Moreover, because of the absence of points, centrifugal masses, springs and bearings, the coil ignition is reduced to a frictionless distribution rotor fitted at the end of the camshaft, with no setting problems and no wear. Bosch fuel injection is also used.

The engine provides a maximum power output of 214 bhp at 6600 rpm and a torque of 179 ft/lb (243 Nm) at 4600 rpm. The engine has a rev-limiting device which limits it to 7500 rpm.

The 5 speed gearbox has an oil pump for lubricating the gears. This is unusual and expensive. The limited slip

226

Civilization is always near Rome

Ferrari Mondial 8/2 + 2

Engine: 90° V8 light alloy block and head. Dual overhead camshaft on each back, where valves in V at 46°. Developed from the 308 with Marelli Digiplex electronic ignition and fuel injection.
Capacity: 2926 cc
Bore; stroke: 81 mm   71 mm
Compression ratio: 8.8 to 1
Injection: Bosch K-Jetronic
Max. power at 6600 rpm: 214 bhp   158 kW
Max. torque at 4600 rpm: 179 ft/lb   243 Nm

Transmission: 5 speed manual gearbox with pumped oil lubrication

Suspension: The Ferrari tubular frame is modified, the rear part carrying engine, gearbox and suspension being removable for easier maintenance. Transverse quadrilaterals, coil springs and Koni oleodynamic dampers

Dimensions:
Length: 15 ft 3 in   4.65 m
Kerb weight: 3225 lb   1463 kg

Performance:
Maximum speed: 142 mph   230 km/h
0–60 mph: ~ 6.8 sec*
Fuel consumption
    at 40 km/h: 21.2 mpg   13.3 litres/100 km
*Estimated from standing 400 m time

Insurance Rating: 7

Derived Data:
bhp/litre (kW/litre): 73   54
bhp/ton (kW/tonne): 139   101
Speed × acceleration: 20.9
Performance Dimension: 15

---

differential is integral with the gearbox. The tubular frame body has a new development, in that the rear end of the chassis frame carrying engine, gearbox and suspension is entirely removable for maintenance operations – a remarkable departure from the old classical GTs.

The body is by Pininfarina, and marked by huge glass areas. The 2650 mm wheelbase, 10 cm longer than the GT 4, has made greater space available for the rear passengers, who also have anatomically shaped seats.

The instruments are all round of course and include electronic innovations. These are rev counter, speedometer, oil thermometer, oil pressure gauge, water temperature gauge. The central console carries a control panel monitoring the efficiency of stop lights, parking lights, engine oil level, gearbox oil level, radiator fluid level, brake system warning light etc.

Standard specifications include air conditioning, electric windows, centralized locking, electromagnetic opening of engine, boot and petrol tank lids, and

steering wheel adjustment for height and reach, together with the normal range of equipment.

With a maximum output of 214 bhp, the performance is vivid.

The new Mondial is named after the Mondial of the fifties, which was so successful in competition, with its 170 bhp from 1984 cc; the idea being that the new Mondial is an expression of the racing pedigree of Ferrari, together with the luxury and comfort of a GT – a high-speed and comfortable executive's express.

MERCEDES-BENZ 380 SE and 500 SE

The performance, handling and ride quality of these cars are all in the impeccable category. Mercedes testing is carried out at the Hockenheim Grand Prix circuit which is an hour's drive from Untertürkheim and it is obvious that the designers have used it continuously and to the advantage of all Mercedes drivers.

Passenger comfort is total; the door height has even been enlarged to make entry and exit easier, just as Giugiaro has been suggesting with his prototype the Megagamma, which Lancia have not yet put into production. Seat belt location has thoughtfully arranged different settings to suit passengers of varying sizes.

The bodyshell is entirely new, 8.5 per cent lighter, and incorporates a much larger glass area than the model it replaces. There is also a wider use of plastic, especially noticeable in the full-length strips along the sides as sill protection, together with deformable bumpers. The drag coefficient is 0.37 and the recession of the wipers beneath the contoured bonnet makes a cleaner line, but aerodynamics and aesthetics are the outer skins of a

body which although lighter, retains the well known Mercedes rigidity in the right places; look for example at the drawing of a section of roof line.

The new all-alloy 90 degree V8 engine is available in two sizes, 3818 cc or 4973 cc. Both engines drive their rear wheels through a new four-speed automatic gearbox. There is a single overhead camshaft for each bank of cylinders driven by Duplex chains, and induction is by Bosch K-Jetronic, the mechanical system of injection. The 380, with a compression ratio of 9:1, develops 218 bhp, and the 500 has an output of 240 bhp. The 380 has a cruising speed of 120 mph or more.

Mercedes-Benz have discovered that the average annual mileage of the S class saloons is 16,000 miles (25,000 km) which is almost twice that of the average of all cars in Europe, and that the percentage of miles on motorways is much higher than average. The new engines are designed to cope with these facts.

The four speed automatic transmission has been

Opposite: *This picture shows the 280 SE, 380 SE and 500 SE. The overhead camshafts of the 280 SE are on the left*

Right: *The power unit for the 380 and 500 with the Bosch fuel injection system in the V, the new automatic gearbox to the left and immaculate engineering pervading it all*

Mercedes-Benz 500 SEL

Engine: V8 all light alloy, cylinders protected by silicon, sohc/bank
Capacity: 4973 cc
Bore; stroke: 96.5 mm   85 mm
Compression ratio: 8.8 to 1
Injection: Mechanical fuel injection
Max. power at 4750 rpm: 240 bhp   177 kW
Max. torque at 3200 rpm: 297.7 ft/lb   404 Nm

Transmission: MB automatic 4 speed to rear wheels

Suspension:
Front: axle with double wishbones, coil springs and anti-roll bar.
Rear: diagonal swing axle, coil springs, and anti-roll bar

Steering: MB power assisted. 2.75 turns lock to lock
Turning circle: 40 ft 3 in   12.16 m

Brakes: Dual circuit, discs front and rear

Dimensions:
Length: 16 ft 10 in   5.13 m
Kerb weight: 3649 lb   1655 kg

Performance:
Maximum speed: 140 mph   225 km/h
0–60 mph: 7.9 sec
Fuel consumption
   at 56 mph: 25 mpg   11.3 litres/100 km
   at 75 mph: 20.9 mpg   13.5 litres/100 km
   urban: 12.9 mpg   21.8 litres/100 km

Insurance Rating: 9

Derived Data:
bhp/litre (kW/litre): 48.2   35.6
bhp/ton (kW/tonne): 138.8   100.8
Speed × acceleration: 17.7
Performance Dimension: 12.3
Petrol consumption/ton at 56 mph (10/F): 6.53   (1.53)
Change in petrol consumption between 56 & 75 mph: 19.5%

matched to perfection with the engine, which can be proved by the difficulty of achieving better results using manual control in the lower gears. Improved fuel consumption being one of the objectives in designing the new automatic gearbox, the 380 returns an overall 20 mpg.

The facia is lower than before, with a new handbrake to the right. The instruments are circular and include a tachometer of course. Seat adjustment is so good with the aid of the new electrical device, that it should be a standard fitting for the driver. All round visibility is without fault and parking is easy in consequence. A happy improvement is the linking of headlamp wash/wipe to the windscreen wipers, which is effected when the lights are switched on.

A high-speed, long distance luxury cruiser which has performance, handling, ride quality and passenger accommodation of this élite order also needs to be quiet – peace and quiet it also provides at all speeds and in all circumstances.

There is surprisingly a long list of possible extras. The car would appear to be perfect without them, but on inspection they all seem to be useful and sensible additions to motoring efficiency. The major service interval is at 12,000 miles, with an oil change at 6000.

Mercedes have always had qualities of engineering design and integrity well beyond the needs and cognisance of most of their owner-drivers. Statistics, as we have said, show that they drive them fast and for longer distances than others, but should they drive harder and faster and longer, the cars would still remain efficient and unperturbed.

The reputation earned in the last twenty-five years by Mercedes-Benz cars, owes more to the chief designer Rudolf Uhlenhaut than to anyone else. He designed the 300 SL gullwinged coupé, winner of the Mille Miglia at 100 mph, the W196 GP car of 1964, one of the most outstanding racing cars of all time, and was responsible for the continuous development of production cars until 1972.

Above: *The new S-class is wider than the saloons it replaces*

Left: *A superb interior comparable with that of the Rolls-Royce Silver Spirit*

Right: *Some generous benefactor interested in humanity more than profit should donate patents of the ABS braking system to all cars and thus save an incalculable number of lives*

Uhlenhaut always road tested the prototypes he had designed, himself. Fangio was a personal friend and from him Uhlenhaut learned to drive to within 2 per cent of the master, on the Hockenheim circuit and the Nürburgring. Uhlenhaut and Fangio set standards for the cars which few owner-drivers will ever need or even imagine, hence our remark that Mercedes have qualities beyond the cognisance of their owners.

It is not surprising that of the current professional drivers of Grand Prix cars, twenty-two use Mercedes for their personal transport, including Lafitte, Ickx, Pironi, Piquet, Patrese, Rosberg, Regazzoni, Reutemann and Alan Jones.

Werner Breitschwerdt was the chief designer responsible for the design and development of the new S class.

The electronic brain of the ABS system

ABS BRAKES

The ABS anti-lock braking system consists of three essential elements:

(a) an electronic control unit

(b) a four channelled hydraulic unit with an extremely sensitive electric motor

(c) four sensors.

The sensors are situated on the front axle stubs and on the rear wheel hubs, between the wheel bearings. The hydraulic unit, which is controlled by an electronic motor, is situated in the engine compartment, and is connected to the standard braking system.

The ABS activates when a wheel is about to lock under heavy braking and consequently prevents skidding. Just before the wheel locks, the system releases the brake and then applies it again, and this happens on each wheel, many times a second. It is cadence braking with more speed and sensitivity than humans can manage, and operating on each wheel separately. Even on dry roads the stopping distance is cut dramatically. The system has been proved by exhaustive tests over millions of miles. Should a fault occur within the ABS system, a light on the facia warns the driver and the normal braking system takes over.

The ABS system is available also on BMW cars.

BMW 528i

PORSCHE 928 S

The Grand category, in this book at least, is for cars which are concerned more with quality than cost. Cars which could possibly, 50 years on, be put beside Birkigt's Hispano-Suizas or a Rolls-Royce Phantom III in one of the best car museums. The Porsche 928 S has a bodyshell which is beautiful and timeless. Its engine produces 300 bhp and 156 mph (250 km/h), plus a marvellous ride with impeccable handling. Every detail of its construction is perfectly designed and made. It will look splendid in the museums, in the year 2030.

The Porsche has a steel monocoque frame, but doors, wings and bonnet are in aluminium, and the rear with deformable polyurethane panels, to save weight. The impact-absorbing bumpers are incorporated inside the shell, which makes the body wider.

The all-alloy V8 low maintenance engine has a single belt-driven camshaft over each bank of cylinders, and a swept volume of 4474 cc. Fuel feed is by Bosch K-Jetronic injection and the ignition is a transistorized contactless system. The engine drives through a

Mercedes-Benz 3 speed automatic box which is installed in the same housing as the differential. The engine and transaxle are rigidly connected by a torque tube enclosing the tailshaft. The final drive ratio gives 26.5 mph/1000 rpm.

The Mercedes automatic gearbox works with exceptional efficiency. Very few professional drivers with a five speed manual could do better. The brakes are superbly progressive, and the steering firm and precise. The handling at all speeds is without fault of any kind, helped by the 60 profile Pirelli P6 tyres, but basically because the whole car is so well designed – ideal weight distribution, wide track and a short wheelbase.

The 928 S is a two seater with space for more luggage behind the seats. The seats give lumbar support together with a secure enveloping feeling, and are infinitely and electrically adjustable. The foot wells are wide and the pedals businesslike. The steering wheel is adjustable and the instrument binnacle moves up and down with it. Some expensive and well made cars make

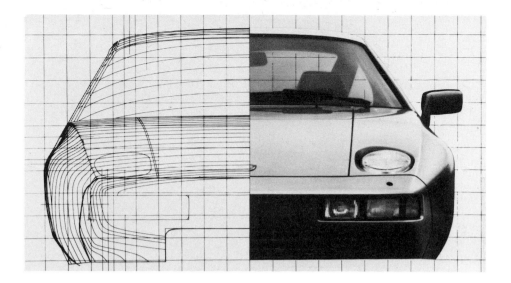

Opposite: One of the most beautiful and fastest cars in the world

Right: Designed with the aid of computers, but also with the Porsche Le Mans minds which brook no mistakes

---

Porsche 928 S (Coupé 2 door 2 + 2 with tailgate)

Engine: V8 with 2 sohc belt driven. All light alloy, front mounted
Capacity: 4608 cc
Bore; stroke: 97 mm 78.9 mm
Compression ratio: 10 to 1
Injection: Bosch K-Jetronic
Max. power at 5900 rpm: 300 bhp 221 kW
Max. torque at 4500 rpm: 284 ft/lb 385 Nm

Transmission: 5 speed manual gearbox rear mounted driving rear wheels (or optional 3 speed automatic)

Suspension:
Front: independent. Double control arms in light alloy with coil springs. Anti-roll bar.
Rear: independent. Upper transverse light alloy link, lower semi trailing arms with coil springs. Anti-roll bar

Steering: Power assisted rack and pinion
Turning circle: 37 ft 9 in 11.5 m

Brakes: Servo assisted diagonally split. Discs front and rear

Dimensions:
Length: 14 ft 7 in 4.45 m
Kerb weight: 3197 lb 1450 kg
Performance:
Maximum speed: 156 (153) mph 250 (245) km/h
0–60 mph: 6.5 (7) sec
Fuel consumption
  at 56 mph: 28.5 (27.4) mpg 9.9 (10.3) litres/100 km
  at 75 mph: 22.6 (21.4) mpg 12.5 (13.2) litres/100 km
  urban: 14.3 (16) mpg 19.7 (17.7) litres/100 km
Insurance Rating: 9
Derived Data: for weight ½ laden (3682 lb) (automatic figures in brackets)
bhp/litre (kW/litre): 65.1 48
bhp/ton (kW/tonne): 182.5 132.3
Speed × acceleration: 24 (21.9)
Performance Dimension: 13.1 (12)
Petrol consumption/ton at 56 mph (10/F): 6.02 (6.27) (1.66 (1.59))
Change in petrol consumption between 56 & 75 mph: 26% (28%)

---

one feel like a belted earl, but the Porsche would keep one happy all the way to a planet and back. This is not just because the seats are the soul of comfort but for many reasons; the quality cockpit finish, air conditioning, cruise control, electrically adjustable and heated mirrors, manual headlight adjustment, four stereo speakers, and a feeling of meticulously functional perfection everywhere.

Porsche produce one single type of car – the sports car. They devote their total resources of plant, manpower and finance to the development and perfection of this one objective. To these resources they add the bonus of their own independent research and design centre at Weissach, which designs everything from fire-engines to complete new cars for other manufacturers.

The 928 S has all the properties of a sports car together with a grand touring quality. Porsche have always used competition in all its forms as a yardstick for development, but it is endurance racing and Le Mans in particular, which they have chosen as the real test, and their wins are legendary. The 924 Turbo is described elsewhere in this book.

ROLLS-ROYCE

The timelessness of a Rolls-Royce motor car is a matter of record. Of all those built since 1904, over half are still working and giving pleasure to their owners. The new Silver Spirit will therefore no doubt last well into the twenty-first century. It is designed and constructed accordingly. The engine has been designed to run over 100,000 miles without major attention. The body is not only aerodynamic, safe and spacious, it has been armoured to withstand corrosion and to remain in outstanding condition for a very long time.

The ride is better than you will have experienced before. The serenity which this provides by the removal of stress and the ease of control it provides, makes a direct contribution to safety.

There is sometimes an element of criticism of Rolls-Royce cars by motoring journalists because they do not look or feel like a Lamborghini or a Maserati. This is absurd. It implies a comparison between two totally different concepts which are irreconcilable. The Maserati will take you to Rome with a feeling of constant excitement, even exultation, at 140 mph (225 km/h). The Rolls-Royce will take you to Rome and back at only 116 mph (187 km/h), but with such serenity that you feel the better for it.

There is no greater symbol of prestige and quality than a Rolls-Royce. Achieved initially through the obsessive perfectionism of Henry Royce, it has gone on continuously. Splendid motor cars have been manufactured over the same period such as Henri Birkigt's Hispano-Suizas, Isotta-Fraschinis produced by Cesare Isotta and Oreste Fraschini, Ettore Bugatti's Royales, Maybach's early, Dr. Porsche's middle period and Uhlenhauts recent Mercedes. Many of them would go faster than a Royce, and almost all were technologically more exciting, but none of them had the serenity which is at the centre of a Rolls-Royce.

The silence of the RR engine when running – take any one at random from a Silver Ghost to the Silver Spirit – is a quiet refutal to the splenetic fuss about how many automotive innovations Rolls-Royce have disregarded. They have used enough.

Rolls and Royce met in 1903, when Henry had just completed his first three cars – all 10 hp 2-cylinders. In the 1904 salon in Paris there were a 10 hp, 15 hp, a 4-cylinder 20 hp and 6-cylinder 30 hp. In 1906 the Silver Ghost was introduced and became known as the best car in the world almost at once.

Rolls-Royce have only rarely entered competition, but in 1913 the Silver Ghost engine, with a lightweight Alpine Eagle body, won the Austrian Alpine Trials. The Ghost engine and chassis was used during the first World War for ambulances, staff cars, armoured cars and not least by the legendary Lawrence of Arabia.

There is total unity of engineering design and principles running through all Royce's work. The 6-cylinder Ghost laid down the basic plan, and the Phantom I (1925–31) was the Ghost plus overhead valves. The Phantom II (1924–35) had an improved suspension system, and the Phantom III changed to a V12.

All the Phantoms had engines of over 7 litres and ohv. Then, with the 20, the capacity was reduced to 3127 cc. Quiet, flexible and impeccable, the 20 was underpowered, and the capacity was stepped up successively with the 20/25 to 3669, the 25/30 to 4257, where it remained for the Wraith, Silver Wraith and Silver Dawn.

Henry Royce had died in 1933, before the Phantom III was introduced, but he designed the 20, the 20/25 and the 25/30, and laid down principles about engine design which were considered hallowed and unalterable, and the same basic design continued through the Dawn (1949–55) to the Silver Cloud I (1955–59).

Royce was concerned with more than the engine. His designs for the whole car were backed by quality control more stringent than any that has been known, before or since. Everything was made with an expensive disregard for anything which might prejudice its impeccability. Connecting rods started as a forging of 8 lb and finished at a polished 2 lb. All rotating and related moving parts were balanced – obviously the crankshaft, con rods, pistons, flywheel and road wheels, but also, surprisingly the gears and even the bevel gears in the differential.

Royce was also concerned with chassis design, which

The Silver Ghost

was rare at that time. Cars until the 1930s were, in the main, engines which propelled the wheels and the suspension was rudimentary. Royce used an open topped water container and the amount of water lost gave an indication of the quality of ride at various speeds. He also measured the moments of inertia by swinging the chassis from overhead pivots, tested the suspension rates of the springs and had a bump-rig which tested the chassis for strength and provided a synthetic ride with a stationary car.

All of these useful devices were carried across the Atlantic to Cadillac by Maurice Olley when he left Rolls-Royce to become famous with General Motors as a chassis designer, carrying out more research on the relationship between spring rates and dampers and ultimately independent suspension systems.

Royce felt that his work was complete with the working chassis, which then went to the coachbuilders, for the bodywork to be built. It was not until 1949, with the Silver Dawn, that coachwork was built by the company. Before that it was made by Mulliner, Park

Ward, Barker and Parrin of Paris (an American).

The Silver Cloud (1955–59) was the last in the line of 6-cylinder engined cars and was the best selling Rolls-Royce up to that time. Including Bentley counterparts, 5897 were built. The new V8 engine of 6230 cc capacity was first produced in 1959 for the Silver Clouds II and III (1959–66). The Silver Shadow (1965–77) used the 6 litre aluminium V8 engine with automatic gearbox, all round independent suspension, four wheel disc brakes, automatic self-levelling and split level air conditioning.

Then followed a series of improvements. In 1970 the engine capacity was increased from 6230 cc to 6750 cc. 1971 Corniche convertible announced. 1972 introduction of compliant front suspension. 1973 ventilated front brake discs. 1975 Camargue model announced, Opus electronic ignition distributor. 1977 rack and pinion steering and suspension modifications. 1979 new rear suspension introduced on Corniche and Camargue models. 1980 larger crankshaft bearings and new oil seals. October 1980, Silver Spirit announced.

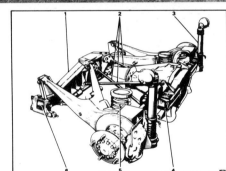

ROLLS-ROYCE SILVER SPIRIT

The engineer responsible for the styling of the new Rolls-Royce Silver Spirit is Dr. Fritz Feller. The fact that he is an engineer determined the priorities, so while the drag coefficient has been reduced, and the ratio of width to height increased, he saw to it that the centre of aerodynamic pressure remained far enough to the rear to provide for stability at high speeds.

He also concerned himself with a design which would cope with all legal requirements, so that the Rolls-Royce can be driven at peace in any country in the world without infringing laws about pollution, bumper strength or virtually anything else in motor cars that is legislated against. The new body naturally passed all crash tests – front, rear, side, roll over and roof drop.

The most important new development in the Silver Spirit is the rear suspension system. When the Silver Shadow was given new front suspension and steering in 1977, the Rolls engineers were aware that it now needed a revised rear suspension system. Having produced a new design it was embodied in the Camargue and

Corniche in 1979, and now it is the most important new feature in the Silver Spirit.

The geometry of the rear wheels' movements has been changed by moving the pivot axes of the trailing arms. The skid-pad cornering power of the Silver Spirit is now above 0.79. The new rear springing system includes self-levelling. Smaller helical coil springs which no longer intrude into the boot area (this is by no means unique at present) carry the weight of the unladen car and changes in load are supported by gas springs which produce a rate rising so progressively with load as to maintain the total spring periodicity almost constant at 56 Hz. The gas chambers crown hydraulic struts which also perform as dampers, and the ride height is adjusted by the volume of oil in the struts.

The diagram shows the rear suspension subframe, which carries the final drive and the trailing arms, together with six diagonal tie-bars and a longitudinal torque arm. The rubber mounts are compliant longitudinally but stiff laterally; hence there is no bump-thump

Above: *Rolls-Royce Camargue, designed by Pininfarina*

Right: *The interior of the Silver Spirit*

Opposite: *The Silver Spirit*

Opposite below: *Rear suspension subframe*
1 *Rear crossmember*
2 *Frame tubes*
3 *Gas spring and strut*
4 *Metalistik mount*
5 *Coil spring*
6 *Metalistik mount*

over cats' eyes or other deformities, because of the compliance of the subframe to vibration patterns.

There is also of course the now safe mascot, but a very important fact about the new body is the fact that the headlamps, exclusive to Rolls-Royce and made by Lucas, are said to be the most powerful in the world, with approximately 300,000 candelas.

The Silver Spirit uses the same 6.7 litre alloy V8 engine as the Shadow, together with the GM Turbo Hydramatic three speed transmission. Carburettors are by SU but the export models use Bosch K-Jetronic fuel injection, and it is understood that Rolls-Royce are waiting for Lucas to develop a fuel injection system for the Spirit. At the same time, there is talk about a 5.3 litre V8 engine using the same crankshaft and block, but with redesigned cylinder heads, ignition and exhaust systems.

The Silver Spirit represents engineering, design and craftsmanship combined, to a standard which has produced once again the best car in the world. The car is beautiful, but it does not fall into the category of 'running sculpture' – the phrase used by Bertone to describe cars like the Lamborghini Countach.

The engine is faultless but it does not produce as much brake horse power as the Mercedes five litre, nor does the Silver Spirit have the capacity of the Porsche 928 S to achieve ground speeds comparable with a small aircraft; but it has retained, to the ultimate, the same quality which was noted by the *Autocar* on April 20 1907, concerning the Silver Ghost. 'There is no realization of driving propulsion; the feeling is one of being wafted through the landscape.'

GRAND CARS: SUMMARY

Here as co-authors we are for the first time in considerable difficulty. We simply cannot agree on our preferences in this group. In a way this is hardly surprising, given that we are now dealing with cars which in their own way are even more emotive than the super sports cars.

We fortunately have no problems, however, on the subject of hand built excellence. The Rolls-Royce remains in a class of its own for finish and, if one is a collector of art for investment, as an expenditure the car is not wholly unjustifiable. Here we have luxury of the sort that we all dream about and engineering with such a long pedigree that one tends to fall into the trap of thinking it reactionary: it isn't.

Turning to the mass produced cars, Mercedes, potentially at least, show dangers of falling between two stools. They tend to follow the example of Rolls-Royce in waiting for any development to be massively well tested before incorporating it, and yet have the difficulty of making a finished product as well, on a mass production basis, as Rolls do it by hand. They would argue that by using more modern methods they in fact do better than Rolls-Royce. We agree that the market for the two cars remains essentially different. The Mercedes 500 SEL we feel competes more with the BMW 735i than it does with the Rolls-Royce. On this basis perhaps Mercedes should think more firmly about more advanced fuel injection methods and keep even their very good automatic system as an option for the more weary!

For style, comfort and performance in elegant combination, the 735i is a true culmination of a range of BMW cars which in general and, by comparison with Mercedes, uses every innovation to its best advantage. This is clearly demonstrated in the data, and yet if one's ideal is the half way house one (of us) would gravitate to the Mercedes.

Then we have three British cars, or at least in Aston Martin's case of British origin; one is made by BL, the Daimler Double Six, and the third in the genuinely grand class is the Aston Martin Lagonda. The latter car, loaded as it is, has a Performance Dimension of 16, very creditable in this company, but child's stuff compared with the staggering figure for the Aston Martin V8 Vantage of 29.6. The Vantage is not a sports car, so we must classify it here and simply regret that we have not had the space to consider it further, partially, we admit, from the decreased interest of not having sufficient data to assess it more accurately.

If we really want elegance then, in combination with devastating performance, we retreat to the pure style of the Ferrari Mondial 8, clearly a masterpiece that could only be Italian. Equally the Porsche 928 S could only be German: here we have sleekness with pure engineering as an art form, and handling to boot.

The choice is yours.

BMW 735

Class 10   Data Summary

Datum Point		Performance	Power Weight	PD	FE
A	Aston Martin Lagonda	29.6	na	na	na
B	Aston Martin V8 Vantage	16.2	na	na	na
C	BMW 735i	18.1	136	13.3	1.87
D	Daimler Double Six	19.1	141	13.5	1.38
E	Ferrari Mondial 8	20.9	139	15.0	na
F	Mercedes-Benz 500 SEL	17.7	139	12.8	1.53
G	Porsche 928	20.4	146	14.0	1.73
Ga	Porsche 928 (A)	18.7	146	12.8	1.55
H	Porsche 928 S	24	183	13.1	1.66
Ha	Porsche 928 S (A)	21.9	183	12.0	1.59

na = not available

Aston Martin Lagonda interior

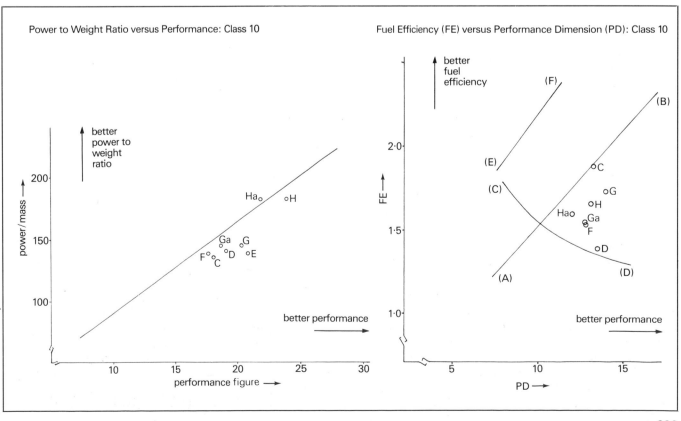

10 Fiat Panda
A Car for the Third World

Robert Mugabe has started near the top with a Mercedes 500 SE, complete with BMW motorcycle escort. Heads of State in Saudi Arabia use Rolls-Royce Corniches and Camargues, or Aston Martin Lagondas. But what about Mr. Third World Everyman? He needs an efficient, unpretentious and above all low-cost car.

In Mexico they are enterprisingly using the one true world car, the Beetle, but with front wheel drive. Other countries may also adopt this because with its unburstable flat tyres, unbreakable torsion bar suspension and a capacity to exist and work in all temperatures from polar low to equitorial high, it is the best ever petrol workhorse. This car wore various military bodyshells during World War II which may prove more functional than the well-known domed body for all the hard work being demanded of it.

But what about a specific design created with the demands of the Third World in mind? Coming late as it does, such a car has the potential advantage of leapfrogging all the good, bad and indifferent experiences which we have had in developing the modern car.

The Panda shown here would make a suitable car for the Third World, especially in its four wheel drive version which has similarities with the Mercedes 230 G crosscountry and station wagon. The Panda has been designed specifically to keep all costs low, especially maintenance and repair.

It was presented at the 1980 Turin Motor Show and is designed by Giugiaro with a wide possible range of interpretations, including four wheel drive and as an off-road vehicle. It represents Italian design concerning itself with the engineering for the whole vehicle, not just bodywork interpretations. The standard 45 Panda production engine is 903 cc capacity producing 45 bhp at 5000 rpm and 6.5 kgm torque at 3000 rpm. The introduction of a 1050 cc is being considered.

The Panda 4 × 4 is a multipurpose vehicle directed essentially at the young as an off-roader for mountains, beach etc and has the same engineering: both vehicles could be further modified and simplified for use in countries in the Third World.

Above: *Simple, economical and quickly repairable*

Opposite top: *Panda facia*

Middle: *Panda new and remarkable washable seats*

Bottom: *The four by four*

Right: *The fabulous Beetle*

Conclusion

We have had considerable pleasure in writing this book, particularly in discussing the relative merits of the feel and look of a car on first acquaintance and its handling ability after more experience, by comparison with the stark realities associated with its performance. Cars are an emotive subject: in what order of preference one puts sex, eating, driving and thinking is something which is a matter for the individual and not really arguable all that logically.

We do not thus feel that a car can or should be judged solely using the type of data analysis we have suggested. If the view we have taken is slightly imbalanced towards this approach it is because we believe that good figures do reflect good engineering and design, and because we wish others to use the same technique – not to the exclusion of, but in conjunction with, more subjective attitudes.

If your own car, or the car you wish to buy, has not been included it doesn't necessarily mean that it doesn't have perfectly acceptable figures or attributes which make it right for you personally. We have succeeded sufficiently if we have encouraged you enough to go back to the chapter on the Performance Dimension and sort out how to work out the data of interest for yourself.

A-Z of Automotive Terms

Note: words in **bold type** within the entries are titles of other entries in this A–Z.

Aerodynamics: the study of the forces exerted by air in motion. A car in motion displaces air and leaves a wake behind it. This creates a drag which consumes power. Drag is also created by friction of air on the body surfaces. The aerodynamic efficiency of the body shape is given a value named the drag coefficient, which can be measured by using a scale model in a **wind tunnel**. A flat plate face-on to the airstream has a coefficient of 1.25. The ideal shape, a tear drop travelling with the point forwards, has a drag coefficient of about 0.03. Most cars are between 0.3 to 0.5.

Air dam: a spoiler placed across the bottom part of the nose of a car to reduce drag and lift. Air flow between the road and the underside of the car is at a higher pressure than that flowing over the top, which tends to lift the front wheels off the road, making them unsteerable.

Alternator: a device for converting rotational mechanical work into an alternating electric current. In its simplest form, it consists of a loop of wire, with its ends connected to a pair of slip-rings, rotating between the poles of a permanent magnet. The magnitude of the voltage induced in the loop varies sinusoidally with rotation, reversing polarity every 180 degrees – hence the name alternating current. The advantages over the direct current dynamo are that the rotor is smaller, stronger, lighter, and can be run at higher rpm. At low rpm, output of an alternator is higher than that of a dynamo.

Ammeter: a gauge measuring electric current. It also indicates whether the charging circuit is operating.

Anti-dive geometry: an arrangement of the suspension system to eliminate nose dipping, maintain adhesion and stability.

Anti-lock brakes, ABS: brakes with a device which prevents wheels locking up and skidding. A Bosch electronic control system is now used by Mercedes and BMW. Sensors perceive excessive wheel deceleration, relieve brake pressure to prevent it, then restore pressure, cycling several times a second.

Anti-roll bar: a torsion bar used to increase stiffness in roll, pressing transversely across the car. Bars can be fitted at front or rear, or both. Excessively stiff bars create roll oscillation known as roll-bar waddle.

Aspect ratio: a tyre term defining the ratio of height to tread width expressed as a percentage. The lower the figure, the lower the profile.

Axle tramp: a juddering movement of the driven wheels. Often applied to live rear axles with semi-elliptic leaf springs. It can also occur on independently sprung vehicles if they are softly damped.

Backbone chassis: a structure down the centre of a car which takes all the major chassis loads, e.g. Lotus and VW Beetle.

Baulk ring: part of the **synchromesh** system, developed by Dr. Ferdinand Porsche in 1947, which ensures smooth gear changes.

Bendix drive: a device for engaging the pinion gear of a starter motor to the ring gear of the **flywheel** and disengaging it when the engine fires.

Bevel gears: gears with a conical shape, used to transmit motion through an angle – usually 90° from one shaft to another; often called bevel spur gears.

Bhp: brake horse power: German PS (*Pferdestärke*), French CV (*Cheval Vapeur*) and Italian CV (*Cavallo Vapore*) are all names for the metric horsepower. Bhp is the measurement applied exclusively to land vehicles and is measured by a horsepower meter which is called a brake, on a **dynamometer**.

Power is the rate at which work is done. Work is product of force exerted F and the distance through which it is moved D. Therefore power = FD/T where T = time.

For engines, horsepower can be calculated by use of the formula PLAN, where P = brake mean effective pressure, L = stroke, A = piston area and N = number of strokes per second. Horsepower = PLAN/550, since 1 imperial horsepower = 550 ft lb per second. When P is in Newtons and the dimensions are in metres and square metres, the answer is in watts. 746 watts = 1 imperial horsepower = 0.986 metric horsepower.

BMEP: Brake Mean Effective Pressure. Mean effective pressure means corrected for all frictional and other losses. It is deduced from bhp measurements, whereas IMEP (Indicated Mean Effective Pressure) is calculated from an indicator diagram produced by a pressure sensor and frictional and other losses are subtracted.

Boost pressure: the pressure of the inlet charge of a turbo or supercharger, being delivered to the engine by the compressor. Usually 5 to 10 psi on road cars.

B post: the front door shut and rear door hinge post.

Bore: a cylinder in which each piston of a reciprocating engine moves. It also means the diameter of the cylinder.

Bottom dead centre, BDC: when a piston is at the bottom of its stroke.

Bowl-in-piston: sometimes called a heron head after the name of the engineer who pioneered its use for petrol engines, bowl-in-piston is actually more common in diesel engines. It means a combustion chamber contained partly in the piston as well as the cylinder head.

Boxer engine: see **horizontally opposed.**

Brake balance: the ratio of braking between the front and rear wheels. A load-sensitive relief valve which releases pressure to the rear. Rally cars can adjust the balance on the move, from the driver's seat.

Brake caliper: disc brake systems have a caliper which is fixed to the wheel upright, and carries a brake pad on either side of the brake disc. When the brakes are operated the pads move together, holding the disc to create a braking effect.

Bucket tappet: a metal cup placed below the camshaft, enclosing the end of the valve stem and spring, in an overhead camshaft engine.

Camber angle: the angle between a wheel's plane of motion and the vertical. Defined as positive when the top of the wheel leans away from the car at the top, and negative when it leans in.

Camshaft: a rotating shaft carrying cams. Its purpose is to create linear reciprocating movement to operate poppet valves, via the cams, part of which are eccentric from the shaft's rotational centre.

Catalytic convertor: a substance which influences chemical reaction without itself being changed. In cars, the use of platinum in the exhaust system which aids the reduction of the oxides of nitrogen into nitrogen and oxygen, and aids the oxidation of carbon monoxide and hydrocarbons into harmless carbon dioxide, nitrogen and water.

Centre of pressure: the side point on which wind forces act. It must be behind the centre of gravity for stability against side winds.

Centre point steering: the orientation of the steering axis so that, viewed from the front, it meets the ground at the centre line of the tyre; this is also named kingpin inclination. When the steering axis meets the ground inside the tyre centreline, this is positive offset, which means heavier steering and kickback. Negative offset minimizes yaw.

Centrifugal force: a body in motion resists any force trying to make it deviate from a straight path. To make a body follow a curved path, it is necessary to apply a force to it. This force is called centripetal force. If a mass is whirled around on a string, it feels as though there is an outward force on the mass. It is this force, equal in magnitude and opposite in direction to the centripetal force, which is called the centrifugal force. It is equal to the mass of the body multiplied by the radial acceleration.

Combustion chamber: the space in a cylinder head or piston into which the mixture is compressed and combustion takes place. Its size determines the engine's compression ratio.

Compliance: the 'give' in the location bushes of suspension systems to prevent road shocks being transmitted to the car body.

Compression ignition, CI: alternative name for **diesel engine** which describes the essential basic difference between it and the petrol.

Compression ratio: the amount by which the mixture inside an engine is compressed, e.g. a compression ratio of 9:1 means that the volume of the mixture when the piston is **BDC** is nine times as great as that when the piston is at **TDC**. High compression ratios mean greater thermal efficiency (i.e. more power and better mpg) but demand high octane fuel.

Constant speed device: also called cruise control. When engaged it will keep a car going at a predetermined speed by opening and closing the throttle automatically to compensate for gradients, etc. The basis is an electronic control unit and a pneumatic actuator.

Constant velocity joint: a joint between two shafts that allows their speed to remain equal irrespective of the angle between their respective axes.

Contact breaker: two spring-loaded electrical contacts on points operated by the cam lobes of the distributor shaft which constitute a make-and-break switch in the primary circuit of an ignition coil. In accordance with the laws of electromagnetism, the high voltage required for ignition is induced in the secondary winding of the coil when the primary current is interrupted by the action of the contact breaker. The contact breaker is one of the weakest parts of a car, and the use of 'breakerless' optical or electromagnetic triggers a great improvement.

C post: the body pillar connecting the floor pan with the roof on which the rear door latches.

Countershaft: any shaft rotating in the opposite direction to that of the main shafts, e.g. in a gearbox the **layshaft**. The term is usually used in the context of balancing, where counter-rotating shafts are used to counteract out-of-balance forces inherent in the engine design, e.g. in a Ford V4 engine a countershaft was used to cancel the out-of-balance primary forces.

Crankcase: a rigid casting in which the crankshaft runs. Previously separate from the cylinder block, is now usually a part of it and contains the upper main bearing housings.

Crankcase breather: a means of venting combustion fumes, usually to the inlet manifold or to the air cleaner housing.

Crankpin: that part of the crankshaft on which the connecting rod big end is attached.

Crankshaft damper: a device fitted to the nose of the crankshaft to reduce torsional vibration.

Crash gearbox: a gearbox with no **synchromesh** so that double declutching is required to change gear.

Crash testing: before any car can be sold, a representative model must be submitted for crash testing to determine whether the car conforms to the very strict requirements on deformability. These tests are performed by MIRA (Motor

Industry Research Association).

Cross flow head: a cylinder head that has its exhaust and inlet parts situated opposite each other so that the gas flow is across the head rather than confined to one side.

Crossover exhaust: an arrangement of exhaust manifolding for engines including more than one bank of cylinders (V6, V8, V12) in which the exhaust pipes from one side are joined to those coming from the other side. This spaces the exhaust pulses equally in the exhaust manifold.

Crossply: a tyre with several plies of rayon or nylon laid diagonally so that they cross the circumferential line at about 40° with alternate layers in opposite directions.

Crownwheel and pinion, CWP: the **final drive** components which reduce the rotational speed of the gearbox output shaft to that supplied to the roadwheels. The final drive ratio is usually between 3:1 and 5:1.

Crush zone: front and rear ends of a body designed to crumple progressively under impact, thus absorbing the energy of a collision before it is transmitted to the central 'safety cage' section.

Cubic capacity, cc: the total of the swept volume made by the pistons in the cylinders.

CVCC engine: Compound Vortex Controlled Combustion Engine. A form of stratified charge engine in which ignited rich mixture in a small auxiliary combustion chamber expands, to ignite a weak mixture in the main combustion chamber. Honda have developed a 1500 cc CVCC engine.

CVT, Continuous variable transmission: stepless variation of the intermediate ratios between fixed bottom and top gear ratios.

Cylinder liners: there are two types of liner: the dry liner is pressed into the existing bore of the cylinder block, like a sleeve. This liner is not in contact with the cooling water. The **wet** liner is used in light alloy cylinder blocks, and is in contact with the coolant.

Dampers: the purpose of dampers is to damp or cut down the oscillations of the car on its springs. Also known misleadingly as shock absorbers. Most dampers are double-acting and telescopic.

Dead axle: in its simplest terms, a bar across the chassis carrying non-driven road wheels. Some front wheel drive cars use this basic form of non-independent rear suspension, e.g. Lancia and VW.

De Dion axle: a development of the **live** rear axle, with the weight of the final drive and differential removed. Originated in the De Dion Bouton. It consists of a light tube, cranked at each end to avoid the half-shafts which transmit the drive. Aston Martin and Volvo 343 have de Dion axles.

Desmodromic: a form of valve actuation which uses mechanical means to open and close the valves, eliminating valve springs. Mercedes used them in the mid 1950s.

Detonation: Also known as pinking and knocking. The combustion of fuel with explosive violence. The octane value of the fuel determines its resistance to detonation.

Diaphragm clutch: a clutch which employs a diaphragm spring instead of coil springs.

Digital instrument: an electronic device with a luminous diode or liquid crystal display, showing facts on the facia instruments by digits. Used in the Aston Martin Lagonda.

DIN: *Deutsche Industrie Normen*, a German Industrial Standard for measurement of power output.

Disc brake: a steel disc usually attached to the wheel hub, with pads on either side which are applied with braking force by calipers and pistons.

Displacement: see **cubic capacity**.

Distributor: a rotating arm which distributes the high tension current to each sparking plug through small carbon brushes.

Double declutching: a method of changing gear which was necessary with crash gearboxes, before synchromesh.

Doughnut: a rubber coupling, used usually in forward driveshafts. Cheaper than a universal or CV joint.

Downdraught carb: any carburettor that is set so that the airflow is vertically down.

Drag coefficient, CD: a non-dimensional constant, applied to a body to describe mathematically its aerodynamic effectiveness. It can be estimated from a number of salient factors, but is usually found from wind tunnel experiments. The Citroën CX has a Cd of 0.3, the Lotus Elite 0.3, and an American record machine Goldenrod has one of 0.12 with a speed in excess of 400 mph (644 km/h).

Drive train: the sequence of components which convey the drive from the engine to the road wheels.

Drop arm: the output arm of a steering box, to which is connected a drag link. These two links transform rotational into linear movement.

Drum brake: a cast iron or alloy drum attached to the wheel hub. A hydraulically operated piston, set in motion by the brake pedal, forces shoes outwards so that their linings bear on the machined internal surface of the drum.

Dry sump: an engine lubrication system that does not rely on a sump full of oil. A high pressure pump feeds lubricant to the engine from a tank. Benefits include a lower mounting position for the engine, increased oil capacity and better cooling.

Dry weight: weight of a car minus all fluids.

Dual circuit brakes: hydraulically operated brakes with two independent circuits so that if one fails the other will arrest the car.

Dump valve: see **wastegate**.

Dwell angle: the number of degrees of distributor cam rotation for which the contact breaker points remain closed during one ignition cycle.

Dynamo: a device that converts rotational mechanical work into direct electrical current. Now superseded by the more efficient alternators.

Dynamometer: a machine which measures work rate or power. There are two types. One measures the power output of the engine (test bed or engine dynamometer) and the other measures the power output from the driven wheels (a chassis dynamometer). In both cases, the measuring technique is similar, the power being absorbed by a water brake.

Electrode: an electrical connector to an electrolyte or the end of a sparking plug.

Eloctrolyte: a substance which conducts electricity by the migration of charged particles or ions, e.g. the fluid in a car battery.

Electronic ignition: an ignition system using electronic switching. There are two categories: those working with a conventional contact breaker, and those that do without it. The switching in contactless systems is done by interrupting a light beam, or using a magnetic pick up. The advantages of electronic ignition are its ability to maintain timing and output constant over high mileages, its ability to produce a strong reliable spark in difficult conditions (fouled plugs, weak mixture and very high revs) and its reduced fuel consumption.

E mark: a plate showing to which European safety emissions or other standards the car complies.

e.g. E10 radio interference suppression
  E11 door latches and hinges
  E12 protection against steering failure
  E15 petrol engine emissions
  E18 anti-theft devices.

Emulsion tube: a device for mixing fuel and air in a fixed choke carburettor. A tube with cross holes. As the air speed increases, the air enters the end of the tube and flows out through the cross-drillings, emulsifying the fuel as it goes.

Epicyclic: a planetary gear train that consists of a centre sun wheel around which revolve smaller planet wheels on the spindles of a planet carrier. The planet wheels mesh with the inner toothed rim of the surrounding annulus. Epicyclic trains form the heart of most automatic transmissions. They can be used as reduction or reverse gears. If the sun wheel is driven by the engine and the planet carrier attached to the prop shaft then if the annulus is locked the sun wheel will rotate the planet wheels inside the annulus, and thus cause the planet carrier to rotate at a lower speed than the sun wheel. If the planet carrier is locked the annulus turns in the opposite direction to the sun wheel, and at a lower speed.

Ergonomics: the study of man in relation to his working environment. In automotive terms, it means designing a car suitable for human use.

ESV: Experimental Safety Vehicle.

Exhaust emission regulations: world ecological concern about the principal **pollutants** (CO, NOx and hydrocarbons) in a vehicle's exhaust emissions has caused regulations in most countries. The solutions may be divided into three categories:

(1) Stratified charge (Honda CVCC)
(2) Lean burn – very lean mixture, high mixture turbulence, simple catalyst, or
(3) **Lambda sensor** and three way catalyst

FIA: *Fédération Internationale Automobile* to which the national motoring bodies of most countries are affiliated, and concerns itself with the integration on a world scale of regulations governing the conduct and passage of motorists. The FISA is a subsidiary of the FIA and governs international sport matters.

Fiddle brake: fitted in pairs to trials cars to enable a driven rear wheel to be stopped, transferring tractive power to the opposite wheel.

Fifth wheel: part of a separate, portable and highly accurate instrument for measuring distance and thus speed.

Final drive: the last reduction gear in the drive train of the transmission system, which includes the differential.

Final drive ratio: the amount by which the rotational speed of the drive is reduced when it passes through the final

drive unit.

Fixed choke carburettor: also called a fixed jet or variable depression carburettor. It consists of a tube with one end open to the atmosphere and the other fixed to the inlet manifold. This tube includes a waisted section called a venturi. The air increases in velocity as it passes through the venturi and its pressure falls. This drop in pressure is used to draw in the fuel.

Flame travel: for the best combustion, the flame should spread out in all directions and its travel should be as short as possible.

Fluid coupling: a coupling embodying vaned bowls of hydraulic fluid rotated by the engine output shaft. It allows the engine to idle freely, but locks up from 1200 rpm onwards and transfers all engine torque with very little slip. Now superseded by the **torque converter** which gives torque multiplication.

Flywheel: a heavy steel disc fitted to one end of the engine's crankshaft in order to smooth out pulsations, dead points and idle strokes.

Foot pounds: the imperial units in which an engine's torque is commonly quoted. One lb/ft is a 1 lb force acting at a radius of 1 ft. The abbreviation can be either ft/lb or lb/ft but when spoken it is usually referred to as 'foot pound'.

Formula 1, 2, 3: at present a Formula 1 car used for Grand Prix races may be powered by a 3 litre normally aspirated, or a 1.5 litre turbo, provided it has no more than 12 cylinders. Formula 2: 2 litre capacity (maximum of 6 cylinders). Formula 3: 2 litre production-based power unit with a power inhibiting air inlet restrictor.

Four link location: two longitudinal lower arms plus two angled upper arms. Used by Ford Cortina, Fiat 132, Talbot Sunbeam and Triumph Dolomite.

Four stroke: Common term for the Otto cycle. The four strokes are 1 induction, 2 compression, 3 power and 4 exhaust.

Four valve head: a cylinder head with four valves per cylinder; two inlet and two exhaust.

Frontal area: the area of a car that hits the air. Total wind resistance is proportional to frontal area × drag coefficient.

Fuel injection: a method of metering fuel to the engine first used by Bosch and Kugelfischer. The first systems were mechanical, but the Bosch D-Jetronic, L and K Jetronic, use electronically controlled solenoid-operated injectors.

Fully floating axle: a rear axle in which the halfshaft does not carry either the vehicle's weight or any cornering loads, being used solely to convey the drive to the rear wheels.

FWD: four wheel drive, meaning that all four wheels are powered. Used on cross country vehicles but also the Audi Quattro. In some contexts (not in this book) FWD or fwd means front wheel drive.

Gasket: a thin laminated joint used for the cylinder head, rocker covers, water pump etc.

Gas turbine: a form of jet engine in which power is generated by the conversion of the kinetic energy of hot gas to the rotation of a shaft. The gases are forced at pressure past diagonal beads attached to the shaft.

Gearbox: a device to vary the speed of the car and its direction – forward or backwards.

Gear ratio: the relative speed at which two gears turn. If one gear-wheel has 100 teeth and engages with another of 25 teeth, the smaller will rotate at four times the speed of the large one, giving a gear ratio of 4:1.

Generator: a generic term covering **dynamo** and **alternator**.

G force: g, the acceleration experienced by a falling body due to gravity: 1 g = acceleration of 32.2 ft per second.

Glow plug: an electrically heated coil in the combustion chamber of a diesel engine to assist starting.

Governor: a device to limit (govern) rotational speed.

Grinding in: seating the exhaust and inlet valves into a cylinder head for a perfect gas tight fit. Also named lapping in.

GRP: glass reinforced plastic used for bodywork.

Gudgeon pin: the pin locating a piston to the little end of a connecting rod.

Gullwing: overhead doors swinging up from roof hinges. Mercedes 300 SL and CIII.

Helical gears: gears in which the teeth are slanted at an angle across the rim and so mesh more smoothly and quietly.

Hemispherical combustion chamber: a combustion chamber that is part spherical in shape. It has a small surface area to volume ratio, thus minimizing heat losses, and has a small **flame travel**.

Heron head: see **bowl-in-piston**.

Hooke joint: a universal joint invented by Thomas Hooke consisting of two yokes pivoting at right angles to each other. Used in most rear wheel drive cars at both ends of the prop shaft.

Horizontally opposed: an engine with its cylinders arranged opposite each other with the crankshaft in the middle. Also known as a 'flat' or 'boxer' engine. The Citroën GS and Alfasud have flat 4s, and Ferrari make a flat 12.

Hydragas suspension: a springing system evolved by Moulton and fitted to the BL Allegro and Princess.

Hydraulic: transferring force or energy by means of a fluid.

Hydraulic tappet: a self-adjusting tappet which uses hydraulic pressure to take up any adjustment. As wear takes place more fluid is used to compensate.

Hydropneumatic suspension: the Citroën suspension system which provides a constant ride height.

Hypoid: a spiral bevel gear in which the bevel pinion drives from below the centre line of the crownwheel. This enables the drop shaft to be lowered, which in turn enables a lower floor level to be achieved.

Idler arm: a passive pivoted link that transfers steering movements to a car's nearside front wheel when a steering box mechanism is used in conjunction with independent front suspension. Not needed with rack and pinion steering.

Idler gear: a gear driving nothing itself but conveying the drive from one gear to another, or interposed to reverse the drive between one gear and another.

Impeller: a device with radial vanes which impels fluid, e.g. in a torque converter. The impeller shaft in a gearbox is the primary shaft from the engine.

Inboard brakes: brakes – usually discs – mounted towards the centre of the car to reduce unsprung weight.

Induction system: the system of trunking which supplies air or mixture to the engine.

Jockey wheel: a wheel, pulley or sprocket included in a chain or belt for tensioning.

Journal: the part of a shaft around which a plain bearing acts. A crankshaft has journals for both big end and main bearings.

Kickdown: a device on cars with automatic transmission which enables the driver to override the mechanism in order to select and obtain full performance from a lower gear.

King pin: A near vertical pin in the end of the axle beam around which the stub axle and wheel are pivoted. With independent front suspensions the stub axle pivots around ball-joints at the wishbones, and king pins are no longer used.

Knocking: see **detonation**.

Lambda sensor: the Lambda sensor detects the amount of oxygen in the exhaust and since this relates directly to the air/fuel ratio, the mixture can be altered via an electronic control unit. A Bosch design.

Layshaft: the third shaft in a gearbox, parallel to the input shaft and the output shaft.

Limited slip differential: a differential which limits differences in rotational speed of its output shafts, usually by clutches which clamp the side gears to their housings when torque is transmitted.

Live axle: a solid axle locating non-independently suspended driven wheels.

Loom: a collection of wires, coded, which complete the electrical circuit of a car.

Low profile: a tyre with a shallow side-wall in relation to its width.

LPG: liquified petroleum gas.

LT: Low tension meaning low voltage.

MacPherson strut: a form of independent suspension in which the hub carrier is rigidly fixed to a strut rising 2 to 3 ft above the wheel centre to a pivot point in the wheel arch structure. The strut incorporates a hydraulic damper and also acts as the steering swivel pin if used at the front, when a ball joint acts as the lower steering swivel. Widely used and named after its inventor, a Ford engineer.

MIRA: Motor Industry Research Association. Based at Nuneaton, Warwickshire. An organization sponsored by the motor industry to carry out automotive research and development.

Moment of inertia: an object's reluctance to be accelerated in rotation, compared to pure inertia which is an object's reluctance to be accelerated in a straight line. The polar moment of inertia (about a vertical axis through the centre of a mass) has an influence on steering behaviour and the limit of adhesion. Imagine a long vehicle with the load placed at the rear. If this vehicle started to skid it would have a large moment of inertia (with the weight of the engine at one end and the load at the other). It would be reluctant to spin, initially, but difficult to stop once it had started. Weights are better kept in the centre, as in mid-engined sports cars which have a small polar moment of inertia.

Neutral steering: a desirable handling characteristic which allows the steering wheel to be turned just enough for the radius of a corner; not more, as in a car with **understeer**, or less as in a car with **oversteer**. Usually obtained by equal front/rear weight distribution and equal front/rear roll stiffness and the same camber angles at front and rear.

NOx: a general chemical formula for the oxides of nitrogen which form one of the major groups of pollutants in exhaust gases.

Octane number: a number which indicates the knock resistance of fuel. Single-cylinder engines known as CFR engines are used to determine octane rating. Petrol is compared to mixtures of 150 octane and N-heptane until a mixture is found which gives the same amount of knock as the test fuel. The percentage of octane in the mixture then gives the octane rating of the petrol, e.g. 95 per cent octane, 5 per cent N-heptane would rate the fuel 95 octane.

Odometer: a distance recorder. Usually operated by a cable drive from the gearbox.

Ohc: overhead camshaft. The camshaft, driven by gears, chain or toothed belt, operates the valves directly through bucket tappets, sometimes rockers.

Ohv: overhead valves. Implicit in the term ohv is the use of push rods to operate the valves through rockers from the camshaft, usually low down in the block. This valve gear limits revs.

Overdrive: a separate unit operated by a switch and not by the gear-lever, usually based on an epicyclic gear. The object of the overdrive is to reduce engine revs for fast cruising.

Overlap: the period at the end of the exhaust stroke and the beginning of the induction stroke during which both exhaust and inlet valves are open.

Oversquare: an engine is oversquare when the bore exceeds the stroke.

Oversteer: a handling condition in which the rear wheels move outwards when turning a corner.

Panhard rod: a rod which runs laterally across the body, being attached to the body at one end and the **live axle** or **de Dion axle** at the other (or the subframe), acting in tension and compression to locate the axle (or subframe).

Parallel links: a pair of parallel trailing links or radius arms, on each side of the car, locating a **live** or **de Dion** axle.

Pinion: the smaller of a pair of gears, e.g. the smaller of the two final drive gears, **crown wheel and pinion**.

Pinking: see **detonation**.

Piston rings: the metallic rings, mounted in the grooves of the piston, that make seals between piston and cylinder. The upper or **compression ring** keeps the gas up in the cylinder chamber while the lower ring controls the flow of oil.

Planet wheel: part of an **epicyclic** gear train, the small gear rotating around the large sun gear.

Plug fouling: an accumulation of combustion deposits which can fuse into a shiny coating and cause misfiring.

Points: see **contact breaker**.

Polar moment of inertia: see **moment of inertia**.

Pollutants: There are four major pollutants from cars.
(1)   CO Carbon monoxide
(2)   NOx Oxides of nitrogen
(3)   NOx Unburnt hydrocarbons
(4)   Lead from the octane-boosting additives.

Poppet valve: inlet and exhaust valves found in all modern car engines, deriving its name from the fact that it pops up and down.

Power brakes: as distinct from power assisted brakes, power brakes rely on a steady supply of high pressure oil for their actuation. (Citroën use them.)

Power/weight ratio: a car's power in relation to its weight. Usually expressed as bhp/ton, e.g. a Fiat 126 has a power/weight ratio of 41 bhp/ton and most F1 cars have a power/weight ratio of 1000 bhp/ton.

Preignition: see **detonation**.

Prop shaft: abbreviation for propeller shaft. A balanced metal tube connecting the gearbox to the final drive with a universal joint at each end.

Pushrod: a rod in an **overhead valve** engine between the cam follower and the rocker arm.

Rack and pinion: a form of steering. A **pinion** or gearwheel at the end of the steering column meshes with a rack (a gearwheel laid out flat).

Radial ply tyre: a tyre in which the cords or plies are arranged laterally, at right angles to the circumferential plane. Their more flexible sidewalls keep the tread flat on the road, improving grip.

Radius arms: arms or rods which locate a live rear axle in the fore and aft direction. See also **parallel links**.

Rag top: a soft top or convertible car.

Rail: slang for dragster.

Rebore: grinding out worn bores of cylinders.

Recirculating ball steering: a steering mechanism similar to **worm and nut steering**. A low friction drive between the worm and the nut is provided by a column of steel ball-bearings running in a helical groove. Used by Mercedes-Benz.

Relay: a switch which allows a small current to energize a device consuming a large current.

Retard: ignition timing which occurs later rather than early.

Rev counter: an instrument which shows the speed of an engine by the revolutions per minute of the **crankshaft**. Electronic rev counters are driven by the distributor. Chronometric rev counters are driven from any convenient place, e.g. camshaft.

Rheostat: a device for reducing or increasing electrical power between source and point of use, e.g. panel lights.

Ride: the movement of a car with wide interpretations. Bounce, pitch, wallow, roll or near perfect.

Ride height: the ground clearance – distance between ground and car. Constant, regardless of load, on Rolls-Royce, Mercedes and Citroën CX.

Ring gear: a gear which is formed like a ring, e.g. the gear on the flywheel, and the internal gear in the annulus of an epicyclic gear train.

Rising rate suspension: the spring rate increases as the wheel moves upwards, either by using rising rate geometry or rising rate springs which have a varying wire diameter. BMW 520, Citroën GS and Opel Senator/Monza. The aim is to maintain stable handling and ride characteristics under maximum and minimum loads – a soft ride on the straight but not sacrificing roll stiffness on the corners.

Road holding: road holding means grip at all times and in all conditions.

Rocker arm: an arm or lever which is in contact with a valve at one end, and a cam or pushrod at the other.

Roll angle: the lean or roll from the vertical caused by centripetal force as a car turns a corner.

Roll bar: a protective metal bar usually in the form of a mild steel hoop above the driver's head in racing cars.

Roll centre: the point of a car about which the body rolls and which is determined by the geometry of the suspension.

Rolling resistance: resistance to forward motion due to friction in tyres and wheel bearings.

RON: Research Octane Number – the anti-knock rating of fuel.

Roots supercharger: an air compressor with mechanically driven rotors, which are either 2 or 3 lobed and so arranged that they are always in contact with each other. As they rotate they draw in air and discharge it. Their advantage is that they provide high boost at low revs, but they absorb power which the turbocharger does not. Roots blowers are frequently used on dragsters.

Rotary engine: an engine which dispenses with a conventional crankshaft and reciprocating motion, e.g. the **Wankel** engine.

Rotary valve: a valve that opens and closes ports by rotating instead of reciprocating. Usually tubes with holes, which are difficult to lubricate.

Rotor arm: a rotating arm in the distributor.

Rpm: revolutions per minute.

Running on: a tendency of badly maintained engines to continue running when the ignition is switched off.

SAE: Society of Automotive Engineers in America which defines various standards of measurement.

Screw and nut steering: see **worm and nut steering**.

Self-levelling suspension: a form of suspension keeping the car at the same height from the road whatever the load. Used by Rolls-Royce, Mercedes and Citroën.

Semi-floating rear axle: the wheel is mounted on the half-shaft and since the inner end of the half-shaft is not required to take side-forces during cornering it 'floats', but the outer end has to support cornering thrusts as well as the weight of the vehicle. See **fully floating axle**.

Semi-trailing arm: a form of independent rear suspension. It is usually used for rear wheel drive cars, the drive shaft having a universal joint at each end. This system gives some of the advantages of full double-wishbones but not all.

Servo: a system for multiplying the driver's effort by power from another source, e.g. the brake servo which uses the low pressure in the inlet manifold to increase the force exerted at the brake cylinders.

Shackle: a semi-elliptic spring is attached to the vehicle frame at each end by a shackle. It is a swinging support.

Shock absorbers: see **dampers**.

Slip angle: the angle between the plane of rotation of a wheel and its actual direction of motion when the tyre is acted upon by a side force as in cornering. A wheel in the straightahead position will respond to side force, like camber of sidewinds, by developing a slip angle causing it to slip away from the side force.

Solenoid: an electron magnet which draws in a soft iron rod or armature when energized by an electric current, e.g. the relay which operates the starter motor.

Solid state: means transistorized. Used because transistors are electronic devices made of solid pieces of matter, whereas

the radio valves involved a flow of electrons in a vacuum.

Sonic throttle: if air flows in a tube and passes through a restriction its pressure drops and its velocity will rise until it reaches or passes the speed of sound, becoming very turbulent in the process. This effect can be harnessed in the design of a throttle, and will give exceptionally good air/fuel mixing.

Sound insulation: presenting a barrier to noise rather than preventing it, with expanded polyurethane foam, bitumen backed fleece, etc.

Spaceframe: a chassis made up from a web of steel tubes. Superseded in Grand Prix racing by monocoque structures.

Space saver tyre: a tyre stored deflated, together with a gas bottle to inflate the tyre.

Sparking plug: the device which ignites the vaporized fuel by the passage of an electrical discharge between two electrodes.

Speed rating: an international code for tyres. Cross ply tyres, with no code letter, have a maximum of 75 to 95 mph. With code S it is 95–110. With radials, SR have a maximum of 113 mph, HR, 130 mph and VR have no specific limit.

Spigot: a projection or lug which locates two parts but does not hold them together.

Spiral bevel: the curved teeth of the spiral bevel **crown wheel and pinion**.

Splines: longitudinal grooves on a shaft which mate with projections on the inside of a cylinder or hub.

Sprocket: a toothed wheel which fits the gaps of a driving chain.

Squat: the rear of a car moving downwards during acceleration. It can be resisted by appropriate suspension geometry. See **anti-dive**.

Squish: squeezing the mixture in a cylinder head to promote better mixing of air/fuel.

Steam injection: see **water and steam injection**.

Steering ratio: the ratio of the rack to the pinion or worm to nut.

Stirling engine: an external combustion heat engine with high theoretical efficiency invented in 1816 by the Reverend Tovert Stirling and still being developed by United Stirling of Sweden.

Stratified charge: this can be achieved by starting combustion in a small auxiliary pre-combustion chamber, e.g. Honda CVCC engine.

Stressed members: sections which form an integral, supportive part of a structure.

Strobe light: abbreviation for stroboscope timing lamp. If a mark on a moving wheel is lit by the light from a lamp, synchronized to flash once for each rotation of the wheel, the mark will appear to be stationary. If the synchronization is not correct the mark will appear to drift to left or right according to whether the wheel is spinning too fast or too slowly. Strobes are used both for ignition timing and balancing wheels.

Stroke: the distance a piston moves during half a crankshaft cycle.

Stub axle: very short axles in carriers pivoted on swivel pins on which the front wheels rotate.

Sub-frame: a mini-chassis supporting suspension, steering, engine and transmission components. The sub-frame is bolted to the monocoque body.

Supercharger: a pump designed to force more air into the cylinders. This is mixed with more fuel, giving more power. There are three kinds:

(1) Exhaust driven superchargers, which are known as turbochargers
(2) Centrifugal vane or Roots superchargers
(3) Centrifugal superchargers.

Swept volume: the volume moved by the piston in one stroke.

Swing axle: A form of independent suspension usually employed at the rear of a car (e.g. VW Beetle). The wheel swings on a shaft having a single joint at the inboard end, near the final drive. A large wishbone straddling the inboard joint provides fore and aft location.

Swirl: the rotational movement of the incoming fuel and air in a combustion chamber, e.g. Audi 100.

Taper roller bearing: a roller bearing in which both the tracks and the rollers are conical in shape. It can therefore be used to take large end thrusts in one direction, e.g. front wheel hubs.

Tapley meter: an instrument for measuring deceleration.

Tappets: small steel cylinders inserted between the push rods and the camshaft cams in overhead valve engines. Tappets shaped like buckets are used in overhead camshaft engines.

Targa top: a simple removable roof panel devised by Porsche for their Targa model. Now found on other cars (Fiat X1/9).

Thermal efficiency: the ratio of the mechanical equivalent of heat available in a fuel to the amount turned into work. It is usually only 30 to 40 per cent for four stroke petrol engines.

Thermal reactor: a device connected to the exhaust system to allow supplemental burning and thus remove the hydrocarbons and CO emissions.

Thermo-electric fan: cooling fan which is electric instead of belt driven and on cold starting is inactive, permitting the engine to warm up more quickly and absorbing no engine power. It then cuts in thermostatically once the correct working temperature is reached.

Thermostat: a restricting valve in the radiator which speeds up the warming of the coolant from a cold start. When a predetermined temperature is reached, the valve opens.

Three-way catalyst: a catalytic convertor which is inserted in the exhaust system and controls the levels of the three major pollutants – hydrocarbons, oxides of nitrogen and carbon monoxide.

Thrust bearing: the crankshaft bearing which takes the thrust when the clutch is disengaged.

Timing marks: marks on the crankshaft pulley which indicate the number of degrees before **TDC**, to be lined up with a pointer on the timing cover. This can be done statically, but is more efficiently done with the engine running and using a **strobe** light.

Top dead centre, TDC: the point at which a piston is at the top of its stroke. TDC of No. 1 piston is the reference point for valve and ignition timing.

Torque: the twisting effort generated by an engine measured in lb/ft or Newton metres (Nm). See also **foot pounds**.

Torque converter: a form of fluid coupling used for automatic transmissions in which input torque is multiplied when starting, usually by 2½. It consists of two halves, impeller and turbine, both with angled blades, with the effect of increased velocity of fluid and consequently torque. When input and output shafts are running at the same speed the fluid changes its direction and impinges on the backs of the blades of the stator, an additional rotor situated between the impeller and turbine, mounted on a one-way freewheel, and begins to rotate with the other two elements. The torque converter then runs as a fluid flywheel with no torque multiplication and very little slip or absorption of power.

Torque tube: a tube which encloses the propeller shaft of a rear wheel drive car.

Torsion bar: a bar of tempered steel which acts as a suspension spring by twisting.

Torsional vibration: crankshafts, camshafts, propshafts, all suffer torsional vibration to some extent. Crankshafts are often designed with a damper at one end to eliminate it.

Tractive effort: the force at the rear wheels. The formula for this is F = GT/R, when:

F = tractive effort
G = top gear ratio
T = torque at the flywheel
R = rolling radius of the wheel.

Track rod: rod or rods connecting the steering arms of the front suspension together.

Trailing arm: a form of independent suspension in which the wheel is fixed to an arm swinging in a plane parallel to the longitudinal axis of the car. The wheel trails behind a fixed pivot point on the chassis, hence the name.

Trailing throttle: driving with the accelerator pedal released, e.g. running downhill.

Transaxle: abbreviation for transmission-axle in which the **clutch, gearbox, final drive** and **differential** are all combined in one unit, connected to the **drive shafts**. All front wheel drive and mid or rear engined cars have a form of transaxle of course, but two FE/RD – e.g. Porsche and Alfa Romeo have a combined gearbox/final drive at the rear.

Transistorized ignition: an ignition system using transistors. See **electronic ignition.**

Transverse link: part of a wishbone split into two separately jointed elements.

Tuftride: a heat treatment applied to steel, and cast iron, to improve durability. A hot bath dip reorganizes the molecular structure. Used for crankshafts of performance engines.

Tumble home: the angle outwards of the upper parts of a car's body.

Turbocharger: a supercharger driven by exhaust gases. It consists of a turbine, driven by the exhaust gases, connected to a compressor; which would appear to be free power. The alloys used have to withstand a heat of 1500°C and they have to be built to cope with speeds of 100,000 rpm, so they are expensive. They improve not only performance, but emissions as well.

Turbulence: a violent random movement of gases in the combustion chamber which speeds combustion and improves engine efficiency. Turbulence is induced by combustion chamber design. Also, turbulent airflow past a car increases its wind resistance.

Twin cam: an engine with two overhead camshafts for each bank of cylinders. One camshaft operates the inlet valves and the other the exhaust valves.

Twin choke: there are two kinds; those in which the butterflies open together and those in which they open in sequence. See also **choke**.

Understeer: a handling condition which means that the steering wheel has to be turned more for the curvature of the bend. Most front wheel drive cars understeer under power but revert to neutral or oversteer if you lift off.

Vacuum advance: automatic adjustment of ignition timing. The economy of running lean works only if the ignition is advanced. With part throttle, manifold depression (i.e. vacuum) is a guide to engine load. The vacuum is fed to a diaphragm which is connected to the advance mechanism, and the ignition advanced.

Vascar: Visual Average Speed Computer And Recorder. A device used by the police to check speed.

Viscous coupling: a method of driving cooling fans that precludes both over cooling, and power wastage when the engine is running below normal temperature. At that temperature a silicon based fluid is allowed into the chamber between the fan and the coupling by a thermostatically controlled valve, and takes up the drive like the fluid in a torque converter.

Volumetric efficiency: this is the ratio of the mass of air induced into the combustion chambers, to the mass of air that they are capable of containing at ambient pressure and temperature, expressed as a percentage. It is measured at maximum torque rpm – 2500 to 3000 rpm usually. Volumetric efficiency is usually 80 to 90 per cent but it can be 100 per cent in a well designed engine.

Wankel: a rotary engine invented by Dr Felix Wankel. It consists of a triangular shaped rotor, moving inside a waisted epitrochoidal housing. The engine is compact and smooth but uses more petrol than piston engines of equivalent size and is heavy on emissions.

Wastegate: the pressure relief valve used to limit boost pressure on **turbocharged** engines. Usually mounted before the turbine, it is governed by either intake boost pressure or exhaust back pressure. Mounted in this position the temperature is remarkably high. It is therefore sometimes placed between the compressor and the carburettor.

Water and steam injection: water injection has been used extensively on aero-engines to cool them. In jet engines it is injected during maximum boost to prevent the turbine blades from melting. There is a theory that it also improves volumetric efficiency.

Watt linkage: an arrangement of three links devised by Watt which allows objects to move parallel to each other. Used for the transverse location of **de Dion axles** and for the dead rear axle of the Alfasud.

Wet liners: cylinder barrels that are in contact with the coolant, fitted in light alloy cylinder blocks.

Wheelbase: the distance between the road wheels, measured longitudinally.

Wind tunnel: a large tunnel into which air is forced at high speed by a large fan to simulate airflow over a car (or scale model) to determine its coefficient of **drag**.

Wiring harness: the mass of coded cables and wires that connect up a car's electrical system. Also called a loom.

Wishbone: part of an independent suspension system. The point is attached to the wheel and hub carrier and the two arms pivot on the chassis to give both fore-and-aft and transverse location. Upper and lower wishbones are used, sometimes of different lengths.

Worm and nut steering: also called screw and nut. A portion of the steering column is threaded and a nut fits onto the thread. As the screw is rotated by the steering wheel the nut runs up and down the thread rotating the drop arm by a spindle.

Yoke: a wishbone-shaped fork to move gears in and out of engagement in the gearbox.

Index